RUMI COMES TO AMERICA

D1548205

RUMI COMES TO AMERICA

How the Poet of Mystical Love Arrived on
Our Shores

Bruce Miller

MILLER EMEDIA
DECATUR GEORGIA

Miller eMedia LLC
615 Sycamore Street
Decatur, GA 30030
www.milleremedia.com

Portions of this book originally appeared in FORTUNE, *Our Deep Dive into the Mysteries of Love, Healing and Success,* by Bruce Miller.

CONTENTS

FORWARD TO THE SECOND EDITION

Soon after I published *Rumi Comes to America*, Reshad Feild's German publishers asked if they could issue a German language edition.

"Sure," I replied. "Go for it."

They then asked to change the title to *Rumi Comes to the West, How the Poet of Mystical Love Arrived in America and Europe*.

That wasn't quite as snappy, but again, I agreed. Since my writing style delights in idioms and figures of speech, I couldn't imagine translating the book into German, but if anyone could do it, they could.

In another email, they asked, "In order to justify the above-mentioned change of title, it would, of course, be great if we had a sort of an 'after epilogue' or an annex saying something about how the story went on, i.e., how Rumi finally came to Europe via the States."

Well, I didn't want to tack on an annex. You either open Pandora's Box or you don't – and I did. Weaving Reshad's European adventure into the bigger story now provides a meaningful bookend to Reshad's richly-lived life. The chapters: "The Impulse," "The Abyss," "Valbella II," "Johanneshof," and "In the Barzakh" are all new material.

The risk with opening Pandora's Box is what comes out. After I submitted the manuscript and implemented most but not all of their suggested revisions, the German publishers rejected the whole thing. My desire for candor may not have been a good fit for their purpose, but rather than an ill-fated exercise, you now get to enjoy a lively teaching story.

Please note, some sections of the new material were drawn from my memoir, *Fortune, Our Deep Dive into the Mysteries of Love, Healing, and Success.*

Please enjoy a spiritual journey in its full messiness, a story that is ever more relevant today.

Bruce Miller, November 2018

INTRODUCTION

Forty years ago, I was given a front-row seat to America's "first kiss" in its Rumi love affair — an experience that launched my young adulthood. Like much of my youth, the memory drifted over time.

Recently, while cleaning out a closet, I discovered recordings of Süleyman Dede, the Sheikh of the Whirling Dervishes in Konya, Turkey, who traveled to Los Angeles in April 1976 to plant this "first kiss." The tapes had never been played, so I decided to find out what was on them. I considered turning Dede's talks into inexpensive pamphlets to defray the cost.

So, I plowed ahead. I repaired an ancient reel-to-reel tape deck, digitized the tapes, located a translator, and awaited the results. After reading the English transcripts, I was shocked to discover that forty years earlier, Süleyman Dede had warned the younger me in Turkish: "Bu kelimeler değerlidir — Bruce, these words are precious. Don't sell them cheap!"

Whoops.

That explains why, rather than a pamphlet, you now have a thoroughly researched, richly illustrated book in your hands that tells the unlikely story of how Rumi came to America.

Why should we care how Rumi landed on our shores? Today, Rumi adorns bumper stickers, t-shirts, trucker hats, and travel bags. An Amazon search pulls up thousands of Rumi titles. Countless celebrities, from Deepak Chopra to Madonna, adore

Rumi. Beyoncé and Jay-Z named one of their twins "Rumi," and even registered a trademark application for the child's name.[1]

What's more, Rumi is Obama's favorite poet. The former President has a signed copy of Coleman Barks' *Essential Rumi* that he received from Richard Holbrooke, Obama's special representative to Afghanistan.

As a brand, Rumi sells fashion accessories, perfume, restaurants, and even yoga wear made from recycled plastic bottles. Once, while I was flying on Delta, I saw Rumi's words float serenely across the in-flight monitor — an unexpected invitation to explore my knee-squished existential predicament.

Today's Rumi-palooza is all the more amazing when you consider that forty years ago, Rumi was virtually unknown in American culture — two or three books at most. How did this happen?

By profession, I'm a brand strategist, and it's my job to stay in touch with the evolving cultural zeitgeist. But even I was surprised when Rumi emerged recently on Coldplay's seventh album. The band has played Rumi's poem, "The Guest House" read by Coleman Barks, to 3 million fans on five continents as part of one of the biggest tours (half a billion dollars) in the history of music.[2]

Coleman told the story:

"When Coldplay's Chris Martin first contacted me, I didn't know who Coldplay was. Finally, I asked my friend and fellow poet, Lisa Starr if she knew. Of course, she did, as did her children, as did everybody else on the planet."

1. "Beyoncé and Jay-Z file trademark on twin names Rumi and Sir." The Guardian. https://www.theguardian.com/music/2017/jul/02/beyonce-jay-z-twins-names-sumi-sir-copyright. July 3, 2017.

2. Coldplay's 'Head Full of Dreams' Trek on Track to Become One of the Top 10 Highest Grossing Tours Ever. http://www.billboard.com/articles/columns/chart-beat/7800960/coldplay-head-full-of-dreams-tour-high-gross 5/19/2017.

Coleman learned that Rumi's poem, "The Guest House," changed Chris Martin's life. He described the effect of the poem on his post-divorce depression after splitting from Gwyneth Paltrow, saying, "It says that everything that happens to you is okay. The idea is to accept what happens to you and not run away from anything — and trust that things will blossom and become colorful."[3]

Coleman continued:

"Lisa and I flew out to LA to record the poem for Chris. A year later, we went to Philadelphia to see it performed. Chris told me beforehand, 'Pay attention when the lights turn out.' Halfway through the set, everything went dark, and my voice came through reading Rumi's 'Guest House' while

Rumi illuminated by Cold Play's digitally-controlled wristbands

69,000 people waved digital bracelets to the music. Pretty heady stuff for a retired English teacher."

It's ironic that in post-9/11 America, a classically-trained Muslim theologian who taught Sharia law in an Anatolian madrassa nearly 800 years ago would become a pop culture phenomenon. One can only imagine how Rumi and his loyal scribe Husameddin would have reacted to American concert-goers waving digital bracelets that synchronously changed color to Rumi's couplets.

Yes, Rumi is cool, and Rumi is everywhere. We rarely question

3. Doyle, Patrick. "Chris Martin on Post-Divorce Depression, Coldplay's New 'Hippie Album.'" http://www.rollingstone.com/music/features/chris-martin-on-battling-depression-coldplays-new-hippie-album-20151119. November 19, 2015.

how contemporary culture got this way, but students of history know to follow the seeds:

Consider the seed Christopher Columbus carried across the sea — in his words, "to carry the Name and doctrine of Jesus Christ into regions so distant." After a grueling voyage, Columbus planted the Spanish flag to claim the New World, naming the outer Bahamas island, "San Salvador" (Holy Savior). Eventually, Spaniards displaced the indigenous traditions of the New World with transplanted ideas of good and evil, Heaven and Hell, and the Virgin and saints. At the cost of the genocidal decimation of the native population, the seed Columbus planted changed the world. Today, Latin America is home to forty percent of the world's 1.2 billion Roman Catholics.

Consider the seed carried by the wandering Hindu monk, Swami Vivekananda. In 1888, at age 25, Vivekananda left his ashram with a water pot, walking stick and two religious books, the "Bhagavad Gita" and "The Imitation of Christ." Living on charity from strangers, Vivekananda traveled throughout India for five years.

In 1893, Vivekananda learned that the Parliament of World's Religions, a historic conclave of religious leaders, would be taking place that year in Chicago. Vivekananda prayed for guidance and received "a divine command" to attend and represent Hinduism and the Vedanta tradition. Supporters arranged money, and the young swami traveled by steamer to Japan, China, and Vancouver.

From Canada, Vivekananda ventured by train to Chicago. Upon arrival, Vivekananda discovered that delegates needed credentials to serve as bona fide religious representatives. Heartbroken, he headed to Boston where the cost of living would be cheaper.

On the train to Boston, Vivekananda met Katherine Sanborn, a former Smith College professor who invited him to live at her farm in Massachusetts. In a stroke of fortune, she invited the swami to meet Professor John Henry Wright of Harvard University. Wright immediately recognized Vivekananda's spiritual station and insisted that Vivekananda persevere in his quest, explaining, "to ask for your credentials is like asking the sun to state its right to shine in the heavens."

With everything arranged, Swami Vivekananda returned to Chicago, but along the way, he lost his contact address. Hungry and tired, he begged for food and directions. With nowhere to turn, he sat down on a curb on Dearborn Street and resigned himself to God's will. Suddenly, the front door of the facing house opened. Out stepped a well-dressed woman who spotted his turban and robes and asked, "Sir, are you a delegate to the Parliament of Religions?"

With fortune propelling his mission, Swami Vivekananda made his way to the Parliament. Channeling the spirit of his guru, the great Ramakrishna, the Swami began his speech with the stirring salutation, "Sisters and brothers of America!" The crowd of seven thousand rose to a standing ovation lasting two minutes.

In his speech, Vivekananda planted a seed — radical for its time — of tolerance for other sects and religions as universal expressions of one truth. American newspapers reported Vivekananda as "the greatest figure in the Parliament of Religions" and "the most popular and influential man in the Parliament."

Vivekananda's seed ultimately touched the great thinkers of the age, from Aldous Huxley and Christopher Isherwood to William James and Joseph Campbell. Yes, a direct line from Vivekananda to George Lucas and Star Wars.[4]

Planting a seed draws a line that changes history — in this case

4. The Vivekananda Vedanta Society of Chicago. "The Arrival."
http://chicagovedanta.org/chicago-vivekananda-arrives.html.

from Ramakrishna through Vivekananda, and into a blossoming of Eastern thought that would lay the foundation for modern American yoga— now practiced by over 36 million people in the U.S.

And let us not forget the mostly-forgotten seed planted by Richard Nixon. His 1972 door-opening visit to Communist China's Forbidden City ultimately blossomed, for better or worse, into 11,500 Walmarts in 28 countries.

The whole of world culture cross-pollinates this way. 800 years ago, a spiritually significant seed changed history when Jelaluddin Rumi's family fled from the Mongol invaders. Rumi and his family embarked on a migration from Balkh, Afghanistan, through Baghdad, Mecca, Medina, and Damascus until finally arriving in Konya, Turkey, a center of learning and spiritual culture in 1228.

For the next sixteen years, Rumi grew to become a highly-regarded, classically-trained Muslim cleric. During this time, the wandering dervish, Shams of Tabriz, waited for the right moment to germinate the Rumi seed which, in Coleman Barks' words, would "forever alter the course of Rumi's life and influence the mystical evolution of the planet."[5]

Rumi died in 1273, but his influence grew for centuries until 1925 when Kemal Atatürk, the founder of the Republic of Turkey, passed a series of decrees that prohibited Sufi lodges and their religious practices. Atatürk later decreed that Turkey is a modern country with no time for "dervish magic." Atatürk's ban still stands today.

In 1976, fifty years after Atatürk and seven hundred years after Rumi's death, that seed was carried again — this time from Konya to California.

When the Sheikh of Konya, Süleyman Hayati Loras Dede, arrived at our modest rented duplex in Los Angeles, I wasn't

---

5. Barks, Coleman and Green, Michael. *The Illuminated Rumi*. Broadway Books, 1997.

paying attention to the "seeds" he had hidden up his sleeve. But in the magic of that moment, Reshad Feild, a British pop singer, with Süleyman Dede, a humble cook, and a group of well-meaning young Americans had all inadvertently conspired to bring Rumi to the West. This book examines how Rumi's spiritual line traversed time to blossom hundreds of years later.

I took my ancient tape deck to a repair shop and began searching for a Turkish translator. After several false starts, I located Sinan Salim in Germany. Sinan was familiar with Sufism, the way of Rumi, and even the local dialect of Dede. Sinan felt that Güneş, our Turkish translator in 1976, performed amazingly well under pressure, but understandably, Güneş could do no more than summarize Dede's remarks. I have spent hours digitizing the talks, stopping every few minutes to clean oxide from the fraying tapes to resurrect the magic of that moment.

If you read Dede's words from the inner heart, you will understand what he meant when he told me, "Bruce, the value of these words is known only to people of a certain station, to the *arif*, the gnostic ones. Gnostics will understand; those with open hearts, those with the active eye of the heart will understand."

I invite you to approach this story with an open, curious heart. You will discover how Mevlana Jelaluddin Rumi bridged the divide of time and space as a seed — a seed planted by his devoted servants, Reshad Feild and Süleyman Hayati Loras Dede.

Bruce Miller

Decatur, Georgia | November 2017

Bruce and Süleyman Dede, Los Angeles 1976

1

THE POSSIBILITY OF A
REAL SCHOOL

For 25 years, from Watergate to the World Trade Center, I had a spiritual teacher. I'm not sure if people have spiritual teachers anymore or if it's even a good idea. As my friend and mentor, Mory Berman, said to me when I was in college, "The height of rascality is sinking low enough to try teaching that which no man can grasp."

Yes, my spiritual teacher was a rascal. Fresh out of film school, I met him in 1974 at a "Festival of Light" in the Masonic Hall above the Baskin-Robbins on Larchmont in Los Angeles. Ironically, the space now hosts a YogaWorks location, often derisively dubbed "the Starbucks of spirituality."

It's hard for people today to appreciate the heartfelt, mostly sentimental phenomenon that characterized the dawn of the New Age. Like so many others, I had a glimpse into a world of pure consciousness aided by a dose of organic mescaline. After this brief lifting of the veils of illusion atop Reyes Peak, 7500 feet above the Pacific Ocean, I had no choice but to seek out knowledge. My thirst inevitably brought me to the Festival of Light.

Amid the hucksters and spiritual dreamers on the program, a balding and bearded Englishman wearing a leather fur-lined vest caught my eye. He stood in the hallway, away from the main stage, demonstrating a dowsing rod to a young woman. I watched in fascination as the tightly-gripped rod curled up to his chest like a psychic erection.

Reshad Feild, 1974

"Look, I'm not doing anything," he boasted to the woman.

I wasn't sure what he was trying to prove.

My curiosity grew when the dowsing rod guy, introduced as Reshad Feild, took the stage. Born as Timothy Feild, Reshad was a British aristocrat, esoteric healer, new age author, antique dealer, mentor to actress Ellen Burstyn, and of course, a dowser. Reshad skipped the spiritual pablum and went straight to the point:

"I am here today to offer the possibility of working in a real school," Reshad announced. "A real school arises where and when it's needed. After 40 days, when the school has fulfilled its aim, the school will disband, disappear and reappear in a different form somewhere else if it is needed."

I liked the hit-and-run quality of what Reshad offered. He painted a picture of a world out of balance and the need for people to dedicate their lives to the service of God and humanity. He told us that individuals were needed to preserve esoteric knowledge and learn to hold conscious energies while the world slid off the rails.

"The purpose of this school is to provide the best possible conditions for people to learn to work with energies," Reshad continued. "We are preparing the groundwork for what is called the Second Cycle of Mankind. This change can come about through the transformation of consciousness needed at this time."

Reshad's pronouncement appealed to my visceral sense that the world was in a creative upheaval. I had come of age in the Sixties — a ten-year span that thrust America into a seismic cultural shift. A few weeks earlier, Nixon's disgrace and resignation had delivered its final dark blow, so a Second Cycle of Mankind seemed entirely plausible. And with that, I signed up.

A group of us leaped into Reshad's mission with a *Field of Dreams* fervor. We spent a month chasing down real estate leads (this was before Craigslist or Zillow). Eventually, a faded mansion in a sketchy area of the Wilshire District whispered, "Lease me, and he will come." We signed the lease, Reshad appeared, and thus began the Institute for Conscious Life.

The Institute for Conscious Life, Los Angeles 1975

I had no idea what I had signed up for, so I hesitated when Reshad asked me, "Bruce, will you be joining us?" I had been working non-stop to launch the operation, so moving-in was the obvious next step. I left my comfort zone in Malibu and answered, "Yes."

The Institute for Conscious Life blended Sufism and the teachings of Gurdjieff with Reshad's esoteric knowledge. Reshad also threw in a few protocols from his aristocratic roots and the

British Navy, including Person of the Day and night watch. Fueling the entire enterprise were Reshad's magnetic charisma and his penchant for the limelight.

One night, after a full day of high drama and heroic effort, Reshad pulled out his guitar. Before his spiritual career, Reshad had sung with pop legend, Dusty Springfield, so most evenings ended with his gallant British tenor. As Reshad sang "The First Time Ever I Saw Your Face," composed by his folk mentor, Ewan MacColl, a dreamy, spiritual longing filled the

Reshad, 1976

room. It was odd to learn that the same MacColl once famously mentored to Reshad, "Mr. Feild, you have to take the emotion out of your voice."

The next day, my Jewish skepticism finally melted when Reshad invited me out to get a sandwich. We walked toward Wilshire Boulevard and into a courtyard restaurant. On cue, Roberta Flack wafted lyrically through the sound system singing, "The first time, ever I saw your face..." As a sucker for synchronicity, I was all in.

Reshad modeled The Institute for Conscious Life after G.I. Gurdjieff's Institute for the Harmonious Development of Man, an intensive school founded outside of Paris in 1922. Gurdjieff was possibly the most original esoteric thinker of the twentieth century. He had sought out remote sources of esoteric knowledge as a younger man, then synthesized his findings into a practical teaching that organized the workings of the cosmos.

"Man is asleep," Gurdjieff proclaimed. "He has no real consciousness or will. He is not free. To him, everything *happens.*

He can become conscious and find his true place as a human being in the creation, but this requires a profound transformation."[1]

Gurdjieff felt that people could awaken from their "sleep-like" state by bringing heightened attention to the subtle impressions of ordinary life. Gurdjieff called this wakefulness "self-remembering." Gurdjieff stated, "There are moments when you become aware not only of what you are doing but also of yourself doing it."[2]

Gurdjieff used the friction of different personalities in his Institute to create heat for the transformational boiling pot — the heat needed to awaken the sleeping self. Reshad's school was unique in that it fused elements of Gurdjieff's work (the friction) with elements of Sufism and particularly Rumi (the love). Friction and love powered the transformative engine of the Institute for Conscious Life.

Reshad originally proposed that spiritual seekers from all walks of life would come to the ICL for forty days, receive a spiritual transfusion, then go off into the world to live meaningful lives — presumably to build the Second Cycle of Mankind.

A steady stream of students and visitors passed through our doors including singer Dusty Springfield, Sufi leader Pir Vilayat Khan, Yogi Bhajan,

Reshad and Yogi Bhajan

1. "G.I. Gurdjieff." The Gurdjieff Society. http://www.gurdjieff.com/about.php.
2. Gurdjieff, Georges Ivanovitch. *Views From the Real World: Early Talks of Gurdjieff as Recollected by His Pupils*. 1st edition. New York: Dutton, 1973.

and Bhante Dharmawara, a Cambodian monk who reportedly lived to be 110 years old.

Life in the Institute was hardly glamorous. Since few people had jobs or income, meals were meager, and the work was non-stop. The day began at 4:30 a.m. with wake-up for prayers. Competition for the bathroom was intense.

"I can't believe I'm doing this," I grumbled as I staggered out of my Army surplus metal bunk, half-heartedly splashed water on my requisite parts, then descended into the basement. At the far end of the foreboding space, a large metal door opened into a walk-in vault where Hassan Immerman, a devoted American dervish, sat wrapped in a blanket. Hassan had traveled through Turkey, Afghanistan, India, and Indonesia, so the flickering candlelight gave his blunt words an ominous tone.

"This is no joke," Hassan warned. "This is serious stuff. If you aren't sure, get out now."

And with that, we linked arms and started chanting, "Allah-Allah."

I had been hanging with this crowd for some weeks, and now it dawned on me: "Holy shit (Allah-Allah). This path has something to do with ISLAM! (Allah-Allah)!"

Being a good Jewish boy, I was in a muddle (Allah-Allah). I decided to go with the flow and fully engage, but not identify.

"Don't get caught in the drama," I resolved. "Don't get attracted or repelled by what is going on."

For the next 25 years, this was my strategy: "I'm not following Reshad, not following Rumi, not following Gurdjieff, nor Muhammad. I am, hopefully, following myself."

My lofty goal, of course, was impossible. The purpose of the school was to create sufficient internal friction for transformation. Friction, by definition, creates identification. The intensity of work created an "I can-barely-hold-it-together" level of stress just beneath the surface, all the time.

Late one night, Reshad's frustration started to boil. I don't know if it was too many gin and tonics or because he was frustrated that the energy wasn't *going through* — not going through us "idiots" as he fondly called his pupils. *Idiots* was a Gurdjieff term for *aspiring seekers.*

"I'm not going to bed until you can love one other," Reshad declared.

It was almost midnight, and we were bone-pleading tired. If exhaustion makes you pliable, our primordial clay was ready to be shaped.

"I want you to love one another," Reshad ordered again.

"Yes sir, coming right up," I grumbled.

A few people made awkward attempts with hugs, staring into eyes, and forced bliss. Fifteen minutes into this, Reshad threatened again.

"I remain true to my word. I will not go to sleep until you can love one another. Bring me my mattress!"

And with that, two strong men went up the stairs and returned, wrestling Reshad's queen-size mattress down the stairs. Denise, Reshad's very pregnant young wife quickly followed, furious to have been evicted from her bed.

I'm not sure we succeeded in loving one another, but the energy finally "went through." It was small compensation because, like a ticking crocodile, 4:30 a.m. would soon return.

Since my plan was not to identify, I made it my practice to "notice." I observed how the play unfolded, how the emotional friction created heat, and how heat was energy. Like lightning seeking the ground, "the energy must go through." And when it didn't, tension and trouble ensued.

At night, the wailing of emotional release would awaken the neighbors. "The energy must go through," I thought.

I also watched the girth of several women expand over the course of a few days. I surmised that the energy wasn't going through; it wasn't too much food. Round-the-clock work, prayer, exercises, and study unleashed a powerful force, a kind of spiritual lightning. This energy had a job to do — it needed to go through.

One moment we would be whirling like dervishes, then Vipassana Buddhist meditation, then Arica exercises, followed by brain-burning Ibn Arabi studies, maybe a fling with Scientology, a little map-dowsing, singing vowel sounds with movements, vortex meditations, walking meditation, a green meditation; it never ended.

NBC News filming at the Institute for Conscious Life

We were young; we had the physical energy, but we didn't have the emotional ballast to live at this pitch. Our only solace was the Astro Cafe — a late-night Greek burger joint on Western Avenue where we could bitch and complain outside the boiling pot, blowing off the precious spiritual energy through a greasy relief valve.

The bitching and gossip at the Astro always focused on Reshad:

"Is Reshad a realized being? Do his teachings emanate from *jabrut* (the unmanifested world) as he claims? Is he orchestrating a divine drama or simply channeling garden-variety anger?" And the primary, but unspoken question: "Why the alcohol?"

One day, the three-ring circus finally made sense. A workshop titled, "An Introduction to the Law of Seven," revealed the grand plan. Each hour of the seminar resonated with a note of the musical octave. We set our intention on the note *Do*, performed movements on *Re*, talked about the illusion of self on *Mi* (rhymes with "me"), had lunch on *Fa*, and so on. The screenwriter in me was fascinated by the dramatic flow of events in our school, and now Reshad had revealed the musical score.

A brainy guy named Doug was scheduled to present the Law of Seven at 2:00 p.m. — on the note *Sol*. Doug had studied with British mathematician, scientist, and philosopher, John G. Bennett. Mr. Bennett had worked with Gurdjieff in his younger years, and then at the end of his life, Bennett made it his mission to transmit this knowledge to the next generation of young people before he died.

Bennett, at age 73, was determined to transmit the inner teachings to the "youth generation." He even attended the Isle of Wight festival, England's Woodstock, for generational insight. To fulfill his mission, Bennett established the International Academy for Continuous

Sherborne House

Education in Gloucestershire, aka "Sherborne House," as an experiment to transmit the "sense and aim of life" to the next generation.

Reshad established a similar school for transformation, named

"Beshara," just down the road from Bennett at Swyre Farm. In many ways, a spiritual cross-pollination flowed between the two esoteric schools.

J.G. Bennett, 1971

On December 13, 1974, in the middle of Mr. Bennett's fourth course at Sherborne House, and a few days before Reshad proposed the Institute in Los Angeles, Mr. Bennett died. I include this background to illustrate a major theme — that "seeds of transmission" propagate history. They propel the story forward. In this particular case, Bennett's pupils served as seeds. They helped move the story from England to America after Bennett died.

Bennett's pupils described the last two days of J.G. Bennett's life:

The day before, I didn't go out. Mr. Bennett was chief cook in the morning. I had to ask for something, and there was Mr. Bennett cutting the cabbage for borscht. I can still feel the silence beneath the noise.

Later, Mr. Bennett spoke about the need for worship and how one should and should not communicate with people who are dead.

In the afternoon Mr. Bennett was on p.m. service: washing up, laying the tables, preparing tea, serving dinner, and washing up again. Afterward, he led a meditation in the ballroom on the Beatitude: "Blessed are the pure in heart, for they shall see God." He asked us, "Why is it the heart, not the mind, or the eyes?"

The next day, Elizabeth (Mr. Bennett's wife) asked: "Can you help; Mr. Bennett does not feel well." He said he was all right and, supported by Elizabeth, he walked upstairs.

One hour later, Elizabeth called a meeting. Her voice is clear and firm:

"Let it be quite clear; he has left forever. Having fulfilled his duty on this earth, he has been looking forward to this day. Whoever wishes to stay up with me tonight may do so."

The theme for the week was Completion.[3]

Doug had studied with Mr. Bennett at Sherborne and had now joined us in Los Angeles to introduce Gurdjieff's two fundamental laws of the universe: The Law of Three and the Law of Seven — also known as the Octave.

What we know of these laws comes from lectures given by Gurdjieff to a group of students from 1915 – 1917 in St. Petersburg, Russia. Later, P.D. Ouspensky turned the talks into the seminal book, *In Search of the Miraculous.[4]* The Enneagram symbol (popularized today for personality typing) was introduced by Gurdjieff through these talks to explain the working of the Octave.

To appreciate Rumi's 700-year journey to America, it helps to understand these two great laws. Mr. Gurdjieff felt that the most complex mechanisms of life are ultimately explained by simple principles observed in everyday events. The first of these is The Law of Three or Law of Three Forces.

According to Gurdjieff, every phenomenon in the universe is the result of three forces: Positive, Negative, and Neutralizing. Three forces define the makeup of atoms (protons, electrons, and

3. "December 13, 1974 ~ On The Death of Mr. Bennett." First published in The Enneagram # 9 - January 1977. https://www.jgbennett.org/december-13-1974/

4. Ouspensky, P. D. In Search of the Miraculous. London: Paul H. Crompton Ltd. 1949.

neutrons), electricity (positive, negative, and ground), natural phenomena like the forces of weather (high pressure, low pressure, and precipitation) as well as actions, events, and human affairs.

In everyday activities, the Three Forces manifest as Active, Passive, and Reconciling, or in human affairs: Affirming, Denying and Mediating. If two countries are locked in opposition, a third country acts as mediator. In marriage,

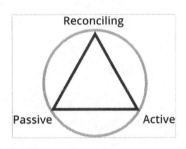

Law of Three Forces

the birth of the child enters the union as a Third Force, bringing a meaningful purpose to the relationship. In Christianity, it's the Father, Son, and Holy Spirit. In Taoism, it's Yin, Yang, and the Tao. In physics, it's space, time, and the continuum. In a sitcom, there's the setup, the complications, and the resolution. In each case, the Third Force reconciles opposing forces as a form of grace.

Even a simple yoga stretch draws from three forces: the active effort to touch toes, the resistant force of stiff muscles and the inner release when you breathe (Third Force) into the tension. Knowing how and when to invoke the Third Force is the key to healing, diplomacy, relationships, child rearing, creating art, and telling a good joke.

The Third Force manifests as an outside force that changes the course of events. The Third Force enters through the grace that follows a prayer, the unexpected guest who enlivens the party, the guy named Johnny who arrives to plant apple trees, or even the creative insight that pops into your head when you run out of ideas. The Third Force sneaks in when you confront the inevitable, accept your fate, and let go of the fear of change.

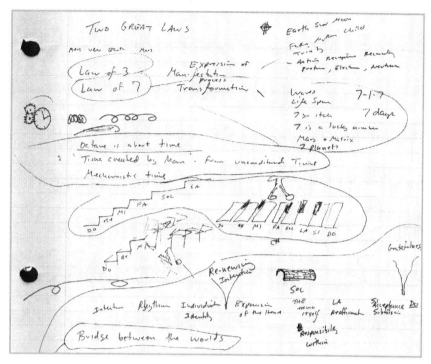

Notes from the Octave class

The Law of Three made sense to me, but the Law of Seven, known as the Octave, was more perplexing. If the Law of Three Forces is about reconciling opposing forces, the Law of Seven describes growth, process, and unfoldment – how things happen.

If I plant a seed, the Octave describes how the plant will sprout and branch out at measured intervals. If I start a term paper, the Octave maps the struggle toward completion. When we make our wedding vows, the Octave predicts the swing from bliss to blame — what Harville Hendrix describes as the natural transition in a marriage from the Romance stage to the Power Struggle.[5] In this way, marital love rides the Octave's vibrational ups and downs. Consider Marilyn Monroe colliding into Tom Ewell's marriage

5. Hendrix, Harville. *Getting the Love You Want*. Holt Paperbacks, 2001.

at the Octave interval in Billy Wilder's classic romantic comedy: "The Seven Year Itch."

Similarly, if you track the narrative arc of Trump's first year in office, the tipping point that would ultimately define his presidency occurred when he tacitly endorsed the white supremacists in Charlottesville — seven months into his first term. And let us not forget the seven-century gestation cycle for Rumi's seed to transplant to the West.

When we go on a diet, the Octave delivers a tempting cheesecake. If we seek fame and fortune, the Octave predicts when our efforts will become thwarted. The Octave reveals itself through seven visible colors, seven notes in the musical scale, seven visible planets, seven days in a week, and the seven groups of elements in the periodic table. After a death, Jews mourn for seven days in *shiva* which means seven. For a Muslim on the *hajj*, the seven revolutions around the Kaaba represent the seven levels of the soul.

As Doug spoke, the exquisite orchestration of an unfolding universe opened before my eyes. I saw how the Institute's daily schedule followed the vibrational structure of the octave. Like acts in a screenplay or movements in a symphony, our daily mix of study, prayer, cleaning, and crisis all melded into a perfectly pitched drama to exhaust our emotional resistance and open the heart.

As a performer, Reshad was an Octave magician. I watched how he lifted the energy to turn complacency into action. Mesmerized by his magic, I became Reshad's Octave student.

Doug explained how the two intervals in the musical scale, where the black keys are missing on the piano keyboard, govern transformation. At these intervals – Mi Fa and Si Do – the vibrational distance between two notes slows (half-steps instead of whole steps) briefly slows the ascent up the scale. Imagine trying to climb the stairs after a few drinks and encountering a shorter rise at the third and fourth steps. Whoops.

The Octave intervals

Esoterically, the slowing is significant (as it would be if you were ascending those stairs while drunk). The subtle energetic lull, particularly in the Mi Fa interval, creates an opening for an unanticipated event to enter, upset the status quo, and disorient the stair climber with the shock of the unexpected. Importantly, this "shock" releases the energy needed for transformation. A divorce, a medical diagnosis, job loss, a heart-melting kiss, a feeling of gratitude, a musical bridge, a Trumpian election, or a wandering dervish named Shams of Tabriz upsetting Rumi's madrassa career – any of these can function as an *outside shock* to shift the energy.

I watched the Institute for Conscious Life unfold this way. A series of small crises would disrupt the normal flow of events: an impromptu wedding, a home birth, the visit of NBC News, a Cambodian monk wanting the walls draped in green, a visit by Governor Jerry Brown

Governor Jerry Brown at the Institute

and his girlfriend Linda Rondstadt – the drama never stopped.

Institute for Conscious Life after morning prayers.

Reshad reveled in his role as orchestrator of the Octave and lord of the manor. As a result, he kept pushing our pop-up operation past the promised 40-day intention. After he extended it another 40 days and again for a third round, I wondered if the Octave would ever intervene.

Then, one day, we received an *outside shock* in the form of a stern letter from the City of Los Angeles:

"To whom it may concern: You are operating a school on property zoned for single-family use. You are ordered to cease operations and vacate the premises."

And, just as promised, the Institute disappeared.

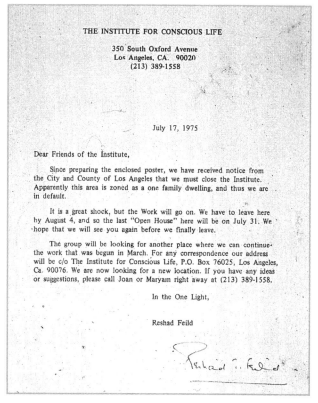

THE INSTITUTE FOR CONSCIOUS LIFE

350 South Oxford Avenue
Los Angeles, CA. 90020
(213) 389-1558

July 17, 1975

Dear Friends of the Institute,

Since preparing the enclosed poster, we have received notice from the City and County of Los Angeles that we must close the Institute. Apparently this area is zoned as a one family dwelling, and thus we are in default.

It is a great shock, but the Work will go on. We have to leave here by August 4, and so the last "Open House" here will be on July 31. We hope that we will see you again before we finally leave.

The group will be looking for another place where we can continue the work that was begun in March. For any correspondence our address will be c/o The Institute for Conscious Life, P.O. Box 76025, Los Angeles, Ca. 90076. We are now looking for a new location. If you have any ideas or suggestions, please call Joan or Maryam right away at (213) 389-1558.

In the One Light,

Reshad Feild

Closing Letter, 120 days after launch.

25

2

THE OCTAVE TURNS

"Maybe, God appears in the form of zoning enforcement," I mused to George, my Communist fellow student.

I crumpled a useless flyer announcing the now-canceled events as we watched the guests stream out of the final open house at the Institute for Conscious Life. I would never comprehend August 14, *Aligning with the Esoteric Geometry of High-Velocity Inner Space*. And tonight's talk, "*Mysterium Conjunctum, The Alchemical Marriage*" was still a mysterium.

"This might be too much energy for one little boiling pot," I remarked.

"Maybe," George replied. "But, I'm troubled by the whole thing. What's your take on this God business?"

I said something stupid about it all being energy, but I didn't pick up on George's real question. He saw life through the lens of social justice and was disturbed by Reshad's *prima donna* way of mixing God with personal drama.

George and his Berkeley contingent left the ICL and moved across town into a duplex in the Silver Lake neighborhood. Their goal was to live a communal, socially-conscious life in a working-class neighborhood — and as far from Reshad as possible. Reshad, his wife, and infant moved to a guest house near the Whisky a Go Go on the Sunset Strip. Everyone else scattered around town.

Silver Lake duplex, Los Angeles

For the next couple of months, our little group was in a holding pattern, waiting for the Octave to turn — which it did when the other half of George's "socially-conscious" duplex suddenly became vacant. Reshad, wife, and baby took that as a "sign" and moved into the other half. Others followed to the neighborhood and just like that, the Institute for Conscious Life 2.0 was born.

Each evening we gathered to hear Reshad read typewritten pages from *The Invisible Way*, his follow-up to *The Last Barrier*, the spiritual best-seller about his Sufi journey to Turkey. One night, Reshad put the freshly-typed page down and seized the pregnant pause.

"I've been deeply contemplating the next step in our work," Reshad announced. "I've been in contact with Süleyman Dede."

Everyone ooh'd and ahh'd, but I wasn't certain who Süleyman Dede was.

The room became very still. "If you're willing," Reshad announced, waiting for the pause, "we can invite Dede to Los Angeles."

Reshad explained that Süleyman Loras Dede was the Sheikh

of the Whirling Dervishes — the spiritual leader from Konya, Turkey of the line of the mystical poet Rumi.

In Reshad's seminal book, *The Last Barrier*, his teacher, Bülent Rauf, (Hamid in the book), made it his mission to push Reshad to his edge as they traveled around Turkey. Bulent gave Reshad the spiritual task to pray outside Rumi's tomb in Konya for three days and three nights —

Rumi's mausoleum

knowing full well that such an act was forbidden.[1]

As is the tradition, Reshad first visited the mausoleum of Rumi's mentor, Shams of Tabriz and then walked to the courtyard of Rumi's tomb. Reshad sat on a bench to meditate, expecting a long spiritual vigil. In Reshad's words:

> I had been sitting on the bench only a short time when I felt a tap on my right shoulder. Opening my eyes required a tremendous effort, and for a moment I could not focus them. When I did, I saw a man in a uniform with a peaked cap bending over me, looking quite stern.
>
> "Yok," he said.
>
> "Yok what?" I replied, not sure what was going on.
>
> "Yok," he repeated firmly, standing up straight and pointing to the gate...

---

1. Born in 1911 into an aristocratic family in Istanbul, Bülent Rauf was an archeologist and prominent scholar of the work of Muhyiddin Ibn Arabi. Bülent translated the Fusus al-Hikam and other works of Arabi, was the honorary president of the Muhyiddin Ibn Arabi Society, and founded the Beshara School for Intensive Esoteric Education in Scotland.

The commotion drew a small crowd and a heated discussion in Turkish as the guards pointed threateningly toward the gate. Despite Reshad's protests about his teacher's special instructions and his long journey, the guards were adamant. Reshad decided to hang on and not move.

I closed my eyes once more, breathed deeply, and tried to pretend that there was no one there. For a few minutes this seemed to work, but then I felt another tap on my shoulder, this time much harder, and then someone shaking my shoulder. I continued my meditation, trying to shrug him off. But then I heard another voice, so kind and gentle that I opened my eyes to see an old man with a gray beard and a blue pinstripe suit standing there and smiling at me.[2]

It was Süleyman Dede — beloved by the townspeople as the "spiritual mayor" of Konya.

Süleyman Dede took Reshad's hands, kissed them, and raised them to his forehead in greeting. The stern frowns of the guards turned to smiles, and all was well again.

I imagined this moment, set up by Bulent and culminating with Dede embracing Reshad, as an initiation — Reshad's entry into the way of Mevlana Jalaluddin Rumi.

---

2. Feild, Reshad. *The Last Barrier.* Element Books, 1993.

We became giddy at the prospect of inviting Konya's Sheikh of the Whirling Dervishes to America — a larger-than-life spiritual figure we only knew from Reshad's book. Reshad dampened our enthusiasm with the challenge:

"You'll have to raise the money and find a translator," Reshad explained. "And understand, Dede's not glamorous. He was a humble cook who fed the poor. He's never been to America."

And just like that, the Octave shifted. If you're doing the seven-fold math, we suddenly stepped into Rumi's grand Octave. A cycle that

Dede in the courtyard of Rumi's mausoleum

started in 1273 with Rumi's death and continued for seven centuries until Dede's visit to America. To appreciate the 700-year storyline, you must follow the official history — but I'll try to keep it short:

Mevlana Jalaluddin Rumi was born in 1207 in Balkh, in present-day Afghanistan. His father and grandfather were noted Muslim clerics. When the Mongols invaded Central Asia (think of this as a world-tilting *outside shock*), Rumi's family began a 2500-mile, several-year journey to Samarkand in Uzbekistan, and then through Baghdad, Mecca, and Damascus. Along the way, Rumi met many of the great philosophers and scholars of the age. He also encountered the brigands, wanderers, Sufis, and impostors who populate his stories.[3]

Rumi's family finally settled in Konya, Turkey where his father, a noted theologian, was invited by the local ruler to establish a madrassa. The young Rumi grew to become a prodigious religious scholar in Konya with an adoring crowd of students.

One day a wandering mystic arrived in search of Rumi who was then 37 years old. In one version of the story, Rumi was on a donkey, riding past the sugar merchants when a man dressed as a beggar reached out from a doorway and grabbed the reins. It was Shams of Tabriz, a great saint who concealed himself like a rough tradesman.

Shams had been traveling for years, seeking someone who could understand his spiritual state. He lost faith in the sheikhs he encountered because none could comprehend the truth of his secrets. Shams said, "Most of these sheikhs are the bandits of Muhammad's religion. They block people's ways."[4]

Shams challenged the startled Rumi with a riddle: "Who was greater, Beyazid Bastami or the Prophet Muhammad?"

Rumi answered that the Prophet was incomparably greater, but Shams pressed further:

"Didn't the Prophet say, 'We have not known Thee as Thou ought to be known,'

Shams of Tabriz

3. Lewis, Franklin. *Rumi Past and Present, East and West.* Oneworld, 2000.
4. Can, Sefik. *Fundamentals Of Rumi's Thought.* Tughra Books, Jan 1, 2006.

whereas Bastami said, 'Glory be to me; how great is my majesty.'"

Upon hearing this, Rumi fainted at the audacity to suggest that Bastami could overshadow the Prophet. While this challenge may seem arcane, Shams threw a heretical wrench into the gears of Rumi's scholarly mind. With an awakened heart, Rumi dropped everything to follow Shams. The two began a three-year *sohbet* — a deep communion of words and silence.

Shams upended Rumi's world like a bolt of lightning — or rather, an *outside shock* that released Rumi from his scholarly life and transformed the theologian into the mystical poet of love.[5]

Rumi dropped everything to follow Shams, leaving students, school, and family behind. His students were not pleased.

Amid the jealousy, Shams disappeared once or twice, and then finally, was never found again.

According to Rumi's son, Sultan Veled (d. 1312), Sham's disappearance threw Rumi into despair:

After his departure, Rumi almost lost his mind. The Shaykh who issued religious rulings became an ardent poet of love. He was an ascetic and became a bartender, but not a bartender that drinks and sells the wine made from grapes. The spirit that belongs to the holy light does not drink anything but the wine of light.[6]

Rumi's love and bereavement for Shams found expression in an outpouring of music, dance, and lyric poems. Rumi's longing was answered with the realization:

---

5. Ibrahim Gamard reminded me of the Aflaki story where after Rumi had been absorbed in *sema* for hours, he received a request to write a legal opinion relating to religious law. Gamard explained: "One shouldn't assume that after Rumi met Shams, he stopped being a religious scholar or having anything to do with religious law, Muslim rituals, and teachings."

6. *From Sultan Veled's Ibtida Name. Quoted from Sorgenfrei, Simon. American Dervish, Making Mevlevism in the United States of America. Doctoral Dissertation, University of Gothenburg, 2013-06-07.*

"Although I am far from him in body... we both are one light."[7]

According to the 14th century Rumi biographer, Aflaki, the grieving Rumi was walking through the metalsmiths' bazaar when the tap-tap-tap of the hammers opened his heart. Round-and-round, Rumi whirled. The rhythmic tapping sounded like *zikr*, the repetition of God's name. According to tradition, this spontaneous movement begat the ceremony of the Whirling Dervishes.

Some years later, Rumi's student, Husamaddin Çelebi, asked Rumi to compose a guide to leave behind to his followers. From this prompting, poetry poured from Rumi's heart — a poetic outpouring that grew to become Rumi's magnificent opus, the *Masnavi*. With six volumes and 26,000 couplets, this multi-layered weaving of mystical fables, Koranic references, spiritual commentary, and bawdy tales is considered the most influential text in the Islamic world after the Qu'ran.

On December 17, 1273, Rumi passed from this world. Worshipers of many nationalities paid their respects — Muslims, Christians, Jews, Arabs, Persians, Turks, Greeks, and Romans. They understood what Rumi meant when he said:

I am neither from the East nor the West. No boundaries exist in my heart.

After his death, Rumi's son, Sultan Veled, started the Mevlevi Order to venerate Rumi's work. For the next 650 years, the Mevlevis performed a far-reaching role in Turkish society, touching every aspect of civic life — politics, the arts, academics, and spirituality.

The Mevlevi's influence continued to grow until 1925 when

7. *" The Quatrains of Rumi,"* p. iiiiv, *translated from Persian by Ibrahim Gamard and Ravan Farhadi).*

Mustafa Kemal Atatürk, the founder of the Republic of Turkey, waged an aggressive campaign to secularize the country to a European model. Until 1925, the Ottoman Empire was an Islamic state in which the political leader, the Sultan, was also the spiritual leader, the Caliph. Atatürk saw the caliphate as backward and corrupt compared to modern civics in the West. Atatürk felt that the Turkish Republic could not be a "nation of sheikhs, dervishes, and mystics [as the] essential aim of the *tekkes* [spiritual lodges] is to keep the people in ignorance and make them act as if they were insane."[8]

Atatürk decreed in his "Law for the Maintenance of Public Order," that all dervish *tekkes*, tombs, and schools must close, including five Mevlevi *tekkes* in Istanbul alone. Dervish practices, the office of "sheikh," whirling practice, initiations, religious garb, and books were forbidden. By Atatürk's order, the spiritual center of the Mevlevi order, which included Rumi's tomb, was made into a museum. Atatürk was quite clear, "Turkey is a modern country that had no time for dervish magic."[9]

Despite the draconian decrees, Atatürk may have been sympathetic and even aligned with the Mevlevis. He reportedly stated to the head of the Mevlevi, "You, have made a great difference in combating ignorance and religious fanaticism for centuries, as well as making contributions to science and the arts. However, we are obliged not to make any exceptions and must include Mevlevi tekkes [in the ban]. Nonetheless, the ideas and teaching of Rumi will not only exist forever, but they will emerge even more powerfully in the future."[10]

Was Atatürk sympathetic to the Mevlevis and prophetic of

8. Barnes, John R. "A Short Note on the Dissolution of the Dervish Orders in Turkey." *The Muslim World* 64, 1: 33–39, (2001).

9. Friedlander, Shems. *The Whirling Dervishes*. State University of New York Press, 1992.

10. "Mevlevi Order & Sema." n.d. International Mevlana Foundation. http://mevlanafoundation.com/mevlevi_order_en.html

Rumi's future popularity? Ibrahim Gamard, a Mevlevi scholar, casts doubt on the motive behind Atatürk's prophecy:

"In my view, Atatürk spoke as a secularist and nationalist, saying that the Mevlevi lodges will be closed and the Mevlevi tarikat [spiritual path] will be illegal, but the books and ideas of Mevlana will still be legal, and as expressions of Turkish genius, will establish new roots and strengthen Turkish culture in the future. All Turks, including Mevlevis, fervently believe Mevlana was Turkish — denying all the evidence that Rumi came from a Persian-speaking family. It is important to keep in mind that Mevlevis in Turkey revere Atatürk, as do most Turks to this day and that they have rationalized the anti-Sufi law in a way that attributes noble intentions to Atatürk."[11]

After Atatürk's decree, the authorities prohibited the sacred practice of whirling and prescribed harsh penalties for illicit worship. Twenty-eight years would pass, until 1953, before the authorities would relent and sanction a modest whirling presentation in a theater. This whirling performance grew to become an annual tourist event but accompanied with police scrutiny to suppress any overt spirituality.

Imagine the shock in America if the authorities suddenly shut down all the Christian churches and penalized overt worship. Today, traditional Sufi brotherhoods are still officially illegal in Turkey. The Mevlevis have survived by establishing an educational-cultural foundation with close ties to the Turkish Ministry of Culture and Tourism. The government stages the whirling ceremonies as cultural displays of folkloric dance — not

11. Gamard, Ibrahim. *Conversation with the author.* See: http://dar-al-masnavi.org/popularity-of-rumi.html

mystical religious practices. The government's uneasy truce with Sufism is all the more awkward because the Whirling Dervish stands as Turkey's national icon and the draw for millions of tourists annually.

Bruce drumming up business at the Sunset Boulevard rummage sale

When Reshad suggested that we raise money to invite Süleyman Dede, I knew nothing of this history. I didn't understand how our Sunset Boulevard rummage sales might release Rumi from modern bondage, or how by roaming the streets looking for restorable furniture, we might restore what Atatürk had banned.

We were young spiritual hippies riding the wave. We spotted a couch on the curb, put it up for sale and made some cash. We doubled our money when we discovered the same couch on the curb a day later. This wheeling and dealing raised $2500 in two weekends — $15,000 in today's earning power — and allowed us to bring Süleyman Dede, Konya's sheikh of the Whirling Dervishes, to America.

Süleyman Dede, or Dede, as we affectionately called him, was born in 1904 in Konya. His home was close to Rumi's mausoleum, which today is still officially a museum, but also a revered place of pilgrimage. At age fifteen, Dede began visiting the center while it was still an active dervish lodge. Three years later, he entered the Mevlevi path. Dede was twenty-one when Atatürk ordered the Mevlevi lodge to be shut down and converted into a museum.

Dede set up a soup kitchen for the poor outside the Mevlevi lodge and spent the next 23 years serving the needy in Konya. Eventually, he received the title "Dede," which means *grandfather* or *master* and is pronounced *Dey-dey*. With this title, Dede began teaching the way of Mevlana.

At the time of Atatürk's decree, Mehmet Bakir Çelebi, the thirty-first hereditary leader of Rumi's family line, was forced to move his family and the formal center of Mevlevi life to Aleppo, Syria, even though the spiritual heart of Rumi would always remain in Konya.

When Mehmet Bakir Çelebi died in 1944, his son and rightful heir, Çelaluddin was just eighteen years old and studying in Syria to become an engineer. The young Çelaluddin wasn't able

Dede's home in Konya

to assume his position as leader of the Order, so Süleyman Dede took on the traditional Konya role. Dede was given responsibility, as the "Sheikh of Konya," to welcome visitors and hold Rumi's sacred presence in Konya.

Consider the delicious synchronicity that Dede — a humble

cook who was not from the official Çelebi family line — was chosen by the Cosmos to carry the seed of Rumi to America. America's New Age wave, coupled with Reshad's book, would soon sweep Rumi to our shore — yet we had no idea what was coming.

As we washed the walls of our duplex with rose water, I imagined Dede kneeling on his Pan Am seat, prayer beads in hand, during the eleven-hour flight to Los Angeles. I thought about Dede's life journey — experiencing Rumi's full flourish as an impressionable 15-year-old, enduring government suppression for over fifty years, and now near the end of his life, receiving an invitation to restore Rumi's legacy in America.

Maybe Dede knew that Atatürk was right: Rumi would emerge stronger again — not in Turkey, but in George's Silver Lake living room.

3

"I HAVE COME FOR THE LOVERS OF MEVLANA"

When Süleyman Dede arrived at our duplex in Silver Lake, I didn't know what to expect — but hardly a diminutive Turkish gentleman in a three-piece striped suit with a pocket watch and fedora hat. I was more startled that our Sunset Boulevard rummage sale materialized a Yoda-like version of Rumi  himself. Dede's humble manner, sly twinkle, and his magnanimous affection took a moment to process. His voice resonated with the velvety tone that soothes small infants. Even Dede's cigarettes were lit like sticks of holy incense or smudge.

Our Silver Lake duplex quickly buzzed with people seeking contact with our munificent guest. Imagine a hothouse in the garden of Mevlana where the fertile ground was being turned for 700-year-old seeds to sprout.

Note: If you wish to listen to the original audio for this chapter, visit youtube.com/ithoutv: *Süleyman Dede in Los Angeles, April 19, 1976.* Additional speakers include Günes, our translator, Reshad Feild, and David Bellak.

David Bellak served as Dede's secretary, personal interpreter, and companion for the journey. After serving as a U.S. Navy deck officer during the Vietnam War, David studied to become a photographer and subsequently traveled the world on a photographic journey and spiritual search. When David visited Konya, Turkey in 1972, he was "found" by Dede, who invited him to lunch. The connection

David Bellak initiated as a sheikh in Dede's in Konya home, 1976

continued to grow as David became Dede's *murid* (student), interpreter, secretary, and assistant – ultimately becoming Dede's *wakil* after completing the 1001-day training, or *çille*, under Dede's guidance.

"During this time I was considered to be a member of Dede's family," David explained to me. "Much to my embarrassment, Dede would remark to his many foreign visitors, 'I have four sons and a daughter, and David is my fifth son.'"

As I worked with David on this manuscript, I began to appreciate the heroic nature of Dede's journey to America. David described the obstacles he and Dede faced to travel to Los Angeles:

After Dede received the invitation to Los Angeles in February, he needed to get a passport and an exit visa — the latter was available for business people, academics, and government officials, but generally not for ordinary citizens, and certainly not an elderly grandfather with no position.

Early on a Sunday morning in early March, Dede came to my room dressed, as always, in his striped three-piece suit, tie, and gold watch chain across his waistcoat. I quickly got dressed as Dede shared his plan while sitting on the bed:

"We'll get a bus first thing tomorrow to Ankara," Dede plotted. "We'll head to the government offices, chatting here and there to find out what we can do without arousing suspicion."

Dede at his home in Konya

Dede and I spent much time discussing how to proceed without raising the suspicions and interests of the government, police or local busy-bodies.

Why would a simple trip to the passport office need such discretion? At one level, Dede did not want to attract any attention from official quarters because someone somewhere could cause problems for no reason whatsoever. At the time, I did not have a clear understanding of the issues. At another level, during the early 20th century, Turkey had undergone major social and political upheavals. The collapse of the Ottomans, the aftermath of World War I, political instability, growing anarchy, and economic decline all contributed to a climate of insecurity. What's more, the Sufi brotherhoods had been dismantled. At that time, they were only being kept alive in secret — "under the table." Paranoia was palpable.

In some ways, I was oblivious to the risks Dede was taking. Years later, I was told that I had been under surveillance at times during my visits to Konya. I recall being escorted by plainclothes police from the city's small rail station on the night of my first visit by train in November 1972.

I also remember bombs going off on Konya's main boulevard on New Year's at midnight across from my hotel. On one occasion, while I was staying with Dede, he awakened me at one in the morning, and with urgency instructed me to come downstairs where they were watching the television news. I didn't understand much, so he "translated" for me. The government had just decreed that anyone hosting foreigners or even visitors from other districts must report the details to the police. Dede told me to move out first thing in the morning, so I did, to the Olgun Palas Hotel.

This was the backdrop for our trip to the Ankara passport office. When Dede suggested that we head to the government offices and chat here and there, I was filled with alarm. "No, Baba. No! This isn't right!"

Dede regarded me with puzzlement and concern. From the earliest days after receiving the invitation from Los Angeles, Dede was excited yet pessimistic, always questioning how we would do this and that, where the money would come from, and, I think, reluctant to get his hopes up.

I wadded some writing paper and tossed it to the floor. His eyes grew big.

"What's that?" Dede asked. "

"Baba, listen, this paper is like throwing a piece of meat," I warned. "Flies will come from everywhere! Going around Ankara is too dangerous. Everyone, all the politicians and officials will be asking questions."

Dede's eyes grew wide.

"You're right!" he exclaimed. "Everyone will wonder who is this old man going to America. What should we do?"

We sat in silence smoking our cigarettes.

Suddenly Dede announced, "Tomorrow we go to Ankara, and we'll think of something; let God direct us. Meet me at the bus station at 9 o'clock in the morning."

And with that, Dede hurried home.

I had now been with Dede, and in his service as a murid, for nearly four years. I was accustomed to how he could materialize results when they were needed. It would be discourteous to inquire about his plan until he asked for my thoughts. Later, I realized that every undertaking with Dede invoked the subtle worlds. This adventure would be no different.

We met the next morning at the Konya bus station for the three-and-a-half-hour trip to the capital, Ankara. During the trip, Dede frequently engaged other passengers, often fielding questions about the tall yabancı (foreigner) accompanying him.

Once in Ankara, we walked through the crowded, smoke-filled streets in search of the passport office. Dede suddenly announced, "Come on, we'll get a dolmuş (a shared taxi on a set route).

Ten minutes later, we were pushing our way through crowded

office corridors, Dede leading the way, and sometimes holding my hand. Finally, we entered a large waiting area, where, in the back, inside a private office, the harassed-looking office director was fielding phone calls, stamping forms, barking at couriers, and shuffling stacks of folders. Without hesitation, Dede walked into her office, interrupted a conversation, and chatted her up about needing a passport.

Deferring politely to his age, but also responding brusquely, the woman directed Dede to the proper office and procedure. But Dede continued chatting away as though ignoring her, talking about his family, how it was his duty to teach this tall yabancı (me) to be a good Muslim, and how he was invited to America to teach Islam. I was embarrassed that Dede kept going on, intruding on this woman's busy day.

After 90 minutes, and several glasses of tea that she had ordered, the woman suddenly called someone in, gave the man a folder of papers, and ordered for him to attend to it.

Soon after, the gentleman returned with the required document. She looked exasperated but relieved. With decorum and humbleness, Dede rose, shook hands with the woman, thanked her profusely, apologized for intruding, prayed for her health, and for her family, bestowed God's blessings, then quickly led the way out.

Back in the corridor, Dede growled, "Come on, let's get out of here." Nothing more was said until we arrived back at the bus station for Konya.

Through grace or wits, Dede managed to get a passport, air ticket, and the exit visa, and now he was sitting in the living room of our duplex in Silver Lake. After we cleared the table, and the room became quiet, Dede shared the reason why he came to America:

"*Efendim*, my good friends. I have come here for the lovers of Mevlana."

Dede seemed simple in his manner, but in a disarming way that instantly melted my concerns that our guest might be grandiose or formal. As Dede spoke, I felt intimately connected to Mevlana.

"Mevlana is universal, embracing the whole world," Dede continued. "In coming here, I said to myself, 'More and more people are loving Rumi, loving Mevlana. *Maâşallah*, with God's will, Mevlana is here in Los Angeles!'"

I tried to connect the dots that brought me to this moment, but instead, I took comfort in the inexplicable — that somehow my path had intersected with Rumi.

Dede continued:

"When I arrived in Los Angeles, I said to myself, 'God has willed it. This place is like the *Dergâh*, the traditional dervish lodge. Mevlana is here! They do *semâ*, whirling, they do *zikr*, invocation, they show *muhabbet*, affection towards Mevlana, and they read the glorious Masnavi. So what are they, if not Mevlevis?'

"*Hazrati* (His Holiness) Mevlana declared seven hundred years ago: 'There are not many people who recognize us today,' Dede explained, 'But, in the future, many more people will emerge who recognize us from the heart.'

"Seven hundred years into the future, I received a letter from Reshad that included a picture of Mevlana. (Dede described a flyer for the Institute for Conscious Life). A rainbow beam of His Holiness Mevlana travels towards this lodge of theirs. At that moment, I felt a bond of heart. I said to myself, 'O God! How great a love is this? They know about many things, but I did not know that it was at this level.'"

(Reading Dede's translation for the first time, I am startled to learn that my innocent flyer played a role in his decision to come to America.)

Dede continued: "I said to myself, 'God has willed! This man, Reshad, is very loyal to *Hazrati* Mevlana.' I decided to visit this man in America. As I am here now, I see Reshad as if a form of *Nûr*, the Light."

The translator asked Dede to explain the story again about the picture and the beam of light.

"On the picture Reshad sent, a beam of light emanates from Mevlana to their lodge. Seeing this, I thought, 'These people revere Mevlana in a genuine way.' There is so much imitation of reverence for Mevlana, even in Istanbul and all around Turkey. People who show the level of affection I find here are very rare. This made me realize, as Mevlana stated 700 years ago, that one day those from the West would understand us. Hence, the Americans who invited me are the ones who understand.[1]

"Many people come to Konya to visit me at great expense. They show such kindness and manners when they visit our desolate house. (The translator interrupts, *Estağfurullah*. Translates as "may God grant me mercy," but used here to acknowledge Dede's humbleness about his house).

"The visitors talk in English, and I talk in Turkish, yet we understand each other. I understand what the visitors are saying by observing their manners and movements.

"So, what do I do with these visitors? Some want to see the archaeological museum and others want to learn about Mevlana. This *fakir* (Dede refers to himself as the *poor one*) is the only one left in Konya, the location of the central Mevlevi lodge, which Atatürk converted into a museum."

---

1. Ibrahim Gamard refutes this prophecy of Rumi's emergence in the West at: http://www.dar-al-masnavi.org/rumi-prophecies.html

Dede slicing bread at home

Then Dede shared a startling bit of history:

"At the start of Republic era, the founding of modern Turkey, Atatürk banned all the Sufi sects."

The translator interjected, "*Evet... evet* (yes, yes)."

"But not Mevlana!" Dede exclaimed.

"Not Mevlana?" Günes asked.

"It was because Atatürk himself was Mevlevi," Dede explained.

"*Tabi! Tabi* (sure, sure)," Günes affirmed. In fact, she confirmed the point twice to make sure.

"Since Atatürk was a Mevlevi himself," Dede explained, "he converted the *Dergâh* into a museum, but he also gave us a chance. Don't mention this to the group: During one month of the year, we were told to perform this ritual of ours, but presented as a show, this praying and favoring of God by order of Atatürk.

"Through this show, people could discover what 'being human' is. They could witness the quality of praying and the type of human that is desired by God.

Atatürk visits Mevlana's tomb, March 22, 1923

"Today, visitors come to our rituals from many backgrounds. I even see Buddhists visit the turning ritual. And then after a while, I see them return as Mevlevis with the manners, morals, and respect of our tradition. And you, you are also welcome to visit us — to come to the source water of Rumi's spiritual spring.

To the translator: "Go ahead, tell them what you intend."

Günes translated Dede's statement that Atatürk was a Mevlevi. This historical quirk meant nothing to me back then, but reading it now, I'm puzzled: How was it that Atatürk, who famously shut down the Sufi brotherhoods, banned their practices, and shuttered their holy sites, could be a Mevlevi? I asked Sinan, my translator, to replay the tape and translate again for accuracy. Sinan's direct translation of Dede came back:

> As known, all of the tarikat were banned after the start of Republic era. But now Mevlana! It is because Atatürk was Mevlevi himself. Since he was a Mevlevi himself, he converted this location into a museum, but he has also given us a chance. (to Günes) Don't mention them about this; during one month of the twelve months of a year, we were told to perform this ritual of ours, this praying and favoring of God (İbadet ve Taat) by the order of Atatürk.

I wish I could have asked Dede to clarify his statement about

Atatürk, but I knew nothing of the history. Recently, another piece of this puzzle fell into place when David Bellak shared a story:

I returned to Konya in the autumn of 1975 for my third visit to Konya and my sheikh. I was unsure as to why, but my heart's voice assured me that I would stay until whatever was being asked was completed. Dede and and his wife, Farişta were warmly welcoming; they even told me to call them Baba (Father) and Anne (Mother).

As time passed, I visited their home most days, helping out or just being there, slowly absorbing Turkish, learning to make tea or running errands. At other times I was about the town exploring and photographing.

On one occasion they were spring cleaning and whitewashing the walls of the small upstairs landing. This required removing the many photographs on display. Dede pointed to the stack of pictures on a table and asked me to help re-install the framed photographs and hangings.

I took each picture, held it against the wall, and asked him where it was to go. Near the bottom of the stack, I picked up a full printed page from a newspaper. Turning it over, I found a photo of Kemal Atatürk, founder of the Republic, staring at me.

I raised it up and blurted, "Dede, why is this picture here? Atatürk did not like people like us! He closed Hazrati Mevlana's dergah!"

I was startled that my outburst may have overstepped the boundaries of the Master-murid relationship.

Dede held the photo for a moment, contemplated silently, then quietly said, "Ataturk was a great man, and he was a Mevlevi."

Without further elaboration, he indicated a new place on the wall for it to be affixed.

I have long pondered why Dede was so clear and definite about Atatürk, a view at odds with everything I had been led to believe — particularly since Ataturk was so reviled in the religious communities, and certainly reviled in Konya.

One day, years later, it finally made perfect sense. I firmly believe that Dede knew exactly what he was talking about. Getting to that conclusion about Atatürk, however, required a great leap of faith and understanding about the process of rebirth and renewal.

At the time of Dede's talk, the Atatürk statement flew past everyone in the room. Dede continued:

"Mevlana said, 'This is the *Kaaba* of the Lovers (referencing the pilgrimage site in Mecca). For those who visit Mevlana, it is the same as *yedi bin yedi yüz yetmiş yedi* — 7,777 pilgrimages to Mecca. For this reason, you need to come to Konya and visit Rumi's *Dergâh* — the house of Mevlana.[2]

"If you choose to come, you should never worry about the money because God will provide for you. Alas, I wish I had so much money! I would pay for all of you to visit! It would cost a fortune, but what would I do instead?"

George spoke up: "May I ask a question? I'm a little clumsy with this, but how should we relate to Islam?"

The translator explained to Dede that these people are Sufis, but not Muslims.

Dede whispered back to the translator, "Yes, they are not Muslims, but they have a strong inclination to Islam. I think they

2. According to Ibrahim Gamard, This is not a quote from Rumi, but from another Persian Sufi poet, Jami (d. 1492), It is the first verse of a quatrain inscribed above the doorway to the mausoleum in Konya.

would find satisfaction in Islam. How should I tell them about this? Can you explain that they already have the state of mind and behavior demanded by Islam? They show love, and affection and they pray regularly. *Kelime-i Şehadet — There is no god but God. Muhammad is the messenger of God.*"

Dede replied to George, "I often ask people, 'Do you want to become a Muslim?' And, the people reply, 'We love Mevlana.' And I respond, 'Mevlana was a Muslim; you can also become a Muslim.'

"Then they ask how can this be done? And I tell them about the Five Pillars of Islam and the Six Articles of Faith, the *Amentü Billahi* prayer. With these, you are a Muslim."

After a back and forth about the details of becoming a Muslim, Dede discussed the importance of charity on the path:

"It is essential that you be charitable with each other, and to people in need, and especially to the people you encounter on the street. The poor people have a share in your earnings."

The translator asked Dede if, according to Islam, one should donate 1/40th of one's total wealth to the poor?

Dede replied, "Yes, it is 1/40th, but do not mention it now — not everything all at once."

I asked David Bellak to comment on these questions about Islam based on his years with Dede:

"This characterizes Dede's approach with his Western visitors and audiences. He understood the emotional and cultural barriers to Islam — that if he focused on Islam, ears, and hearts would close. So, he focused incessantly on love (Aşk/Ishq), the desire of God that his creation should remember and come to Him. Dede sought to clarify, beyond the misrepresentation in the media, how simple the way of Islam (submission) is."

Dede speaks to guests in our Silver Lake duplex.

Dede continued, "Let me tell them a story for the sake of humor. One day, a spiritual leader, the *imam*, arrived at a village and saw that the villagers were not attending the mosque.

"He asked the villagers, 'You are Muslims; why don't you come to the mosque?'

"They replied, 'We are shepherds and farmers. To pray in the mosque, we must take off our shoes for ritual ablution. If we take the time to remove our shoes and wash, the sun will continue to rise on our fields. If we abandon our herds, the animals will trample the crops, causing great harm.'

"So, the imam told them to come to the mosque with their shoes on. And with this, they came to pray regularly wearing shoes.

"After a while, the imam got assigned to another location. A new imam came to the village and saw people praying with their shoes on.

"The new imam scolded them, 'You malignant ones, how dare you enter with the same shoes you wear in the barn!'

"The villagers replied, 'This is how we were taught by the previous imam.'

"So, the new imam summoned the former imam for an explanation.

"The old imam explained, 'I got them into the mosque with their shoes on! Your job is to get them to take them off.'

"This is how we come into Islam," Dede explained. "With or without our shoes."

David Bellak comments: "This story also illustrates Dede's approach. In the years I knew him, I can count on one hand the number of times he was adamant on how his visitors must approach the Islamic rites. More importantly, he was perceptive at 'reading hearts' — knowing what was contained therein."

Dede continued: "I have a second story that illustrates this differently."

"A Buddhist who had fallen in love with Mevlana arrived to visit us in Konya with his entire family.

"The Buddhist said, 'I love Mevlana so deeply that I traveled here all the way from Thailand.'

"So I asked the Buddhist, 'As you know, *Hazrati* Mevlana was a Muslim; are you a Muslim too?'

"I had the feeling, a knowing, that the Buddhist was a *true* Muslim. But, to clarify, I told him about the Five Pillars of Islam and the Six Articles of Faith. I told him that if he fulfilled these, he would become a Muslim.

"This man could speak several languages including French, so I found a French-speaking student from the Islam Studies Institute who taught the Buddhist visitor how to pray, how to wash for the ritual ablution and the Al-Fatiha prayer — the entire training in five days! Then he learned the *Surah al-Ikhlas* and I told him, 'My Son, you have become a Muslim. You can go now.'

"Eight years later, I received a letter from him. He wrote, 'We have found a true guide, a *murshid* in Indonesia. We are part of a group there, eighteen people in total, and we are fasting through the month of Ramadan.'

Dede turned toward the translator: "Tell them about this as you wish. The people in this room are in a true state of being Muslim. From my perspective, they are all shining, *mücella*, or polished. Looking into their being, I feel as if I see myself in them. Even further, I feel ashamed."

Startled by such an admission, the translator replied, "*Estağfurullah!*"

Dede paused to consider. "Maybe, don't tell them about this, but look, these people are so clean indeed! Is this not what being a Muslim is?

"Thank God, thank God! All of you, say: 'Thank God!' "*La ilaha illallah, Muhammed-ür Rasulullah,*" let's hear it! *Eşhedü enla ilahe illallah,* come on! *La ilahe illallah, Muhammed-ür Rasulullah!* (*Crowd joining*).

"So, what are these people now? Muslims! They have just told the *Shahada* — the Muslim profession of faith.

"Our Holy Book, the Holy Quran, accepts the legitimacy of all prophets in history. Not once is a separation considered between *Hazrati* Muhammad, *Hazrati* Jesus or *Hazrati* Moses. All of the prophets that have come since Adam are believed to be Muslims — but with different laws. Nevertheless, they were all Muslims.

"Therefore, a Muslim will not say anything critical of any prophet. We cannot say such things. It's impossible because the laws associated with each prophet are good. However, since the last prophet is Muhammad, *peace be upon him,* we act in accordance with his laws.

"When *Hazrati* Jesus arrived, he declared his laws to his people.

You know this story. Many people had faith in him and became his followers. Before Jesus, people followed the laws of *Hazrati* Moses. According to the Quran, 'The truth of the Bible, the Torah, and the Psalms are embodied in the Quran, including all the laws of all the earlier prophets, who were the most beloved servants of God."

The translator whispered that she was shy about translating.

Dede leaned over and asked, "What is there to be shy about? We are not telling lies here. We tell what we have heard from our parents."

The translator replied that she was concerned whether her translation was thorough.

"You translate very well," Dede assured her. "I can read it from their eyes. I see their faith and understanding."

David adds to this passage:

"This is another example of Dede's capacity to read hearts. In the Mathnawi, Rumi alludes many times to the polishing of the heart, which, when clean of all defilement, then reflects the Truth of the Divine."

A woman asked: "There are some things that concern me in the Quran where it mentions that there is a time for killing and a time for peace. I was wondering about the Muslims killing the Christians and feeling justified. I'm sure that it is my ignorance, but I would like this clarified."

The translator translated the question to Dede, explaining that the participant must be confused.

"No, she did not mention a misunderstanding," Dede said. "She was clear in her question. I will provide her with an answer.

"*Efendim*, my good fellows. There were wars during the times of *Hazrati* Jesus; people killed each other during the times of Moses as well.

"The human is such a sacred being. Everything that has been created by God in the perfection of Cosmos is assigned to the order of humans. Air, water, fire, what we eat and drink – all these countless blessings have been given to us. Even the angels are assigned to the order of humans.

"Why did God do so? God desired it, and so God willed it to be. It is because God is autonomous in everything — this is how God willed it to be.

"By the time God created the souls of humans, both demons and angels were subject to humans. But Satan picked some people and misled them. Despite this, whatever we see and experience in this Cosmos of Perfection is meant to be for humans. It is for us! It might be that we wish not to be humans. God, on the other hand, says: 'Be human! I have given you everything. I have provided you with wisdom, ideas, with food and drink. I honored you with many blessings. It is for you to get to know me, love me, avoid evil doings and be afraid of my torment.'

"Regarding war, in any given country, always, everywhere, at any given moment — even now — there are people who are occupied with *eating* their own. We will not call them humans. Hence they are demons disguised in the qualities of a human."

The translator reminded Dede of the question and the particular passage in the Quran about the killing of Christians.

"By no means!" Dede countered. "There is no such thing! It is not about people killing Christians. The book says: 'The laws of Christianity are no more applicable. Now is the time for being a Muslim, hence become a Muslim yourselves. Show your faith in this book.'

"There is no such thing in the Quran ordering to kill Christians, by no means! There are English translations of Quran; she can go ahead and read those."

The translator asked the questioner, "Did I understand correctly? Did you say that it says in Quran to kill the Christians?"

"It says that there was a time for killing," the questioner replied. "And then I correlated that with the Muslims killing the Christians."

"Dede says that there is no such thing in the Quran. And it never says, 'The killing of Christians is justified.'"

David intervened to clarify that the related word in Quran should be *"kafir"* (non-believer) not "Christian." The translator explained this to Dede.

"It seems that she has misunderstood it," Dede replied to the translator.

"My daughter, *'kafir'* refers to people who deny the existence of God," Dede explained. "We do not deny the existence of God, neither do the Christians! If someone denies the existence of *God the Truth* from pure spite, rejecting to acknowledge God, this person will become a *kafir*.

"In the Quran, however, there are no instructions to kill the non-believers. The Quran says instead to handle them with *hilm*, with *softness* and beauty. Demonstrate the existence of God. Ask them, if there were no God, how could all these blessings come into existence all by themselves? Tell them with softness, and then also by showing that you feel offended. Tell them that they were ill, but they have healed. Tell them that *God the Almighty* performed the healing with the force and power of God.

"If this person still keeps saying, 'I will not acknowledge that God!' — only then does this person become a non-believer. The book does not order killing them. By no means, there is no such order for killing.[3]

"It is not only our beloved prophet Muhammad, peace and blessings be upon him, who expressed it this way, but all the prophets of history as well. In the Bible of His Holiness Jesus,

3. Kabir Helminski offers a thoughtful discussion on the Quran passages in question: http://www.huffingtonpost.com/kabir-helminski/does-the-quran-really-adv_b_722114.html

there is no order for killing the people. He advised loving and showing compassion instead. The same with Moses and David.

"Do you know how a human can be killed? Only if a human commits such a crime that even animals would not commit. The divine laws prescribe the eradication of a human if this human killed someone else. Because this human will damage and harm humankind further, they will hang him, execute him, or eradicate him accordingly."

Dede leaned toward the translator: "Have they been satisfied with the answer? This is the point. In Islam, there is no such thing as killing someone because he is Jewish, Muslim, Christian, Buddhist or some other communion.

"With the will of God, *Eyvallah*. Thank you! Accept it as it is!

Selim asked, "What is the way or *tarikat* of Mevlana?"

"The way of Mevlana is identical to your way of being here," Dede replied. "*Tarikat* means a *yol* (Turkish word for road or path). This follows the path you have chosen — through whirling, wishing for goodness and peace, loving humans and bestowing affection and love on others. This is what Islam is about; there is no such other thing."

"It's hard to know how to go about this process of loving everybody," Selim pointed out.

Dede gestured toward Reshad, "Look at the illuminated face of this person for the sake of God! Have a look! It is shining! Is there supposed to be a better state of Islam than this? Have a look! O God, O God! Come here; I will kiss you on your cheeks! Come over here! I am passed out by the love of this person!

"The love of this gentleman, this friend and brother, has brought me here. Because I deeply admire him, I decided, under any circumstance or cost, I will travel to America, and I will meet him."

Reshad, sounding weak, offered regrets: "Apologize to Dede

that I did not eat dinner. Tell him that I have not eaten today, and I will not eat until my body obeys me."

Dede was startled to hear this and replied, "Now, I will say something. Reshad has received an inspiration that is of his own consignment. He does this as he finds fit. But I should quickly note as a poor, helpless person myself..."

"*Estağrufullah,*" the translator intervened.

Dede continued: "Fasting is to be performed, but not by torturing the self-psyche, the *nafs*. Suppose someone gets upset and begins fasting as an act of protest and continues until death? We have heard of such people. This is forbidden in Islam! Since this body is sacred and is required to perform invocation, one is obligated to feed it. The annual fasting (of Ramadan) is meant to cleanse your self-psyche. This is all about cleansing our psyche and not that God will become bigger or smaller because of our actions.

"Is this not so? The purpose of fasting is to cleanse your self-psyche and to understand the plight of those with hunger. Otherwise, it is self-torture. God tells us to eat and drink from the blessings of God. In all God's books, in the New Testament, the Torah, in Psalms, and in the Quran, it says, 'Eat and drink, but do not waste.'"

Reshad jumped in, "Before you translate, I would like to say that I do not speak Ottoman Turkish, but in 24 hours, I do. If you open your heart, you will hear his heart. You will hear it completely."

Reshad continued: "Twenty-two years ago, I started on this path. Some of you have been on it a few months; some a year or two. It is only One — One Life."

Switching gears again, Reshad chastised: "Why is it when I asked you... I asked you to record all this. Who did I ask to do this?"

Someone told Reshad that the talk was being taped.

Reshad changed the subject: "When I started this journey, I was very young, just ten years old. I knew I knew nothing. But then, I thought I knew something..."

Dede interjected: "Where does it originate from, that Reshad *Bey*, Reshad *Efendi* has given his heart since the age of ten? As God the Almighty created the souls, God has assigned each of them with a rank, with a duty. The duty of our brother Reshad was given to Mevlana's path. He was told to lead this path; he was told to be a Mevlevi, and God created him.

"We can follow this path if we choose, or not if we choose. It's all up to you. If we choose not to do it, you are accountable in the eyes of God.

"Since God has bestowed Reshad with this blessing, it is his duty to perform this." Dede turned to the translator: "Relate this exactly and without retouching!"

After Günes translated, Dede asked her: "May God be pleased with you! Where did you come from, my daughter? I will pray for you."

Günes said she needed a prayer as she will be traveling to Istanbul.

Dede replied, "In the truth of God, I will pray for you in such a hearted way. As you will be traveling to Istanbul, when is it?"

"I will be traveling on June 1," Günes replied.

"I will provide you with prayers before you go," Dede replied. "Sometimes, people ask me to pray on behalf of a sick person in the presence of Mevlana. I am neither a so-called 'breath healer,' *Üfürükçü*, nor a 'prayer healer,' *Okuyucu*."

Günes again said that she needed a prayer.

"Look, my daughter, I have witnessed the effect of prayer so many times. Each year, my wife and I go to the thermal springs. Last year, Hasan, a rich factory owner who owned a Cadillac also visited the springs with his wife. After sitting with him for three or four days, I asked him why he came to the springs.

"He replied, 'Do not ask about it, Dede.'

"'What is it?' I asked.

"He said, 'I have been given everything by God — so much money, factories to run.' He was a paint manufacturer.

"'But, I do not have any children,' he explained. 'I was told that God would give me a child if I came to this Turkish bath. That is the reason I am here.'

"I told him; 'My brother, please come to the presence of Mevlana and give your prayers. May God provide you with a child, *Inshallah,* if God wills!' I said this because I have numerous experiences involving deaf-mutes who began to speak from such prayers.

"So I told this man, 'Come to visit us in Konya. We will pray together and wish a child for you.'

"He responded, 'My good fellow, my workers have gone on strike. I must return to my factory. Please, pray on my behalf!'

Dede in prayer in Konya

"So, I sought refuge, *niyâze,* in the presence of Mevlana and prayed: 'Oh God! Your Holiness Mevlana, you are universal. For the sake of you, may you bestow a child to this servant of yours, Hasan. He assigned this request to me, and I am forwarding it to you. May God be my witness!'

"Seven months later, Hasan wrote, 'My wife is pregnant.'

"I replied, 'If it's a boy, name him Hüsamettin and if a girl, Kerra, a *red-hot cinder.*'

"We continued to write letters. Hasan sent a thank-you saying, 'It was due to *barakah* — from the spiritual abundance of your prayers that this happened.'

"I wrote back saying that it had nothing to do with the abundance of *my* prayers; it was due to the abundance of Mevlana, that great Sultan. Hence God will accept your prayers; they will not be rejected."

Dede mentioned his struggle with smoking to explain how God accepts our prayers.

"I pray every day until the evening. I performed the pilgrimage two times so far. I pray, 'O God, this cursed thing devastates me,' yet I keep smoking. My prayers are not accepted.

"I prayed for Hasan. I became the means, *vasıta*, for it. God accepted my prayer and gave him a child. I have various experiences in this way. Therefore... I am missing my point..."

The translator reminded Dede that he was going to pray for her.

"I will gladly pray for you. That you will fulfill your wishes and become attained.

"And now for everyone, I pray for you. May God be with you! May God fulfill your aims, answer your wishes, and protect you from evil — that you become *insan-ı kamil* (perfected human), to become exactly the humans that God wants! This is our invocation.

"You are like a mirror to look at. I read everything from your mirror appearance. When I give these talks, they all originate from your soul."

Dede interrupted the translator while she was speaking.

"Tell them about my cigarette situation as well," Dede suggested.

"Tell them that your prayers were not accepted for quitting smoking?" Günes asked.

Dede corrected, "Not that the prayers were not accepted, but rather... that I could not be content with myself with my situation.

In a way, it is like the saying: '*The Lover is not to be discredited; he has an addiction; what is he to do?*'"

Dede gestured to the group.

"Genuine dervishes, the state of these people; they are genuine dervishes. I am the one sitting on the Post, but I could not become a true dervish. These people, they are all dervishes! They are the type of dervishes that God favors."

Dede pointed out someone in the group, "This one does it in the same manner that His Holiness Moses did it.

"I am seventy-four years old. I have witnessed many such miracles in my life — the prayers of Mevlana are *admitted*. He said it himself, as do all of the holy books which say: *"Those who show affection to us, those who join under our wings...* (to the translator: 'Tell this next bit as you find fit') *...they will all have bodies of glittering gold. Similarly, those who join under my sikke, my precious metal, those who follow my path, they will all become golden.'*

"This is not gold that money is made from; the precious metal here indicates a precious state. If you show affection to His Holiness Mevlana, you will become gold."

Reshad intervened, again in his fasting voice: "*Estağfurullah...* Please hear. This is particularly for you all. Mevlana and Jesus are the same person. There is no difference. There is no difference. I'll try to put it into English."

Reshad continued, "When there is the Second Coming — which can be now because there is only now — all the sins, which is a lack... What is a lack? It's a lack of knowledge. Prior to that, we have to be quite clear, since we are not our bodies, but our bodies are necessary for what has to be. If our bodies do not obey us; if our emotions do not obey us, and our thoughts do not obey us, we will demand that they do obey us. And when they obey us, that is the Second Coming. Mevlana is... How can I put this to you... Hazrati Mevlana is the secret, but you have the secret, but you just don't know that you have the secret."

Reshad turned to the translator. "Could you explain... Mevlana is the secret; they have the secret, but they just don't know they have the secret?"

"Dede was saying more or less the same thing," the translator replied sweetly, "about half an hour ago. He said that every human is a Muslim in essence."

Reshad changed the subject, addressing Günes. "When I heard your name, I said, 'Yes, she is the one. The last one was thrown out."

"Why is that?" Günes asked.

Dede jumped in before Reshad could answer.

"Yes, all religion is the religion of the Muslim. 'Muslim' is just a name. The holy books say, 'Any child born from the mother is born Muslim.' Thank God, we are all Muslim! God be praised.

"Don't you say, 'Thank God?' Thank God for our health! Thank God for our sight! For our hearing, talking! Thanking God means praising God. Thank God, that You have given us these blessings. O God, we thank you!

"Is that not so? God has given us sight, hearing, gathered us here, and let us talk in this way. This is what His Holiness Mevlana says:

"'All thankfulness and appreciation, all gratitude and indebtedness, for the creation of humans, creation of the djinns in compliance with humans. Now that I, the Adam (human) am provided with language, and since such a long time has been giving its response, we will be thankful, that God the Truth has given us this language.'

"Look, how beautiful it is that we have gathered! How we have loved each other, shown each other affection. Would we be here if we did not love each other?

"If we had a single discourteous, nâdân, person among us, I would not be able to speak further. Nobody would be able to speak. How am I able to speak? I more or less guess and feel what you want me to say. This makes me happy. I thank God that we can be together and enjoy good conversation."

Reshad interjected: "In America, there's no conversation. Nobody ever talks to each other. Conversation *yok*."

Reshad continued, "I have been trying since I came to this country to encourage conversation — to get people to actually talk to one another."

"Even if there hasn't been conversation, there will be now," Dede assured.

Everyone laughed.

"These people entered this community — *uşşak halakası*, this ring of Lovers," Dede explained. "If that were not so, they would not have been able to participate, and not a single word would have been spoken.

"See, this tall man here, he is following everything. He has been coming for three days. If he did not get a taste, he would not have joined us even if we forced him with a stick."

Dede pointed toward another person: "What a gentleman, have a look. Like a lion! He has Love! He has affection! He gets up all of a sudden, and dances!"

Dede asked Ayisha, "Go find my wallet and bring it here; there is a piece of paper — wait a second, here, there is this. (He pulls a bank receipt out of his pocket.) I would like to read a poem to you. Yes, it is on a bank receipt; I had to exchange money on the way here. They would not allow me to get here without foreign money. We paid a load of money to be able to see these beloved ones."

"I will knead the bread," Reshad offered metaphorically. "Dede will bake it."

"I have delivered you further," Dede said. "Let *it* bake you! Thank God, he has baked himself already. Anyhow, I cannot locate it."

Since the poem was not on the receipt, Dede shared it from memory:

"Come to the lodge of Mevlana; see such enjoyment! Mevlana says, 'There is Love, there is Affection; there are Words and Songs. There is *kudüm* (drum), and there is *ney* (reed flute).'

"In our path, there are songs; there are words, there is Affection, there is Love, there is Love! Such is our dervish lodge.

"It is not what *raw* people would imagine it to be.

"It is a lodge of Love; we have an endless Love, we see everything Good; we see nothing of Bad, *inshallah*.

"This is our path. If God wills, may it be your path as well, if God wills, *inshallah*."

Reshad jumped in: "If it is not possible for them to go to Konya, to the lodge, maybe it's possible for the *tekke*, the dervish lodge to come here."

This was not correctly translated for Dede. The translator forwarded the reverse in Turkish: "Instead of the lodge coming here, is it possible for us to get there?"

Dede replied, "Look, *Hazrati* Mevlana says, 'Those who come from my blood are my children. But my true children are those who follow my path.' Lodges are everywhere. Masjids, mosques are everywhere. Wherever you pray, it is a masjid there.

"*In a house, in an idolatry house, in a ruined house, in a drinking house, I call you. O Beloved Friend!*' he says. God is there, wherever you call upon God.

"Thank God, that you already have a presence (referring to Reshad) to teach and counsel you, to advise you here. You are bonded to such a person. This man has given his heart to *Hazrati* Mevlana.

"I would tell you: 'Whatever you need to look for, look for it here.' This person is capable of presenting Mevlana's work and showing the true path. When someone has been given this grace, *Lütuf*, they should take it from him and act accordingly.

"Since I am a guest here, this quote would count for me too:

"Those seeing once will not see it (him) again. Neither will they be able to give its (his) worth for a purchase.

"Estağfurullah."

"Mashallah," everyone replied in unison.

Dede at home in Konya

Dede continued: "I came from Konya for the sake of Reshad's love. Likewise, if you wish, you can visit me. Thank God, you are here! Everyone gets what is predestined, *nasip,* for them.

"This is a spiritual dining table. A predestined dining table was drawn and you arrived to receive the blessings. This is how a spiritual dining table works.

"A human needs a spiritual guide, a teacher to help enlighten

69

the soul. If a student does not go to school and does not sit at the desk, can this student learn something by oneself? A student needs a school to become a human — to gain the necessary attributes. The school is here; the teacher is here."

Reshad interjected again with unexpected pathos: "I only want the Truth. That is all I want. To find the Truth, it is necessary to die... in life..."

"Excuse me, excuse me!" Dede interrupted emphatically. "To die does not mean to eradicate for good. Humans carry so many problems; these problems even come to mind while praying. You have to withdraw from your problems. With this withdrawing, comes the state described as to *die before dying.* You should withdraw from your problems and follow this path. This is how it works. This is how the Cosmos revolves. The Cosmos is structured in this manner. If you keep attending this lodge, you will learn many things, and your hearts will be filled with Light and Love. Every human needs a teacher, a mentor, a spiritual guide."

Dede quoted, Ni- yazi Misri, a sixteenth-century Sufi poet:

"Do not give your heart to every guide, that you might be misguided on your path,
Become One with the Absolute Guide, to guide you to the furthest destination."

Reshad jumped in again to admonish. "I was watching ten to twelve people go to sleep over the last fifteen minutes. Don't do that. You will miss the great opportunity of being awake. You have the chance to listen. You were offered this a long time ago. You weren't able to receive it the first time, so you were offered it a second time. This is a great chance to be awake — to listen in the heart. Never be complacent. Never think you know anything.

If you knew what Dede knows, *estağfurullah*, what I know, you wouldn't go to sleep. So, listen. God sends. Be careful."

Dede whispered to the translator, "What does he say?" The translator explained, and Dede concurred, "Thank God, it is the Truth."

Reshad's reprimand continued: "During my birthday party, I had to get on my knees to apologize (to Dede for the group's behavior). I had to do the Stop Exercise in the middle of my birthday party. Dreadful. I think it was the worst evening in my life. But for me to have to do the Stop Exercise![4] Do you know you can kill somebody doing that? There were eighty people there, and I could have killed the whole lot — just because of the chaos and the horror and the ridiculous nonsense for what it was all about. Because nobody would listen."

Ibrahim Gamard recalled the birthday party referred to by Reshad and what happened after Reshad yelled, "STOP!" The party was hosted by my parents in Malibu:

"In the midst of all the tension and embarrassment present in the room, Dede stood up from his couch and began to turn slowly in the manner of the Mevlevi shaykh near the end of the Samâ'. The room became hushed, and there was an extraordinary feeling of transcendent peace and love in the room. After at least five minutes, Dede sat down and, though much tension remained, it was much reduced by this devotional and simple, but spiritually profound act.[5]

Reshad continued:

"If you come quietly, you will have all the energy you need —

---

4. Gurdjieff would yell, "Stop!" requiring his students to freeze in their tracks for a moment of self-observation. Reshad used the exercise as a wake-up amid chaos.

5. Gamard, Ibrahim: "Memories of Süleyman Dede Effendi." http://www.dar-al-masnavi.org/dede.html.

everything you need. One or two hours of sleep a night is quite enough. If you will listen, God brings somebody like Dede. Don't go to sleep.

"Why am I going on a fast? And I will remain on it even if it takes me forty days until my body obeys me — it is because I want to be able to listen *so completely!* That it's not for me."

Dede changed gears: "Let us stop with our talk because this ocean is endless. Even if all trees were to become pens and all the oceans were to become ink, they would not suffice to capture it all. Let's put a pause here. We can listen to music too. Good? Would you mind?"

Despite Dede's wish to shift the octave and close the evening, someone asked another question about Islam:

"Help me understand how true believers, both Christian and Muslim, can love God on one hand and commit murder with the other. I cite Beirut as our most recent example."

Dede replied politely: "Since the time of Adam, our System of Cosmos has been structured in this manner. No timeframe is offered for deliverance by God from these things. They continue since the time of Adam. Why do you wonder about the *why?* They want to kill, and then they kill. It is essential that *you* do not kill!

"If the state needs an executioner, do not be that person! This would be my answer. Suppose a court sentences a person to be executed. An executioner will be needed for the firing squad, or to put the rope around his neck, to kick the stool away, maybe with a blade instead. Is this needed? According to the laws, maybe yes. But you don't need to be that person!"

Dede whispered reflectively: "In this Cosmos, people exist who kill. Christians kill Christians, Muslims kill Christians, whoever kills whomever. Let us not be those people. Whoever these people are, it is not of our interest. We are not related to them. Why wonder about them? This is the nature of the Cosmos.

"Does it not happen in America as well? One person earns much, another little, another wants to have it all. It is like this for everybody!

"My son, we dervishes are content with our states of being. We do not want to hurt anybody, do bad things, or kill people. We do not want to seize another's possessions. Be as yourself."

The translator apologized again for her translation. She explained that this meeting benefited her immensely, but she was concerned that she was not capturing the essence of what was being said.

"What is your name?" Dede asked. "I have not asked your name all this time."

"Güneş" (it means "Sun").

"There you go!" Dede offered. "This is why you rose here like a sun. We thought that sun would be the single one up in the sky, but it landed on earth and came to us!

"I am born into your fire!" Dede proclaimed. "Now, we will perform music. Then we will perform an invocation; we will do whirling. Let us freshen the hearts! Let the heart be filled with

Love! Let us not spend our time in *beyhude*, in vain. Our spiritual talking is done and we will listen to music. The ear and the heart need music. The whirling is for the human's enjoyment! It's food for the soul, a healing for lifeblood, to take our illnesses away, resting our bodies, resting our souls."

While people gathered their instruments, Dede told the translator how Mevlana taught astronomy at the Karatay Madrassa. He explained, "Mevlana transferred what he could from the stars to the flowing waters in the fountains. The sounds from the water provided musical notes to relax the minds of the students."

"And now, let us enjoy the music," Dede announced.

Actor Kedric Wolfe demonstrates his ball-bearing whirling shoes in Malibu.

While preparations continued, Dede told the translator about Reshad's birthday in Malibu:

"They took me to a heavenly place," Dede recollected. "There was lamb, rice, and many other servings. I believe they were drinking as well. A very nice day! The location overlooked the Pacific Ocean; what a beauty! I thought I was in Heaven!"

Dede pointed to me: "This boy, this tall person; he was there. I believe it was him. This fellow. What is your name?"

"Bruce," I replied.

"Bruce, Bruce (*sounding like Brux*)," Dede attempted. "I cannot pronounce it well."

"Yes, tricky to say in Turkish," I replied. "We hosted you at my parent's house in Malibu two nights ago."

Dede turned to the translator. "It was a heavenly house. You should have been there — grilled lamb, a feast. By God's chance, I met a lawyer. Do you see, my daughter, how great God's work is? Just have strong faith, and the rest will work out for you!"

Günes reminded Dede again that she needed a prayer.

"Let me pray for you," Dede offered. "If you have troubles, let them come to me."

David told Dede that I was the one who created the poster of Mevlana and the rainbow of light. Dede gestured to kiss the backs of our hands dervish style.

"This is what we Mevlevis offer to each other," Dede explained. "We kiss each other for the greatness of God! Where did you find that picture? How did you create it?"

"I just did it," I replied shyly.

"There is something that makes you do it!" Dede exclaimed. "God *made you* do that!"

We laughed together, but Dede's explanation of *who's doing what* perplexed me for the rest of the evening — and continues to this day.

Dede in Malibu

4

"LET US BE LOVERS!

The next night, a public crowd crammed into our little living room. Dede, Reshad, and David sat together up front. Günes, our sunny translator, sat close to Dede. I ran the taping equipment from a corner while others served cups of tea. Part of the ritual *adab* was to whip out a cigarette lighter for Dede without missing a beat, so several guys jockeyed to be quick on the draw. Few people knew what to expect from a Turkish spiritual leader, but hardly an avid smoker.

(If you wish to listen to the original audio, visit youtube.com/ithoutv: *Audio: Suleyman Dede in Los Angeles, April 20, 1976)*

§

"Let them drink!" Dede began. "May God the Almighty open our hearts so that we can witness the cosmos of Truth, *inshallah*, if God wills.

Dede receives a guest with Reshad and David Bellak.

"May God give healing to our suffering ones, curing to our diseased ones, and fulfillment to those in debt.

"And, may God connect us to each other through our hearts and our souls! And, may God, the deity of the Sufis, illuminate your hearts so that you may discover the cosmos of Truth.

"What a beautiful community. Since we share sincerity in the Light, we connect with each other. You have come from many locations far and wide to create this chance to be together.

"As you have practiced goodwill towards me, may God accept you as the beautiful ones with goodwill as well, *inshallah*."

Dede gestured to a woman who just arrived: "A cushion for this lady is needed; she is not comfortable."

She smiled and bowed.

Dede replied, "You are welcome, you have arrived with enjoyment. Please, please, please." He gestured for her to sit.

Dede continued.

"Greetings my good fellows; you have arrived in joy, and have brought good fortune! You have brought divine love, affection, and loving.

"When you travel such a distance, God blesses you with each new step you take — a thousand merits for one step, a thousand merits for another step."

Dede leaned toward the translator: "How are you going to explain the merit? Explain it like 'God will be content with you.'

"For the lovers, the path of God unfolds more quickly and effortlessly than you realize. God leads you on the wings of Gabriel, the *Salawat (invocation)* of God, and the Prophets. The lovers will not realize how it even happened!"

The translator apologized for speaking with her back toward Dede.

"*Estağfurullah*, it is fully okay," Dede replied.

"My friends, we have traveled by plane for eleven hours. Through the sunlight of Shams of Tabriz, it seemed like an hour or even a minute, so quick was our arrival. With our thankfulness and praise to God, we have flown here. And, I said to myself, 'Gabriel, the closest archangel to God, has taken us on his wings.'

"O God! As if we were floating in cotton, or floating on the sea, transiting through such a cosmos, we arrived in no time. After eleven hours, we had no difficulties, and we arrived in joy, in cheerfulness, and in pure eagerness.

"The individuals who are in Love with God the Truth, in Divine Love, will have neither exhaustion nor sorrow in their hearts. As Galip says: *'For the adepts of Love, how hard would it be to find the charm Dilârâ! If you are Majnun, oh heart, how hard would it be to find Layla!'* [1]

"If you have Love, Love, Love... there is no sorrow; there is no gloom! However, as we discussed during the meal, those lovers,

---

1. Reference to the love story of Layla and Majnun. https://en.wikipedia.org/wiki/Layla_and_Majnun

those whirling ones, those butterflies, will lose their minds when they see the light. They will fall in love with that light. They will keep approaching the light, hitting their wings, until they eventually break. It is love that makes the lover do this. That whirling one, that butterfly is in love with that light.

"*Inshallah*, may you fall in love with the Light, become mortals within that Love. And become lovers! Love is humanity's primary quest; it is the mandate of the Divine. If there were no love, the mandate of the Divine would not be fulfilled. Accordingly, let us be lovers, let us be the whirling ones, let us release gloom and sorrow."

Following this long introduction, Dede turned with a twinkle to the translator, challenging her to translate it. Everyone laughed.

Dede continued: "There was once a poet named Yunus Emre (1238-1320) who served in the dervish lodge for forty years. His job was to bring logs from the mountains to heat the cook stove. Out of deep devotion and loyalty, he would select perfectly straight logs, load them on his back, and carry them to the lodge. It was solely love that inspired him to do this.

"When you attend these gatherings of love, it's the same as being in the company of God the Almighty in the Garden of Truth. There is no gossip, no lies, no pursued profit, and no financial interest. These gatherings are gardens of lovers.

"When one enters a garden, there are so many things to see: roses, hyacinths, basils, as well as violets, and unique flowers with different colors and scents. The flowers open one's heart. We are in a similar garden every time we attend one of these gatherings."

Dede offered to answer questions.

"May God give ease to my tongue. If you have difficulties, I can respond to the best of my abilities. I can offer advice by my authority, my ability, and my force."

Someone asked: "When we pray in this different language, do

we have to understand these ways? When the way of Mevlana comes to America, will the turn of the dervish adapt? Will the tradition change accordingly?"

Dede remarked to Güneş, the translator: "Ask this sister, to whom does she pray? Does she pray to God or to moonlight? Better not ask it in that manner, but rather ask if she prays to God or not; let's first hear what she has to say about that."

Güneş asked the questioner, "Dede wants to know to whom do you pray when you pray?"

Everyone laughed.

Dede answered: "God has the capability of understanding everyone's language, everyone's tongue, everyone's prayer. Moreover, when you lean toward God silently, without letters, without writing, only as 'O God, O God — God will immediately respond and say 'Oh my servant, what do you want?' Be it English, German, French, Turkish, Arabic, or Persian. God is familiar with every language since it is God who gave us these languages!

"Therefore pray in your own ability, as you normally would do by yourself. God knows already that you will pray. God asks for your prayers already, and thus you can pray to God."

Dede leaned over to the translator, saying, "This next part... it is important that they grasp this.

"Pray to God while walking on the road or standing. This is written in all the books – in the Holy Quran, Holy Bible, Torah, and Psalms. All the holy books have declared: 'If you want to pray to me, to invoke me, do it in the manner you prefer – while walking on the road, while standing, or shouting, or just by allowing it pass through your heart.'

"When prayers are offered with this attitude, they will be well-received. God always hears these prayers and shows a curiosity and thirst for them. God prefers prayers this way: 'Let my servants never forget me while they are on the move, while they are standing, while they are sitting, while working, even when they are busy.' Hence, God the Truth will accept their invocations and fulfill their wishes immediately. In such a case, God is in love with us. I have been explaining this for some time.

"Observe how God created us as humans. We have these hands, these eyes, these arms, these ears. Look what God has done for us, how holy we are among all creation. As humans, we have been given countless blessings. We have been given wealth, a spouse, children, strength, ability, breathing, clean air, the sun.

"You might think that animals also benefit from these gifts, yet the animals are provided for us. We milk the cow and eat its flesh. From sheep, we get milk, and wool, and use its skin – all for our benefit. We are the beloved servants of God, *inshallah*. A human being has to know oneself. Each of us should be aware that we are blessed beings."

From another questioner: "In the duality in which we live in this world, we come across many teachers, and they give us many different meditations, prayers, and techniques. Is one better than another?"

"Such an evaluation is not our responsibility," Dede replied. "Since God knows every language, God will accept everyone's praying in their own way.

"As Muslims, as Mevlevis, we follow a path. We have Affection, Divine Love, Security, Bliss, and Happiness. These move us along the path. We have Mevlevi music and Rumi's words. This is the Mevlevi way. Love of humanity, peace, fair conduct in life, and goodwill are all on our path. We show reverence to all other paths, and to the members of each religion and to their temples – yet we are Mevlevis ourselves. Talk to us about Mevlana, about God, about the Prophet.

"This reverence is how we interpret a Buddhist bowing in front of a statue of Buddha, or a yogi seeking refuge in God in a seated posture. Surely if he aims towards God, he is praying to God. We show reverence to all religions that recognize God as one.

Anyone can pray in any language and in any form! A Buddhist, a Christian, a Jew, a Muslim — God will not reject their prayers.

"Yet our path is the path of love, and if you follow this path of Masnavi... Well, I don't want to promote religious propaganda; I am just sharing the truth. If you set your mind to this path, and follow it, and embrace these ways of praying, God will be satisfied.

"We have the music, the words, the dialogue, and the goodness. We have the means to open the window of the heart. Affection and loving give pleasure to every human; it enchants and brings ecstasy. This is our path.

"If you wish to aim towards God by means of the Mevlevi path, you will have two *wings*.[2] I cannot say if other paths have even a single wing since I do not belong to them. Yet, I show them reverence because they remember God.

"And, don't you worry; I understand your English too! Whatever you say, I understand it."

Aside to the translator: "Tell this bit quick, then I will go on.

"If we did not show affection to each other and God did not love us, would God have gathered us in this place? You have come from such distances, spending money, taking a cab, and expending energy. What is this about, coming here? It is to see each other, talk to each other, laugh together, and love each other. What does this say? That we are beloved servants of God, *inshallah*! Since we have gathered, there is no such a thing as a *foreigner* here.

"We are all loyal to the Beloved. We have gathered for affection, to learn something new. We are not here to criticize, to blame, to show disrespect to people of any religion or nationality. We are here for affection. All is good; all of this is good!"

---

2. *God... teaches by means of opposites so that you will have two wings to fly, not one.*"
from Barks, *The Essential Rumi*. The two wings are also referenced in the Masnavi as *fear* and *hope*, and *knowledge* and *conjecture*. Dede might also have been referring to *Mevlana* and *Muhammad*.

A guest entered from the back.

"Sit down here," Dede gestured up front.

Someone lit the guest's cigarette while Reshad offered coffee.

Dede addressed the guest: "Excuse me for sitting and smoking. I have many faults. And no coffee, please."

Dede noticed a couple in the rear of the room. "Oh, there you are! How are you doing? May God give you well-being! Since we have last seen you, we have become very cheerful.

"We have become very cheerful indeed! It's because you have shown us goodwill and have responded to us beautifully. You are held in the throne of my heart, and there you reign."

Reshad told the couple's story: "Dede, their son was suddenly very ill. He was in the hospital with five surgeons waiting to operate. And, they telephoned me. What was it, 6:15 in the morning? I was in bed, and all I could do was pray. I prayed very, very hard. A short time later, the boy left the hospital needing no operation. He had a blood clot in his head. God sometimes creates a situation like this, so a couple like this can sit here."

Dede continued: "There are experts among healers and doctors, yet God is the ablest healer of all. Through Mevlana, Reshad prayed to God, 'For the sake of Mevlana's people and that beloved servant of yours, allow that this child be healed. Let him be spared from his operation and his illness.'

"Since he prayed in this way, God has given your son a healing."

Dede continued: "Now, I hope this doesn't sound like boasting, and I hope you won't be saying, 'Dede came here and said these kinds of things. But, let me add a story.

"I had a friend, a sheikh, who was very ill in Istanbul. I visited his lodge on a Friday to check on him. The doctor told me that he should be left alone with his wife because he was likely to die by night or the next morning.

"But, I explained that I would sit with him anyway, even if he was going to die. I sat and meditated and prayed to God, asking, 'Let God heal him.'

"They informed the sheikh that Dede had arrived. Since he loved me deeply, the news boosted his morale. So, they took him out of bed, helped him sit, and invited me in. I was concerned that he would die next to me and I would be held responsible, saying, 'Dede came, and the man died.' But since he insisted, I entered his room.

"I told him, 'Muhittin Efendi, my brother, I want to pray for you. Let me take your illness away, but I am not going to take the credit for it.' He wondered what I was going to do. I replied, 'I will take it and throw it into the waters of Sarayburnu[3], and when it gets mixed with those waters, you will get better.'

"So, I prayed, 'O God, Mevlana is your beloved servant. Since Mevlana is universal (Alem şumül) and every word of his comes from your words of Truth, and because you love him, O God, may you give healing to this man.'

"Seven months later, the man was healed.

"God loves Mevlana as a successor of the prophets. The Quran claims this, and all of the four books claim this. The saints of God are representatives of prophets; hence these people are the messengers of God. Therefore, when we hold them within, God the Truth will accept our prayers and heal those in need.

"Seven months after the doctors discontinued his medication to prepare for his death, the sheikh went on a pilgrimage to Mecca.

---

3. A promontory that separates the Golden Horn and the Sea of Marmara in Istanbul.

"After the pilgrimage, when he arrived in Konya, I asked him what happened. He said; 'Dede, you prayed for me, and then I was healed. I was able to make my pilgrimage.

"Yet beware, it was not Dede who made this happen. I held Mevlana within and prayed accordingly. It was not my power; I did not have the ability and force to cure his illness. However, I prayed in the right way. I held Mevlana and sought refuge in God. God accepted my prayer, just like that."

Dede turning in his home in Konya

Another question: "Could you explain what it means to talk to God through Mevlana?"

"As a beloved servant of God, God accepts our prayers immediately when offered through Mevlana," Dede explained. "Let's say a doctor, an expert doctor is about to operate on a patient, and he takes the scalpel. Where is the patient's suffering? Maybe in his heart, his stomach, or somewhere else. He locates this point, applies the scalpel, and removes the infection. Similarly, since Mevlana is a beloved servant of God, the *scalpel of Mevlana* is applied precisely where the patient needs healing. This advice comes from the way of Mevlana: Visualize Mevlana; take him into your heart. God will provide what you need, *inshallah*, if God wills."

Dede paused for a moment. Then he made a profound observation:

"Rumi wrote the Masnavi 715 years ago. At that time, Rumi

prophesized that the world of Islam would forget him. But he also felt that years and centuries later, the Western world would come to appreciate him and understand him better. This came true today.[4]

"Now I observe that in Africa, a recently modernized civilization, there are people who are connected to Mevlana with strings in their heart. This indicates that Mevlana carries a certain type of goodness. They read his works and sense this already. There are thousands of various works, but today's sultan, today's president..."

Dede asked the translator: "Who is the president of America at the moment? Say it again?"

Dede is told the name, Gerald Ford.

"Okay, let's assume this man, Ford, is the president today. In the same way, Mevlana is *our* president today – *the owner of today.* There were many other saints before his time, and they were suitable for then. I am talking about the *owner of today* — the one who informs this time.

"Let me offer something helpful. If you have a translation of the Masnavi, whenever you run into problems, open the book by saying *Destur*, 'I seek your *permission.*' You will find the answer right away. If you feel troubled, or depressed, or sad in any way, open the Masnavi at random and read the first lines you come across. Even if it turns out to be a story, you will find the answer, and he will guide you to that."

"I tell people this all the time," Reshad agreed. "The Masnavi is way beyond the *I Ching.*"

An anecdote about opening the Masnavi: One morning we were all gathered in prayer following *zikr*. With respectful presence, Reshad cracked open the Masnavi to receive the day's

---

4. See Ibrahim Gamard's discussion on this prophesy: http://www.dar-al-masnavi.org/ rumi-prophecies.html

message. Reshad paused, then chuckled, turned to Dede and said, "We keep getting this reading."

The translator translated this to Dede, who casually reached across Reshad's lap, flipped the book to another page, then closed his eyes to resume his prayer. We all looked at each other. Did he do that? Back to the talk:

Question: "It is said that Mevlana and Jesus are the same. Could you elaborate?"

"Such a fine question!" Dede replied. "Mevlana said, 'I am the Jesus of my time. I am the Moses of my time, and the Mohammed of my time.' This is how he says it. 'I am Mahmoud of this time. I am the Ahmed of it, the Jesus of it, and the Solomon of it.' He is not separate from any of them. All of his expressions are derived from them. He is the sultan, the *sultan of today*.[5]

"We know about the President of America today and the stars on the flag. The states all answer to a single president. In similar fashion, Mevlana has absorbed Jesus, Moses, and Mohammad. He absorbed all of them! He is today's equivalent of all the prophets. What the prophets instructed as the path is also shown to us by Mevlana, the *sultan of today*.

"Mevlana is not with us anymore, but his works are present. In his works, he says that he is Mevlana of the time, the Jesus, Moses, Solomon, Adam, Idris, Noah, Hud, Saleh, Abraham, Ishmael, Isaac, and Jacob of the time, all of them! He states: 'I have what you are looking for. It is my flag that sways today.'

"I have been spreading a lot of propaganda for Mevlana, but I have told only the truth. This is a product of experience; his miracles are visible to the eye. Over the years, people have come into this state and have become aware of this truth.

5. This quote is likely attributed to Aflâki's chronicle of Rumi's life, completed in 1353 (eighty years after Rumi died).

"Hence my recommendation: You don't have to travel far. Simply read it and a birth will take place in your heart."

Dede took a sip of coffee, then reached for a cigarette. Someone flicked a Zippo to life. Dede bowed with hand to his heart: "Mashallah."

"Recently a young woman came to visit me," Dede continued. "She was an English teacher in Istanbul visiting from Australia. She told me, 'In Australia, there is a community of lovers of Mevlana.' The English scholar, Nicholson, translated the Masnavi to English and traveled to Australia where a growing number of people began to read this work.

Dede with guests, Los Angeles, 1976

"After learning of this, I came to a realization with this helpless mind of mine, with this narrow mind of mine (the translator interjects "*estağfurullah*" twice, indicating Dede is not so), that when seven hundred years ago, Mevlana said, 'I am Jesus, I am

Moses, I am the Mohammad of the time; I have what you are looking for,' that Mevlana was telling the literal Truth."[6]

Dede took another sip of coffee.

Question: "How does the heart of the human being come into the realization of God?"

"By orienting yourself to God, obeying God, by doing things that God will favor," Dede replied. "This is how the heart opens. My heart is not so open; I would not know so well. But it occurs to me that if you work for God, if you obey God, and stay away from what is forbidden, God will open your heart. This will become immediately visible inside you.

"God is in your heart already. Regardless of religion, doctrine, or race, all of humanity carries God within their hearts. However, opening the heart is not like opening the door and going down the stairs. The human being must go through a spiritual awakening. When you love God, act in accordance with God's will, and follow the path God wishes, your heart will surely open. You will become content and cheerful."

It was time to close the evening. Reshad asked Mufrida to lead the group singing, *Ya Salaam*. Dede followed with a quiet prayer.

It seemed that the evening was over, but soon an animated discussion arose. David wanted Dede to go to bed whereas Dede felt otherwise:

"What shall we do?" Dede asked with concern. "Why would we go to sleep now? What time is it? Look. These people have come from far places!"

"Dede, you have traveled far, you're not feeling well, and you need your rest," David reasoned. "And, it's after ten o'clock."

"Okay, it is past ten o'clock," Dede countered. "But how am I

---

6. Dede is likely referring to Aflaki's account of Rumi's funeral: "If you Muslims call Mowlânâ the Muhammad of your time, we recognize him to be the Moses of our era and the Jesus of the age." "Shams al-dîn Ahmad-e Aflâkî, 'The Feats of the Knowers of God'," translated by John O'Kane (Boston: Brill, 2002, p. 405).

going to let these people go? I cannot do that! I have been healed now. Today I was not feeling well, but now I am healed! Their arrival has been my medicine. I am now healed. Thank God! In the truth of God, there is no mistake!

"Let's sit for another ten or fifteen minutes; it would be a dishonor otherwise. There's no such thing as illness; please sit. I am not going to get ill or something; it is okay."

Dede turned toward the group and continued: "All *djinns* and humans appreciate and praise God, showing indebtedness and gratitude. God gave language to Adam and the measure of time with that.

"God will award us with favor. Why did we come here? To find healing! To find well-being! To find force! To find energy! Is that not so?

"We have been in a sleep for years. I have been in a sleep for years. I could not learn anything essential! Instead, I have been lying down, eating, drinking and sleeping!

"How are we going to find another day like this one? Those who see it once cannot see it one more time. They cannot give a price and purchase it afterward.

"Who knows when we are going to meet each other again? Let us sit, my son. It will be all right. God is with us as we are talking about God. Since we expect everything exclusively from God, God will spare us, *inshallah*. God spares us because God watches over the people who set foot on this path."

Dede asked the translator jokingly if she understood Arabic. Then, Dede motioned to me, asking, "What was the name of our friend here?"

"Bruce, Bruce," people replied.

"Bruce, it sounds nice," Dede complimented. "Okay, anyhow, you make these recordings on a daily basis. What are you going to do with them? Sell them?" (Huge laughter) "Who do you play them to? You collect them every day. Do you do it for *Barakat*, abundance?"

"*Barakat* by the meter," Reshad laughed.

"Bravo, bravo! But mind you, these are precious. Don't sell them cheap!" Dede warned.

The crowd laughed.

"Amin!" I responded, not knowing what to say, nor realizing that forty years would pass before the talks would see the light.

"The value of these words cannot be measured," Dede explained. "Their value is known only to people of a certain station, to the *arif*, the gnostic ones. Gnostics will understand; those with open hearts, those with the active eye of the heart will understand.

"Imagine taking a beautiful dress to the Tellal Pazarı flea market in Konya. Who would buy it? They wouldn't know its value. Instead, such a dress must be displayed beautifully in a shop window, illuminated with light, so that it stands out.

"Similarly, these words contain a chemistry; not to be sold in the flea market, but by a jeweler."

Someone popped another question: "I would like to ask Dede, what impresses him the most about American customs?"

David: "He's only been to Los Angeles (laughter)."

Dede: "From my perspective, America is magnificent in its art. And, I love the people. In America, I have not witnessed a single thing that I don't enjoy. I was so impressed visiting the house in Malibu.

"In Konya, the winter is not over; the heating stoves are still at work. But here, there are orange trees, pine trees, fruit trees, blooming trees — all that green. There were even date palms! And, I told myself: 'This land is a taste of Heaven!'

"Everyone I have met follows the path of Mevlana which may explain the fact that I have not experienced anything unpleasant so far. Look at these faces; they are all beautiful!

"When I arrived, I saw black people like this one over there, all with curly hair. I adored them so much! I asked one of them, a well-dressed man with a cart, what he does and he told me that he was a porter. How I adored this, adored all of them! You have beauty, cleanliness, and goodness in your land, thank God.

"Today, Reshad complained about the air pollution from all the traffic while we were at the beach. I didn't think so at all! What people perceive as smog felt like illumination to me.

"I enjoyed the splendid sand on the endless beaches; there is no such sand in Turkey. The sand in Florya doesn't compare. You could bury thousands of people under it. Unfortunately, I was ill, and if I had felt better, I would have buried myself in it. I wanted to bury myself in the sand so that God could ease the pain in my feet. I was not feeling well at that moment."

David Bellak remembers that day at the beach and how Dede's pain persisted into the night:

"Dede was not feeling well, but he refused my repeated attempts to get him upstairs to bed, insisting it was his duty to stay with the murids (students) who had invited him to America to learn about Mevlana. Eventually, he acquiesced. Once in bed, he pleaded with me to massage his legs. Soon he was asleep. I gently covered him, then slipped out of the room to chat with some young women in the room next door.

"Suddenly the door burst open. Dede entered wide awake in his pajamas, saying 'Davut, Davut, come look.' His eyes were wide with excitement exclaiming, "'There are angels everywhere, like a cinema in my room!'

"I jumped up to be with him. He described how he was asleep, but awoke to find the walls alive with angels, moving and dancing and shimmering with light. The room was dark, and the door closed.

Eventually, I ushered him back to bed and sat at his side as he continued to describe the angels with wide-eyed wonder."

Dede continued to describe his reaction to America:

"Your land has such beauty. I have been to Europe and Arab lands, visiting many different cities. But your land is very beautiful. May God spare you to your land!

"It is essential that you visit our lodge, the lodge of Mevlana. *Inshallah*, I will write a poem to give to each of you as a present. Please read it and let it be remembered as 'The Heirloom of Dede.'"

Dede leaned over and whispered to Günes: "They can visit me in Konya."

The translator reminded Dede that it would be difficult.

"Then they can come here regularly and have conversations with each other. Let me be finished, after which I will leave. They are sending me away to bed already!

Dede continued: "Okay, give me a pen, please."

Dede took the pen and paper and wrote down a traditional Mevlevi hymn:

Come to the lodge of Mullah, look and see: What an enjoyment there is!

For each sorrow of the beautiful-faced, there are a thousand sorts of remedies,

Unlike the legend of the misled, there is no infusion of hypocrisy (zerk-i riyâ),

There are songs (avâze), kudül, ney, tambur and chanters (nevâ),

Fall onto the soil, you, searcher of the Face (appearance of God),

See, that among the people of purity (meşreb-i pâkin),

there is neither thirst (cevdet), nor generosity (Sahâvet),

You will be given one sip and the breeze of its scent,
At this height, like Gabriel, there resides the secret of God the Guide
(Hüdâ).

Dede explained to Günes: "Some people simply say: 'Let us see God,' but God is not a man; how can you see him? God is not a tree. Since God is hidden within everything, God is a secret; God is hidden. While translating, please consider this part accordingly."

Dede continued with his poem:

They will bestow a chalice; its color is of wine (mey),
Like the dew (ruhsar) on a fresh rosebud (gülter), it sparkles light as
the color red,
Take the wine in this jug; sip it all at once; allow your body to spirit
away,
Inside it, there is a gospel (beşâret), one that never runs out (tecelli-yi
bakâa),
That is devoted to the ones who carry this grace (erbâb-ı kerem).

To Günes: "I would like to stay longer, but I believe the people are ready to go."

"My good people, I would like to ask permission to leave. My good fellows, and with the will of God, thank you very much! You have served me, and accordingly, may God serve you as well!

"Inshallah, may you stay in good health! Please, stay seated. Inshallah, inshallah."

Masha'Allah

5

THE SEED IS PLANTED

The next day, in a touching ceremony, Süleyman Dede initiated Reshad as a sheikh of the Mevlevi. Dede wrapped the ceremonial wool hat, or *sikke*, while we sang a haunting melody, the *Tekbir*. Once wrapped, it is called the *destar*, the head covering of the sheikh. Dede kissed the *destar*, placed it on Reshad's head, performed prayers, and signed a Mevlevi document giving official permission. The deed was done. The line of Mevlana had come to America.

Dede wraps the sikke.

Reshad exhibited a newfound gravitas with the title. Having had no academic or religious credentials, becoming "The Mevlevi

Sheikh of North America," conferred a position of spiritual authority.

Later that evening, Dede summoned us to the small garage that we had outfitted as a prayer space. Dede gestured from one side of the room to the other: "Stand here, cross your arms, bow, turn, now do this, now do that." He was initiating us into the whirling ceremony, or *sema*.

Dede teaching the sema in our converted garage. Günes stands behind him.

Ibrahim Gamard shared his memory of the moment:

> *This wonderful elderly gentleman was darting around the room with the excitement of a little boy, moving semazens here and there,*

98

marking the outer boundaries with chairs, and teaching us respect for the invisible center line extending from the pôst, the place from where the shaykh represented Mevlana. I remember feeling very affected by Dede's joy and enthusiasm. I thought that he must have been thrilled by the religious freedom available in America since the Samâ' had been illegal in Turkey for decades. But in America there were no such restriction or interference. Samâ' could be done anytime![1]

Each night, we continued to practice the *sema* in the garage prayer space. The young couple and their 12-year old boy who earlier had a blood clot healed through prayer were among the guests. David Bellak remembers the couple sharing their son's experience:

"The morning after the sema of the previous night, the couple approached me wishing to speak to Dede about their son who was known to 'see' things and have sensitivity to energies. I arranged for the boy and his parents to visit Dede and share the boy's experience. The boy described an extraordinary sight he was given as Dede and I entered the sema space dressed in our black cloaks. Dede wore the traditional headpiece or destar of the sheikh.

"The boy said that he saw a very old, bearded man with a very large headdress above Dede's head. The boy's vision of the man remained in the prayer space, even after we returned to the house. Dede questioned the boy closely about the details. The boy had no idea who or what this figure was. After Dede described the image of Rumi, it seemed clear that the boy had seen Mevlana."

---

1. *Gamard, Ibrahim. "Memories of Suleyman Dede Effendi." http://www.dar-al-masnavi.org/ dede.html*

Reshad was now a sheikh and we were initiated in the *sema* — well sort-of. With just a few rudimentary lessons under our belt, we had a public presentation of the *sema* planned for later in the week. This was new and exciting, but I was intrigued by something more telling the next morning.

At breakfast, the cooks served Reshad an all-American meal of eggs, toast, bacon, coffee and orange juice. Without warning, and in a flurry of Turkish, Dede pointed at Reshad's bacon, gesturing that something was wrong. In deference to his Muslim faith, the cooks had served Dede's plate bacon-free. A flurry of words through the translator ensued.

"Tell Dede that I humbly apologize for the bacon," Reshad offered sheepishly. "I'm sorry if it offends him and I will remove it from my plate."

More translation and more shaking of Dede's head.

"Dede explained that he would like bacon, too," came the translation. He was promptly served.

In another version of the story, Dede reached into the fridge, nicked a strip of bacon, and devoured it.

Either way, was this a gracious accommodation, or was Dede demonstrating that Rumi's message must adapt to the time and place? Probably both, as he later said, "I come to plant Mevlana's message of universal love in this soil. The way of Mevlana, of Rumi, will grow in the West in its own way."

That afternoon, I lugged cases of lighting equipment up the grand stairway of MacArthur Park's neo-gothic Elks Hall. As I strung cables and hung spotlights, I sensed that something meaningful was about to happen.

When the lights came on, five young American dervishes unfolded their arms, lifted their hearts, and whirled to the ritual cadence of Mevlevi music. For the first time in history, men and women performed the sacred rite together in a public performance. Was this the *Mysterium Conjunctum* Reshad had promised — the Alchemical Marriage, the reconciling of opposites?

Ibrahim Gamard was one of those dancers. He recollects:

That sema was the most blessed one my wife and I ever experienced. I remember, just afterward, walking up some concrete steps leading outside from the auditorium to cool off. I sat down and looked up at the stars, and it felt like the whole sky was opening up to me beyond the physical dimension.[2]

"The seed is planted." Men and women turn together in the historic Elks Temple at MacArthur Park, Los Angeles.

Afterward, someone asked Ayisha, one of the whirling dancers, the one question that trumped all others in the school: "Did the energy go through?" Ayisha answered coyly, "Maybe, my lunch went through." But she knew; we all knew: This was the moment that Rumi took root in America.

2. *ibid*

At the time of Dede's visit, the Movement for Spiritual Inner Awareness (MSIA), founded by the new age visionary John-Roger, reached out to interview Dede. This newspaper interview took place after the whirling performance:[3]

Q: *Why have you come to America?*

DEDE: *I came here to visit our Mevlevi friends and to visit my friend, Reshad. I am happy to have found love, prayer, and Mevlana here. For what purpose do you do this interview?*

Q: *I am doing this for all the people who can't be here today to share with us and have this beautiful experience.*

The interview

DEDE: *God be with you in all your endeavors, and I hope that you will be able to let everyone hear about this. Then I will be very happy. God will be pleased also. You are taking many photos, but please don't take them when I am not in a dignified position.*

Q: *I have never seen you in a position that was not dignified. (Laughter).*

DEDE: *I like you very much, and I know that you aren't going to do anything like that, but I have met lots of newspaper and magazine reporters who would do that on purpose.*

Q: *My work with this newspaper is to bring the things that I find*

3. The Movement Newspaper, MSIA, May/June 1976.

to be valuable in my life, things that would be worth sharing, to the people who read this publication. In one way, I see my interviews as part of my diary, and I am sharing what I do each day with the readers; it's not that I'm an editor or a writer — just a person.

DEDE: I am very happy that you feel this way. I like you very much. And now I am ready to answer your questions! (Laughter).

Q: Do you believe that it is necessary that turning to God actually be done physically, or can one do this turning to God in some other way?

DEDE: If they didn't turn inwardly all the time, they couldn't turn outwardly. They couldn't even turn twice; they would be very dizzy. God helps them to turn that way, as a whirling dervish.

Q: Can a person who has "really turned" stop turning?

DEDE: Why not? If he wants to and doesn't feel it anymore. It's a feeling, and you turn as long as you feel it. If you stop feeling it, then you don't turn. If you are too old to "turn," or sick, you can do the "zikr" (chanting God's name), and this will give you the same satisfaction. But you can take it or leave it; it's all up to you.

Q: How old were you when you first got involved with Mevlana?

DEDE: Fifteen. I was going to school, and I started going to the monastery, as I was fascinated with the Mevlevi Dervishes. When I was 18, I entered the monastery and worked in the kitchen. I worked in the kitchen for 23 years. Usually, one works in the kitchen and cooks and does the hard chores for three years before one is eligible to become a Dede. However, that doesn't mean that after three years you become a Dede. At that point, your superiors judge whether you're worthy of ever becoming a Dede. I had no idea that I would become one, I just enjoyed being there. After 23 years, they gave me the title of Dede, and I received a meditation cell and didn't work in the kitchen anymore. Now I have other duties, such as teaching Mevlana. I also write poetry and make music. I'm happy that you have asked me this question. No one has ever asked me about this!

Q: If someone is having difficulties living in a monastery or ashram or other school structure where they have had great inner and outer growth, but now no longer wishes to deal with the personality aspects of the other students, what would you suggest?

DEDE: I would ask and pray that they stay. Those that stay have fidelity and faith and reach their goal; others don't. I would ask them to stay and go on if it's been a place of growth. There were many times that I would say to myself, "What am I doing here? Why do I go through this? Why don't I just leave?" But then I heard deep in my heart that God was talking to me and telling me to have faith and to trust in Him and stay. So I stayed and had trust. But there were many times that I wanted to leave. Suffering is part of life. We must learn how to suffer without falling to pieces. This is part of our training – to be strong.

Q: I have always looked at the negativity and pain that was being brought to me as what I had given to others and that I was being given an opportunity to even the score.

DEDE: Only a few chosen see the light of God, and you saw the light of God, and you're there. You're repenting. Don't ever think that it was you and your willpower that took you there and showed you the Light; you should stay there and turn toward God and be repentant.

Q: I have a friend that once told me, and I have not forgotten this: No one said that it was going to be easy, but that God loves His own and all will return to His home.

DEDE: Eat as much as you want, enjoy as much as you want,

never waste. Be very honest; never kill anybody nor bring harm to anyone. God never said to deny anything for yourself or to torture your body – not in all the sacred books. He said, "I gave everything to you so that you may enjoy them, just as long as you don't abuse anything, waste, or harm your neighbor, or commit any insult or crime." God never said to deny yourself anything.

Q: If a person is harming another person without being conscious of it, do you suggest interfering with that person's natural flow? When does one step in? Who decides the punishment?

DEDE: You have to warn this person and give him three chances. If he continues to do the harmful action, either consciously or unconsciously, you just let the person go. There isn't anything else you can do, but you should make him aware of what he's doing if it's possible.

Q: How does your wife assist you in your seeking?

DEDE: She has been with me all the time. In fact, we were married and had our first child when I was working in the kitchen. Later my superiors took my entire family into the monastery.

Q: Do you recommend that married couples have children?

DEDE: You should get married and have children; a tree without fruit means nothing.

Q: When I asked this question, I received the thought that children are the gifts that God gives to those who love.

RESHAD: Ever since Dede has come to my home, we have eaten well – on many levels.

DEDE: I eat "well" in my house only when I have guests. If there is much work in my house, which isn't very large, and someone complains, I remind him that this is God's gift and not to complain.

Q: I sometimes have the thought that as the world develops technologically, God becomes more difficult to see; material things get in the way. Is this because God wishes only those that are strong?

DEDE: *I like your question. In a way, it is a test. God created everything and gave all these beautiful things to man for his enjoyment, but it's also a test when one is enjoying life fully, not to forget God, but always remember Him. And when one is enjoying, one should never waste, nor forget his brothers.*

Q: *There seems to be an epidemic of terminal illnesses in this country. What can be the best way to support someone suffering one of these illnesses?*

DEDE: *Moral support is the most important for these people, and be careful to explain the importance of the shortness of this life in relation to reaching God – that this life is temporary.*

Q: *It appears that time is going by faster and faster – Do you have any thoughts about this?*

DEDE: *First, nobody can stop time; we must accept that. The universe turns and the days fall, one after the other, and they turn, too.*

We don't feel that there is enough time to accomplish all of the things that we want to accomplish. So we must benefit from the time we do have and make that time valuable. Enjoy every moment. Make the most of each moment in each

"The Movement" interview

day. If you are happy and had a good day, then you lived that day fully. You should always try to be happy. If you are sad about everything, then you have wasted your time, and haven't lived your life fully. You should never complain about anything, no matter how difficult the situation. Can I ask you something now?

Q: Anything. I don't know that I'll have the answer, but you may ask.

DEDE: Who showed you the way of Mevlana for the first time?

Q: Actually, the first time was when I was young. I saw through examples – people who were not nice to one another; it was by their negative examples that I first questioned. Then my wife showed me the right day. While in the middle of a very negative day, I noticed that she was very centered. I saw that she knew something that I didn't, and I wanted to find out what it was. Anything was better than where I was at!

DEDE: I congratulate you for having such a wife. I would like to meet her.

Q: Thank you for the compliment, and I must also congratulate myself for having seen this.

DEDE: I congratulate you, not only because of your wife, but because you were able to see "the right way." I listen to you as if listening to music. You are very, very lucky to have a wife who knows the meaning of patience more than anything else and has the light in her heart. You should be proud of her and pray to God. Thank God for having such a wife, and even do sema saying that "I have a beautiful God," because that is also praying.

RESHAD: Dede, I've been praying for months, and months, and months, and months to God for some indication of what was intended for the people in our group. What is the next step? What would be of the most service? It seems that a tekke in the way of Mevlana is intended, and now, inshallah, it will take place.

Dede reads the interview in the publication.

DEDE: *Everyone should know that this is not my doing, or Reshad's doing, or anybody else's doing. It's God's doing. I always wanted to come to the United States and to travel, but there was no way to be able to afford it. But I wished this so strongly – God willed that this should happen. I am very happy to have come here and to have met everyone, but it was not my doing, or your doing, or anybody else's doing; it is God's doing.*

RESHAD: We had no money to speak of, but someone suggested a rummage sale, and we raised $2500.00 in two days. If that wasn't Allah, I don't know what is! Money has come in from different centers as God has produced all the ways for Dede to get here — through hard work, not wealthy patrons.

DEDE: One should be proud of one's poverty. So much evil comes because of money. If you're poor but honest, then you are the best type of person possible. Honesty is the main thing in the world.

Q: Is it a rare situation that a rich man can be a holy man? I was wondering if God could make an exception for me!

DEDE: A person must never, never forget others; one must never forget charity and helping others and constantly sharing. If you are poor, you must never lose your faith in God. God will see to it that you will have enough all of the time. David calls me a "king," and I feel like a king, and we don't pass away like the other sultans — totally forgotten. If I can bring one little light to the hearts of people, then I will be remembered forever. No matter what, no matter how difficult life gets, have faith in God, and God will see to it that you are not left alone.

TRANSLATOR: I can't tell you how I have benefited in the last three days. I mean it! I'm not joking!! (everyone laughs).

RESHAD: We know that, but again, God sent you. How else could we have heard the words in this language?

DEDE: There's a good translation of Masnavi by Nicholson. Whenever you feel troubled or unhappy, you should read that.

Q: Do you foresee the Turn being taught widely here?

DEDE: Only God knows.

Q: Is there anything that you would like to share with us?

DEDE: Whatever I say, anyway, are not my words. They are Mevlana's words that are inspired in my heart. I am very happy with what I have seen around here. I hope that someday you will be able to put a book together about the people that you have met. I'm ready to die now; I do not have much time left, but I will die peacefully.

§

As I edit this interview, Dede's humanity comes through strongly. Beyond sacred and profane, he saw God's manifestation as a seamless, beautiful whole; even the LA smog "felt like illumination" to Dede.

David Bellak shared a story that illustrates Dede's pragmatic approach to spiritual life:

One night in winter 1975, an older man arrived at Dede's home. Dede asked me to let him in. I did not understand their conversation, but the back and forth was emphatic. As the man left, Dede gave him some paper money.

After the older man left, I politely inquired about him. Dede seemed annoyed if not cross. He said the man was collecting money to build another mosque in the neighborhood.

Dede suddenly snapped, "Why do we need another mosque? There are too many around here. Look up there, at the corner, and another over there (gesturing across the darkened cemetery)." He then added, "They should collect money to build a cooperative or a beer factory to give people work so they can eat! We have enough mosques!"

6

THE SCENT OF THE ROSE

By week's end, the love fest was coming to an end – two glorious weeks of whirling, initiations, bacon, and the scent of the rose. And now a big crowd assembled for Süleyman Dede's final night. The tireless cooks, working in a tiny kitchen, wanted to be pragmatic as well as festive in feeding the crowd, so they committed a grievous error.

Somewhere along the way, Dede mentioned that he liked pizza. We didn't know if he was embracing all things American or if he was referring to *lahmacun*, the traditional pizza of Turkey. It didn't matter because the well-meaning cooks covered both bases. They created a homemade pizza for Dede and ordered take-out for everyone else. When the pizza guy rolled up with boxes of pepperoni, everything appeared to be moving smoothly, that is until Reshad burst out of the house to confront the boxes of evil pie. If the present moment is a palpable substance, Reshad cleaved it open like an angry thunderbolt.

The hour-long scene, in front of guests and Dede, went down like this:

EXT: SILVER LAKE FRONT PORCH – EVENING
RESHAD
(Loud, chastising, and angry. Repeat as needed.)
"HOW COULD YOU? HOW COULD YOU, ON THE FINAL NIGHT THAT OUR GUEST, THE SHEIKH OF THE MEVLEVI, WHO HAS GIVEN SO MUCH, WHO HAS TRAVELED THOUSANDS OF MILES TO BE WITH YOU, HOW COULD YOU ORDER PIZZA!! MY GOD, WHAT WERE YOU POSSIBLY THINKING? AND AFTER ALL THAT I HAVE TAUGHT YOU ABOUT THE GUEST! THE GUEST IS THE MOST IMPORTANT, AND TO ORDER PIZZA, DON'T YOU UNDERSTAND WHAT WE ARE WORKING WITH? IT IS THE QUALITY OF VIBRATION IN THE FOOD. WHAT WAS THE PERSON THINKING WHO MADE THIS FOOD? WHAT ABOUT THE ENERGY OF FOOD? DON'T YOU KNOW HOW SENSITIVE I AM, HOW SENSITIVE OUR GUEST IS, HOW SENSITIVE WE ARE IN THIS WORK? YOU REALLY BLEW IT. YOU REALLY BLEW IT BIG TIME!"

I can't remember if the tirade played out for 20 minutes, maybe 30, or was it an hour? I tried to put on my zen face, but Reshad's anger twisted my equanimity into a knot.

There's a particular kind of pain — call it a force field — that you endure with public chastisement. What's worse, in a Sufi school, you don't get your turn on the witness stand. You can't offer an alternative story, apply logic, or explain your intentions. You simply deal with the flood of feelings that arise from your gut.

As often the case with Reshad, you could choose between two reactions: inner work or emotional abuse. Neither was satisfying.

Inner work required remaining present, breathing quietly, and letting the energy move through — yes, the energy must go through. Emotional abuse came from tightening, reacting, and feeling the injustice. Enduring a tirade was not about justice or right and wrong. When your shit got stirred from the bottom of the pond, the experience was simple fluid mechanics. The challenge, in the spirit of Archimedes, was to remain buoyant.

There was a third possibility: challenging Reshad. But, that didn't seem possible when your spiritual teacher was also a father figure.

For years, I wondered: Was Reshad's pizza tirade over-the-top? Was it emotional abuse? Or was it a conscious shock precisely applied to allow the energy to go through — a wake-up call because we had fallen sway to the "glamour" of hosting our VIP guest and had fallen "asleep" on his last night? Maybe it was both: Over-the-top abuse allowed the energy of the octave to go through.

There is a Sufi expression: "may you never recover," and the "Pizza Night" was a pivotal turning point, one of many such shocks. Over the next 20 years, these splits in the path would emerge again and again, culling beloved friends from the school.

Pizza Night was one little octave within the bigger octave of Rumi emerging in America. Like a series of nested Russian dolls, one octave inside the other, the Rumi project was unfolding from the planted seed. Dede made it clear: Rumi in America was all God's doing — a necessary next step in an unfolding Cosmos.

In the *Last Barrier*, Reshad used the metaphor of the rose bush to explain how the sacred drama played out, something he learned from a sheikh in Istanbul who described how the line of prophets unfolded. As the sheikh told it:

"Once there was a rose bush. It was carefully planted so that the roots grew deep in the soil that had long been prepared to receive

it. These roots were Abraham. As the rose grew, it was necessary that it be correctly pruned, otherwise it would eventually go wild and would not fulfill the intention that the gardener had for it. The stem, through the good earth, deep roots, and pruning, was straight and strong. That stem was Moses. One day the most perfect red rose appeared in bud. The bud was Jesus. The bud opened; that bloom was Muhammed." [1]

Next, the sheikh reached for a vial of rosewater and invited Reshad to savor the scent:

"Take it," he said, "and tell me what it is."

The sheikh's message: The scent of the rose was Rumi. This is what Dede meant when he said, "Mevlana has absorbed Jesus, Moses, and Mohammad — Mevlana is the *sultan of today.*"

As I reflect on Pizza Night, the most immediate question is why did Reshad choose to destroy such a beautiful rose on Dede's last night? An executive chef would have given a stern glance to his cooks, "Pizza? Bad call," and let the show go on. The teaching moment could come later in the kitchen — but not in front of the guests.

But a spiritual teacher is not an executive chef; he's a magician. There are black magicians and white magicians, but they don't wear identifying hats. A magician works with energies. A magician can *do.* "Doing" is a Gurdjieff term which means to understand the laws of nature, resist the octave's mechanical influences, and use the tension released to transform energies. The magician senses the energy of the octave moving through the moment like the opening of a rose. He knows that the scent of the rose is the most intoxicating of all. To this end, he is not afraid

1. Feild, Reshad, *The Last Barrier, Element Books,* 1993.

to blotch the painting or crush the rose. His actions are inspired from a higher world.

Maybe, Reshad was a magician — or maybe his emotional filters simply had no check valves. Either way, the energy of Rumi was coming to America and, pizza or not, it had its own job to do.

The sheikh in Reshad's story wasn't finished:

The sheikh smiled and beckoned me to come and sit in front of him.
His presence was overwhelming. He took my hands in his. "Listen to
me carefully and on your journey remember what I have to tell you.
Now mankind needs the smell of the rose. One day he will not even
need that." [2]

The story of the rose confounded me. How could we possibly grow beyond the eloquence of Rumi's poetry? Why would we evolve beyond the scent of the rose?

The rose is part of a larger story — a 700-year transmission from Balkh to Konya to Atatürk to Dede to Los Angeles to Coleman Barks to Coldplay and to whatever comes next. Each step of Rumi's grand project unfolded like a birthing process, each precipitated by an outside shock.

Dede's visit to Los Angeles ended on a discordant note, but the Mathnawi is filled with ribald stories and raucous conflict. Consider the central act of the story: Shams of Tabriz disrupts the local madrassa and, to the student's shock and dismay, spirits the headmaster away to become the poet of mystical love.

Transformation is often cloaked in in the cloth of chaos, as J.G Bennett explained:

"There is a very high wisdom that knows how to use chaos for

2. *ibid*

creation and how to bring harmony out of conflict. We must be careful not to criticize what we cannot possibly understand."[3]

Planting seeds can be a messy business. Consider the tale of Larung Gar:

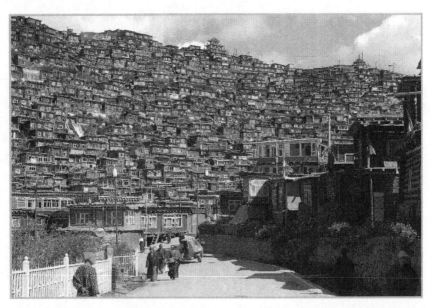

Larung Gar Buddhist Academy

In 1980, the monk, Khenpo Jigme Phuntsok, accompanied a small group of the faithful to take refuge in a vast, barren stretch of mountains in Sichuan Province, China. Khenpo set up camp, planted the "seed," and secretly practiced Dzogchen meditation with his group while they hid from the Communist Chinese who were engaged in the violent destruction of traditional Tibetan culture. Khenpo's humble enclave grew for the next 20 years to become one of the largest and most influential centers for Tibetan Buddhism in the world — 40,000 monks, nuns, disciples, and

3. Bennett, J. G. 2017. Transformation. CreateSpace

residents, plus hundreds of temples and dwellings — all from one man planting a seed.

Today, the Chinese are destroying Larung Gar. Similar to Atatürk dismantling the Sufi brotherhoods, the seed that Khenpo Jigme Phuntsok planted will be forced to move on, and take root again in another time and place.

Süleyman Dede planted a seed that had been germinating for 700 years. With perfect synchronicity, the first tendril appeared 14 days after Dede's visit in the form of Coleman Barks, a young University of Georgia English professor who was attending a conference in Maine hosted by Robert Bly. Coleman recollects:

"Bly's conference was about poetry, music and mythology and whatever Robert had been reading lately," Coleman recollected. *"At that point, Bly had been reading translations of Rumi, and he had a stack of these that he gave to me. Bly said, 'These poems need to be released from their cages.'*

"And so I began doing that, just on my own for seven years. Every day I would sit with A.J. Arberry's translations trying to feel the interior of the poems and to rephrase them. I never thought of publishing them. I just let them pile up."[4]

By planting the seed, fortune released Rumi from his scholarly cage a second time — the first when Shams reportedly threw

4. *"Coleman Barks, Foremost Rumi Translator, Talks about the Persian Mystic's Timeless Appeal and His Own Spiritual Life." SF Gate. http://www.sfgate.com/living/article/Coleman-Barks-foremost-Rumi-translator-talks-2537796.php*

Rumi's books down a well, and now with Robert Bly challenging a young Coleman Barks. Seven centuries after Shams confronted Rumi in the marketplace, this major octave was about to shift gears.

Dede's 1976 visit began what I called the "Mevlevi Spring," a Rumi love bubble of devotion, creativity, and generosity that lasted for two and a half years. Also during this time, Coleman Barks began his poetic magic turning Arberry's scholarly translations into contemporary free verse.

"Every afternoon, after I finished teaching," Coleman recounted, "I'd go into a restaurant and work on poems — have some tea and work on those. From 1977 to 1984, there are seven years when I wasn't even thinking about publishing. So, that was a kind of practice I did."[5]

While Coleman was sipping tea with Arberry, I was scouting the neighborhood to stage our first full performance of the Whirling Dervishes. I found a baroque former movie palace — the Ukranian Cultural Center — on Melrose Avenue in Los Angeles.

The major challenge was to create the traditional costumes. Niki Mantas remembers making the patterns:

We created the patterns from pictures and film footage. The VCR hadn't been invented yet, so it must have been 8 mm.

I remember trying several prototypes. One problem was to get the skirts to unfurl without causing a fluttering wave, so rope with little lead curtain weights was eventually sewn into the hem. Worked like a charm.

The sikkes were my responsibility. I tried to find milliners in

5. Colker, Vicki Goldsberry. "Interview with Robert Bly and Coleman Barks." C/Oasis: Writing for the Connected World, 2002. http://www.sunoasis.com/blyinterview2.html

Vancouver to see if I could apprentice with someone, but I never found one.

There were several artisans who worked with felt, but their advice and my efforts led to something that looked, at best, like dryer lint in the shape of a bird nest. I knew I would never master the technique, so I made a pattern, guessing the height and taper from pictures. I measured heads big and small and used basic geometry to figure the top and bottom circumferences. Then I racked my brain to figure out how to determine the two rays that would carve out the right segment and curve in order to draw a template. I found some beautiful camel hair coat material through my aunt, who was a tailor for Oppenheimer in Chicago.

The assembled sikkes needed a cardboard lining to stand up, which was a cheesy approach, but these were desperate times. We were a week away from the first public Sema, so cardboard forms it was. Each sikke was custom-fitted to keep them from flying off.[6]

Working around the clock, we pushed through our physical exhaustion, partly out of our belief in Gurdjieff's "Greater Accumulator" — what he described as an unlimited reserve of cosmic energy available when one is freed from emotional limitations. In truth, we were driven by the simple reality that the show must go on.

6. *Interview with Niki Mantas, April 26, 2017.*

Sema at the Ukranian Cultural Center, Los Angeles, 1976

With the clock ticking before the performance, a huddle of young dervishes gathered around me, chanting in prayer, as I hot-wired 4-gauge stage lighting cable into the too-small breaker panel. More than prayer, they shielded my illicit handiwork from the prying eyes of the building manager. It was a trick I learned at film school: keep one arm behind your back when "tying in" to avoid a killer jolt to your heart.

While we turned in Los Angeles, one thousand miles away, a young seeker named Jonathan living in Boulder, Colorado had a vision. Following an inner prompting, Jonathan started to paint Rumi's likeness on a bed sheet. Jonathan took this synchronicity as an omen to encourage his Sufi group to invite Reshad to Boulder.

The "next step" that Reshad and Dede prayed for had emerged.

The Boulder group offered us a magnificent house in downtown Boulder for the first Mevlevi *tekke* in America.

We accepted the invitation, packed a U-Haul truck, loaded up children, a newborn, and a caravan of cars and headed across the desert toward Boulder — but not before Reshad told our Armenian landlord neighbor that Sufis always return a space in better shape than they found it. Reshad offered our services, *gratis*, to paint the seven-bedroom duplex, while we simultaneously loaded the truck. Yes, the Greater Accumulator.

Thus began the Mevlana Foundation. Fifty years after Atatürk shut down the Konya *tekke*, a dervish lodge was born in the West.

Dede, Reshad, and David Bellak – Boulder, 1978.

Two years later, in 1978, Süleyman Dede returned to America to consecrate our dervish lodge, our Mevlevi *dergâh*. People traveled to Boulder from various parts of the world to sit with Dede, our living link to Rumi.

My friends reminisced:

"I remember my first encounter with Dede. My heart burst open, and I seemed to melt into thin air. The powerful effect of love made me speechless for days. What an amazing experience. What an incredible time in my life."

— Barbara

"I was pregnant. Dede placed his hand on my head and said a prayer. I felt such silence through my body. Then he said that this child was a boy, and the next one will be a girl. I had NO plans to have any more children, but, he proved to be correct — my next child was Alisha."

— Judith

"I was cooking a pilaf for about a hundred visitors by myself. Dede passed by the kitchen with his interpreter. He stood there for a moment watching me. Then he said, 'May you never recover.' Only now do I know what he meant."

— Jonathan

"I remember coming down the stairs, turning the corner, and walking down a path towards Dede who was sitting at the end. When I reached him, he uttered the name, 'Sultana.' That's how I got my Sufi name. So much love emanated from him."

— Aleta

"I wondered why he never gave me a name. Then one day he called me over and said, 'I haven't given you a name because you already have your name... Susan, which means love. Not wishy-washy love, but fiery Love.'"

— Susan

"Dede wanted to talk to us privately, so he took us to my parent's bedroom, as the house was full of guests. He kissed both of us on the forehead, told us to sit down and listen. Ken and I had had a serious disagreement that morning and were still angry with each other. I thought we hid it well, but obviously not in Dede's eyes. He took both our hands and proceeded to talk to us about love and understanding and forgiveness. What he said was very pertinent and specific to what Ken and I had experienced... as if he had been present with us that morning. We walked out of the room radiating love for all. We were in awe of his incredible love and wisdom."

— Lima

"I had the pleasure of making bread for Dede. After I finished kneading the dough, Dede offered to give the bread-to-be a blessing. I knelt at his feet with the dough and looked up into his eyes. As he met my gaze, I felt an amazing energy emanate from him. It was like looking into the entire universe. The experience may have lasted 10 seconds, but it has been with me forever."

— Penny

"Dede said that when he passed, he would always be with us in our hearts."

— Vic

"Dede gave me a Sufi name, but it was in a lucid dream. He told me that I should wait to use it. 'Not yet,' he said. I'm still not using it because I have not had a follow-up dream."

— Jinny

"During one of the zikrs with Dede, my state moved so that whole room of people were doing zikr inside of me — a gift from a conscious man. It repeated and has repeated, but that was the first taste. Reshad was sitting behind me; he leaned forward and said into my ear, 'That was the fourth dimension,' which in no way *describes the situation. Wily old fox, I wonder what he was seeing."*

— Hajah

Dede was known for appearing lucidly to all manner of people, as well as for his premonitions, deep intuition, and appearing far from Konya in unexpected places. David reports that upon arriving in Konya from Scotland, Dede's wife Farista Hanim asked David nonchalantly if he had seen Dede — in Scotland!

"No," David replied puzzled, "Why?"

Farista Hanim said that a few weeks previous, one of Dede's *murids* in the Netherlands reported seeing Dede walking in the city. In fact, over the years, Farista Hanim described numerous such "sightings" by people from abroad.

Many of my friends have received visitations from Dede in their dreams. Ron Lemire recollects:

Not long ago I had a dream of Mevlana, Dede, and Reshad, and it reinforced the knowledge that when we meet such Souls with an open heart, we are always in the company of Friends.

David also received Dede in a lucid dream which he recounts:

In December 1978, I returned to Konya from London in quite a state of turmoil. As I entered Dede's house, I burst into tears and fell to the floor at Dede's feet. He calmed me down with a glass of tea. As we sat, I lamented, "Dede, I wish you had a telephone in your house so I could phone you from London!"

Laughing, Dede replied, "I know you – you'd like to put a telephone in my grave!"

Several years after Dede's passing, I had a dream in Edinburgh where I seemed to be in a large Victorian drawing room in London.

In the dream, the phone started ringing out in the hall. I heard someone answer it.

A moment later Reshad bounced through the door prancing like a pixie, singing, "It's for youuuuu."

I went out to the hall and answered the phone with the usual "hello." Dede replied in clear and unmistakable Turkish:

"Oğlum, sen nasılsın? (Son, how are you?)"

Completely shocked, I replied excitedly, "Baba, ben iyim SEN nasılsın? (Father! I'm fine, how are YOU?")

Dede replied with great satisfaction and strength of voice, "Ben çok iyiyim! (I'm really well!")

"EYVALLAHHHH!!!" I shouted back, abruptly waking myself up.

At that moment, I drew an immediate connection to Dede's statement years ago about the telephone in his grave. The impact — so powerful and real — has never left me.

§

And with that, Dede's Boulder visit came to an end. The first *tekke* in North America had been consecrated. Dede posed for a group photo, headed down the walk, and turned to face us proclaiming:

"Even though I leave you now,
know that Mevlana is in your heart."

Dede departs the tekke, Boulder 1978

7

THE BLOOM COMES OFF

———— ✺ ————

The peak of every wave follows with a trough. Each spring tide comes with a corresponding ebb. After Süleyman Dede's 1978 visit to Boulder, the Mevlevi Spring ended. The wave of love that had washed onto our shore quickly pulled back with a dramatic undertow.

Take this as a parable: It was around this time that NASA engineers noticed that the orbit of Skylab, America's first space station, was decaying faster than anticipated. More importantly, NASA had no way to control where their 77-ton loose cannon would crash. To save money, NASA neglected to build in any control or navigation mechanisms to return the orbiter safely to earth. They assumed that the Space Shuttle would arrive in time to boost Skylab into a higher orbit. And that didn't happen.

As Skylab's orbit decayed, a worldwide Skylab frenzy grew. Congress demanded answers from NASA on how they intended to avoid casualties and disaster. People hosted Skylab parties wearing silly protective hats. The San Francisco Examiner even offered $10,000 to the first person to deliver Skylab debris to its office.[1]

"I need to get out of Boulder," I thought, not necessarily connecting the end of the Mevlevi Spring with Skylab's precarious descent. "It's time to leave the Sufi circus and start a real life."

I should add that I was 28 years old, the critical life juncture – and octave-multiple of 7×4 – called Saturn's Return. On July 11, 1979, with Skylab rapidly descending, the NASA engineers fired the station's booster rockets. They hoped that by sending the crippled space station into a tumble, it would fall harmlessly into the Indian Ocean. Well, almost. The bulk of the craft crashed into the outback in Western Australia. Kaboom, the Skylab story was over.

As I was plotting my exit, the kitchen phone rang in the Boulder *tekke*. It was my mom. She jumped straight into it:

"Bruce, I just received the most amazing phone call," she began. "Two guys found Skylab in the Australian Outback and approached Hill & Knowlton in Sydney. They

The space debris from Australia that restarted my adult life.

want me to turn it into an event, and I need your help."

My mother, Nann Miller, known in the PR industry as the "P.T. Barnum of public relations," famously staged enormous publicity stunts that earned her a place in the Guinness Book of World Records — "World's Biggest Root Beer Float" (Hires Root Beer),

1. Long, Tony. "July 11, 1979: Look Out Below! Here Comes Skylab!"
https://www.wired.com/2011/07/0711skylab-reentry-space-junk/

"Biggest Ice Cream Sundae" (Knudsen Ice Cream)," "Biggest Group Portrait" (Los Angeles Olympics), and so on.

I spent two seconds to consider the opportunity, and just like that, I was crossing the desert in a rental truck to receive a crate of space debris and restart my adult life in Los Angeles.

Around this time, Reshad also left Boulder. He returned to England to try his hand at normal married life with two small children, but his marriage quickly unraveled.

Bruce moves to his new life, Utah desert.

Further proof that all orbits were declining, the Colorado Sufi group that had sold us the house for the Mevlevi *tekke* sued us for what could be termed "breach of spiritual contract." In the proverbial sense, "Rumi had left the building," and now they wanted their house back.

We spent the next months, not advancing Rumi's message of unconditional love, but dealing with lawyers and depositions. Since Reshad didn't want his name besmirched in the courts, we agreed to a "kangaroo-court" arbitration overseen by Yogi Bhajan's representative in New Mexico.[2] The Sufi plaintiff happened to be a former student of Yogi Bhajan and, not surprisingly, we lost the suit and relinquished the *tekke*.

With all things going downhill, more would come. Reshad would soon lose his Mevlevi title, official permission, and privileges. This was unfortunate because Reshad took great pride

2. Yogi Bhajan (d. 2004) was a spiritual teacher, and entrepreneur, who introduced Kundalini Yoga to the United States. He maintained a community of American Sikhs in Espanola, N.M.

in his designation as a sheikh and his signed official permission. Reshad recounted the story of the document:

> *"Süleyman Dede sent it to me; it's a copy of the original. Dede said, 'Look, people will argue with you; they will deny you and on and on. But you take this document, and they can never argue again.'*
>
> *"That's Dede's signature and seal on the statement saying that he came to Los Angeles and initiated me. It's true that I have been denied many times since by many people because I don't behave like people expect me to behave."*[3]

As it turned out, Süleyman Dede's signature and seal were not permanent. Dede ended Reshad's tenure as a sheikh of the Mevlevi Order – maybe because Reshad wasn't a Muslim, or because of his excessive drinking, his rocky marital life, or because he was too much of a loose cannon to represent Rumi's legacy. We may never know for sure, but Dede's doubts about Reshad began to form from the beginning. David Bellak remembers Dede's reaction to the Pizza Night:

> *After the pizza tirade, Dede spoke to me about it. He was shocked, saddened, and clearly upset at the way Reshad behaved — that Reshad could conduct himself in a way so contrary to the precepts of Mevlevihood. Dede had no idea that he could act in such a manner.*
>
> *Dede asked me about it again when I was helping him to bed. Since I had no background in the particulars, having met Reshad briefly on only a few occasions, there was not much that I could offer.*
>
> *After Dede's return trip from the States, he began to receive letters*

---

3. Lee, Virginia and Walker, T. Mike. "Reshad Feild: Sufi and Healer," *Yoga Journal*, October 1982, pp.26-32, https://tinyurl.com/ydch9rc5.

of concern, particularly from people distressed about Reshad in the Vancouver community because of his behavior. By this time I was living in London, and continuing to return occasionally to Konya. On each trip, Dede would ask me to retrieve the letters from abroad he kept in a small pine box under his divan, waiting for me to translate.

At one point, while going through and reading the letters, Dede became clearly upset. He said something in a harsh tone that I didn't understand. I asked him what it meant. His reply was cryptic, even startling:

"It means, ben, ben, ben! (me, me, me)," Dede snapped sharply.

Everything Dede heard through these letters created the impression of Reshad being all about himself.

Ivan Rhodes, a student of Reshad who had become very close to Dede, remembers the growing tension among Reshad's Canadian students:

"Several students had been complaining about Reshad from multiple directions," Ivan explained. "Unfortunately, I was one of them. Finally, Dede felt compelled to respond.

"Dede had high hopes for Reshad and hoped Reshad would continue to grow, but in the end, Reshad was unable to respond appropriately to the role. Dede didn't reject Reshad; at a certain point, Reshad rejected Dede, rejected the guidance coming through him. Maybe, Reshad thought he was beyond Dede's guidance. But, in almost any kind of relationship, that won't let a relationship work.

"One time, I came into the room when Murat Yagan[4] was talking with Reshad, and Reshad turned up the juice – turned up the spiritual energy or presence. You could feel it. It was physically demonstrative.

"Tears began to come down Murat's face. He said, 'Okay, Reshad, I can see you can do this. You can stop now.'

Murat Yagan

"And then Murat said something that stuck with me. He said, 'Reshad, how come none of your students can do what you just did?'

"Maybe Reshad thought he was the only one in the universe who could do what he just did. Maybe, he thought it wasn't his job to teach anyone else to be able to do that. Murat was insistent that if Reshad could embody presence, but not be able to teach it, there was something amiss with what he was doing.

"In the end, Reshad could not accept any kind of authority – in this world at least. That's my impression. I don't wish to demean Reshad in any way; we all have our weak points and weak moments. And I never lost my love for Reshad, but watching people suffer under his tutelage was, in many ways, difficult and demeaning."

4. Murat Yagan, a teacher from the Kezbah Caucasus tradition and author of I Come From Behind Kaf Mountain was actively working with students of Reshad in Vancouver at the time. Murat had become very close to Dede.

When I shared this chapter with my friend Jinny, she replied from Africa where she was helping to build a Montessori school for children:

> *"In spite of his personality and immature emotional intelligence, Reshad was an instrument. He brought people together for life. He served a great purpose in spite of his flaws. There's a paradox in that the bigger the person, the bigger the flaws. Suppressing one's expression to hide one's flaws is like a living death. Whatever you think of Reshad, he didn't suppress anything."*

Despite being terminated by Süleyman Dede, Reshad was unapologetic, perhaps because he saw his teaching style as an example of Sufi unpredictability. Around this time, he offered an enigmatic riddle during a *Yoga Journal* interview:

> *"I'll give you three definitions of a Sufi," Reshad challenged.*
>
> *"One is: 'A Sufi is the son of the moment.'*
>
> *"Second: 'If you find a Dervish, he is non-existent.'*
>
> *"And the last one: 'There is not room for two sheikhs in one house, but there's room for twelve dervishes under one blanket.'"*[5]

Unfortunately, the two sheikhs, Dede and Reshad, would no longer share the beautiful space created for Mevlana. With his marriage on the rocks, Reshad left England and landed in Santa Cruz, California to teach at the invitation of students there.

I flew up from LA to join Reshad for a talk where he and I shared a motel room. On the last night of my visit, Reshad was invited to a private dinner with a dinner date hosted by the

5. Lee, Virginia and Walker, T. Mike. "Reshad Feild: Sufi and Healer," Yoga Journal, October 1982, pp.26-32, https://tinyurl.com/ydch9rc5.

organizer. As we prepared ourselves, Reshad called to me from the other room. He seemed road weary and maybe even soul weary.

"Bruce, I've been on the road for a long, long time," Reshad lamented as he pulled himself together for the dinner. "A long time. But, you get used to it; you get used to being on the path."

I felt honored to receive this man-to-man candor from Reshad, but his picture of the "path" unnerved me — a path engineered by a cunning God who seemed to pull no punches when it came to fate. I would have been devastated to leave a wife and two small children behind in England. Reshad's "path" felt more like one of sadness and emptiness than one of spiritual adventure, but I also marveled at his comfort suffering the slings and arrows of fate.

Some people ascribed Reshad's fate to a karmic path called the "Way of Blame" — the path of the *malāmatiyya* — an intentional path described by Shams of Tabriz and others:

> *Rumi's teacher and companion, Shams-i Tabriz (d. 1248) referred to the malāmatiyya as "those who try to draw people's contempt upon themselves by outwardly blameworthy actions."*[6]

The straight-up term for *malāmatiyya* is "mess-maker." The great mystic Ibn 'Arabi (1165-1240) took it further. He saw the path of blame as a deliberate concealment of one's mystical state:

> *As for the great ones among them, the name [malāmatiyya] is ascribed to them because they conceal their states and their rank with God when they see that people criticize their acts and blame what they do because the people do not see the acts as coming from God... But were the covering to be removed and were they to see that the acts belong to God, no blame would attach to him upon whose*

6. Schimmel, Annemarie. *The Triumphant Sun, A Study of the Works of Jalaloddin Rumi.* SUNY Press, 1993.

hands they appeared. In this state, all those acts would be noble and good.[7]

Gurdjieff's students also felt that their teacher's *malāmatiyya*-like behavior was a kind of teaching mask. J.G. Bennett writes about Gurdjieff:

My wife and I both observed an extraordinary change [in Gurdjieff]... For a few days, we caught a glimpse of the real Gurdjieff, and that all his strange and often repellent behavior was a screen to hide from people who would otherwise have idolized his person instead of working for themselves.[8]

Was Reshad's *malāmatiyya*-like behavior evidence of a mystical state or a coded pathology from the DSM-5? Should we drop the pretense and call it what it appeared to be: garden-variety bad-boy behavior? Not sure. Since I'm a Loyalist on the Enneagram, Reshad's blameworthy behavior didn't force me from his side — at least for now.

Tonight, I was to be his squire — the shield-bearer at his side for the dinner with his Santa Cruz host and his date. But as his dinner date went on and on, I realized that my squire shield was powerless against the love-smitten gaze growing between Reshad and Penny, the red-haired twenty-something sitting across from him at the table. While the two made goo-goo eyes, I pondered Reshad's inexplicable ease in turning the page from one life chapter to the next, from Los Angeles to Boulder to Devonshire and to Santa Cruz — and now from wife two to what

---

7. William C. Chittick, *The Sufi Path of Knowledge: Ibn al-'Arabi's Metaphysics of Imagination* (Albany, NY: SUNY Press, 1989), pp. 374-375.
8. Bennett, John. *Witness: The Autobiography of John G. Bennett*. Omen Press, 1974, p. 243.

appeared to be wife three. It was especially unsettling to a stick-it-out guy like me.

But I didn't have the full script. I wasn't in on the full *malāmatiyya*. I didn't realize that after Süleyman Dede's visit to Boulder, and after his let-down from Reshad, Dede invited his son Jelaleddin Loras to tour the States so that his son could become the successor.

Surprisingly, what I shrugged off as Mevlevi melodrama back then is studied by serious academics today. As an example, I found this passage in a recent book by William Dickson, Assistant Professor at the University of Winnipeg, titled *Living Sufism in North America: Between Tradition and Transformation*:

> *Following the completion of his schooling [Dede] handed his son a one-way ticket to America, while his mother Farişta Hanum stood with a packed suitcase for him. The message was clear, and Jelaleddin landed in New York in December of 1978 with instructions from his father to train Americans in the Mevlevi path. He currently lives in Hawaii and acts as the president and spiritual director of the Mevlevi Order of America, working to continue his father's legacy of teaching traditional Mevlevi whirling, meditation, and prayer. Like his father, Jelaluddin continues to teach women to turn, in contrast with traditional Mevlevi practice of teaching only men.* [9]

After Jelaleddin arrived, he made his way to Seattle. I was still living in Boulder, deep into legal cleanup, when the phone in the *tekke* kitchen rang. It was Reshad.

9. Dickson, William Rory. *Living Sufism in North America: Between Tradition and Transformation. Suny Press 2015, p104.*

"Bruce, listen to the sound of my voice," Reshad commanded with gravitas. "If there is any way you can meet with Jelaleddin, even if for five minutes, just to look into his eyes, I would *strongly* encourage you to do this."

I'm Mr. Six, a Loyalist, but obedience to one's teacher is something else — a tenet of traditional Sufism. Reshad called it "characterized obedience." Contrarily, he also taught us to "live in the question" — to not take things at face value and to listen within. Swimming between these two currents — questioning and obedience — describes the zig-zag path shaped by the Octave. When to push, when to let go, when to question, when to obey — this yin and yang invite the creative force, Gurdjieff's Third Force, the energy that moves the story forward.

On the questioning/obedience scale, I lean far toward the left. I've seen the pendulum swing back sharply from blind obedience to deliver its collateral damage. If the ultimate goal is to become responsive to your own inner guidance, a safe-and-sane Sufi needs to listen, check within, abandon one's bias, then "do." When you rise to the level of a magician, you abandon the foreplay and just "do."

For now, I had no issue looking into Dede's son's eyes, except for the small fact that I was living in Boulder and Jelaleddin was in Seattle. As synchronicity would have it, Republic Airlines was launching service with a promotional $49 round-trip from Denver to Seattle. The bad news was it would take 5 hours to get there with stops in Missoula and Spokane.

As the plane nose-dived into the mountain-encircled airstrip in Missoula, I tried to remain present and awake. I had been taught the importance of "carrying the line" to become an energetic vector of the Third Force, to embody the presence that opens the doors of possibility. Or as Reshad would sing to us in his lyric:

Go on your way, be easy,

Go on your way, be free.

Carry the line you're given,

Take it to a waiting world.

Yes, that seed-carrying business.

I did my best to carry the presence at 30,000 feet. I rented a car in Seattle and drove to the house where Jelaleddin was staying. I collected myself at the door because I was carrying the all-important line from Reshad. I knocked on the door and was let in. Jelaleddin looked up. He was eating dinner while watching Franco Zeffirelli's *Romeo and Juliet* on TV. Having been on a plane all day, I was famished, but I was too shy to ask for a bite.

"So, who are you?" Jelaleddin asked.

"Bruce, from Boulder. Reshad sent me."

"Okay. Hi," Jelaleddin nodded.

Reshad hadn't mentioned that Jelaleddin couldn't speak English. With that, Jelaleddin went back to his dinner and TV, but I had looked into his eyes, chalked one up for characterized obedience, then drove back to the airport.

Years later, I learned from my wife, Karen, that Reshad also sent her to meet Jelaleddin. She surmised that Reshad was trying to inoculate his students from choosing sides in the coming Mevlevi split — but the split occurred regardless. As Reshad was forced out from his official role, students felt compelled to choose between Reshad and Süleyman Dede — but now through the proxy of his son.

The split culminated when Reshad invited Jelaleddin and his entourage to his house in Aptos, near Santa Cruz. My wife, Karen recollects:

We had been told all week that Jelaleddin would be visiting us as a guest of honor, so we cooked and cleaned all day in preparation. We had never cleaned so diligently — windows, crevices, the garden, everything.

Jelaleddin arrived with a small entourage right before dinner. We were asked to go downstairs while Reshad and his visitors had dinner together upstairs.

At the appointed time, we were invited back upstairs to join our guests for zikr. Jelaleddin was our special guest, so he was invited to lead. The zikr went well, and the energy picked up, even becoming jelal, a more forceful zikr.

Suddenly, Reshad started intoning loudly over the Arabic, "Lord Jesus Christ have mercy on me..." Over and over, Reshad sang the Christian prayer. I didn't know what to do, so I stayed with the zikr, but I could see that our special guests were becoming uncomfortable.

The tension continued to build while we chanted. At a certain point, it became too much, and Jelaleddin abruptly stopped the zikr. He was visibly upset.

Reshad strongly defended himself, saying, "I'm a Christian; this is how I pray."

I was new to all this and didn't understand what was going on. In fact, all of us were young; I don't think anyone understood what Reshad was doing.

Unsettled by the proceedings, Jelaleddin and his group got up and left the house.

Reshad gathered us together and said something about our guests being too attached to "religious form." We accepted the explanation without understanding the spiritual turf battle at play.

These events — the lawsuit, the divorce, Reshad's Mevlevi title,

Skylab, the splitting of friendships, and now the great *zikr* battle — all seemed isolated at the time. In retrospect, a messy alchemical process was at work: *nigredo*. In alchemy, *nigredo* describes the blackness by which the inner fire activates and matter starts to putrefy.

"Everything that has lived, dies; everything that is dead putrefies and finds a new life."[10]

The bloom was off the rose. The Mevlevi Spring came to an end. Its closure also marked the beginning of the Islamic world's long descent into turmoil. Within a few weeks after Dede's departure, army troops implementing martial law for the U.S.-backed Shah of Iran fired submachine gun bursts into a crowd of thousands, marking the point of no return for the Iranian revolution, the hostage crisis, and most importantly, the emergence of a radical Islam that still defines our politics today.

A few years later, Süleyman Dede also left this world. David Bellak remembers:

A letter was on the kitchen table when I arrived home from work. Dede had passed from this world to join the Beloved ten days before on January 19, 1985. Though not unexpected, it was nonetheless a shock. The tears were many and quick to come.

My then-wife and I agreed that I must leave for Konya at once. My immediate concern was that Dede would just disappear — his legacy consigned to history — and be quickly forgotten. I felt that no one in Turkey really had any idea of his contribution and the efforts he had made to convey Rumi's teachings to so many people in lands

10. *Antoine-Joseph Pernety, 1758*

distant from his home in Turkey. I was distressed that I hadn't been notified immediately, but why would they? No one was aware of the nature of our relationship. Our link was between hearts. There is a well-known saying, "From the heart to the heart is the way," kalptan kalba yol var.

David and Dede in 1984

Arriving in Istanbul, I called upon Dr. Celalud'din Çelebi, Rumi's hereditary heir and head of the Mevlevi order, to pay my respects. Dr. Çelebi assured me that Dede had carried out his appointed duties and would be buried according to the rites of Islam. The perfunctory nature of our meeting heightened my concern that Dede would be forgotten by history.

I continued onward for the 12-hour bus journey to Konya. After leaving the bustling bus station, I left my bag at my home of years' past, the small ancient Olgun Palas Hotel where Ali Bey, the manager, welcomed me. Then I left on the familiar 15-minute walk through the old neighborhoods to Dede's little home.

When I last saw Dede in the summer of 1984, my wife and I had come with our infant son. During that visit, Dede was a shadow of his former self — weak, pale and gaunt, nearly blind. We sat together quietly, and although I tried to say a few words here and there, I felt inadequate and unprepared for the obvious. I gently placed my son in Dede's arms, which clearly pleased him.

Looking now at the photograph, I see something I had missed at that moment. Dede's face seemed peaceful but empty, as if he was already connected by an invisible cord he appeared to be holding in his hand — a cord to another place.

It was during an earlier visit in the winter of 1981-82 that I sensed this day was not far off. The premonition revolved around the circumstances of

Dede with David's son.

the local blacksmith, Halil Bey. It was nearly impossible to walk to Dede's home without passing Halil Bey's nondescript mud brick space with the handmade horseshoes lining the walls. During my early visits to Konya, Halil Bey would be my touchstone — my uncle and mentor — when Dede was away.

Unexpectedly, Halil Bey came to the room where my wife and I were staying. Usually positive and smiling, Halil was crying and distraught with tears in his eyes. He explained that earlier that day his landlord had given him 30 days' notice to quit the shop he had occupied for 26 years. We did our best to comfort him.

Halil Bey

"I have been shoeing horses all my life," he sobbed, 'What will I do now?" I know no other way to make a living."

Later in the evening during that visit, I couldn't help but notice Halil's darkened door as I walked briskly to Dede's home to bid farewell. When I told Dede the news from Halil, Dede looked crestfallen. I had never seen him like this before — shocked and distressed. Dede was an especially insightful and intuitive soul, so I guess he sensed that the world so familiar to him was coming to an abrupt conclusion.

"Davut," he said with almost a whimper, "What will happen to me? They have taken my dervish away from the door; there is no one else, and you are going. What does it mean?"

Today, as I write this, I still struggle to make sense of Dede's words: "They have taken my dervish away from the door."

I remember once asking Dede a question while we were walking, "Sir, who is Halil Bey?"

Dede replied, "Halil Bey tam bir derviş" (a perfect dervish).

I had assumed that Halil Bey and Dede were simply neighbors, a friendship of the Way, nothing more nor less. Yet, Dede's words – a perfect dervish – opened a world to me. By definition, a dervish is one who sits at the threshold between the two worlds.

And now here we were, three years later – at the threshold between worlds.

Straining with his weak voice, Dede asked, "Davut, how do I look; what do you see? Tell me, son, is this a fatal sickness (ölüm hastası)?"

I feigned cheerfulness, unable to confront this reality, but I knew it to be true.

And now, it was two years after taking that picture of my son. After the 12-hour bus ride to Konya, I headed straight to Dede's home in the Old Town, just over the wall from the Hacı Fettah cemetery. The concern I felt when I first learned of Dede's passing was that his final resting place would be little more than a marker, and that is what I found — a small wooden board in the freshly turned earth with his name.

My immediate reaction was, "This isn't right. Dede should have something to reflect his stature and worth." I didn't know what I could do to bring about an appropriate tomb, but I was determined to try, for it only seemed right.

I let myself in through the walled garden door, and into the little mud house that had been home for Dede and Farişta Hanim and their five children over many years. Farişta was there alone as I came through the door, her face taut and strained, but peaceful as always. I kissed her hand in greeting, tears welling up in my chest.

No, I must be the brave son for her. Tears would come later, and still do.

I do not remember many of the words we shared, but I hold a clear image of our being together, experiencing the same absence.

Unsure of what to say, I sat on a chair next to the divan that had been Dede's "corner." Farişta Hanim began to speak:

"Davut, it was in the evening, about this same time. Dede was there as he always was, but for days he had been unable to eat. I tried many times each day to feed him."

Farişta Hanim preparing a festive meal with stuffed vine leaves

Farişta Hanim's voice was strong, yet emotional. They had been married sixty years. After a pause, she continued.

"I was trying to feed him yogurt with a little water, but it was hard for him to swallow, plus he didn't want anything. He just wouldn't eat."

She paused again, then continued:

145

"I went to the kitchen to get something, and when I returned Dede was still sitting there, in silence. Suddenly, he sat upright and spread his arms just like in the sema, with his head moving, whispering the name of God so silently (Allah, Allah, Allah). And then, right before my eyes, he fell over... and was gone."

When I started this project, I searched the official Mevlevi histories and Rumi Web sites in Turkey to find information about Dede. I was startled to find no mention of the man who had held Mevlana in his heart for the benefit of so many. According to Kabir Helminksi, who visited Dede annually during his final years, Dede was held in high regard by Mevlevis, Bektashis, Jerrahis, and others.[11] But from my inquiries, Mevlevi officialdom seemed to regard Süleyman Dede as just a simple cook.

I contacted Ibrahim Gamard who confirmed this:

"The current head of the Mevlevis, Faruk Çelebi Efendi, told me that every Ramadan, Dede came to cook for the Çelebi family in Istanbul," Ibrahim said. "Faruk knew Dede for nearly 30 years, but he does not recall that Dede had special knowledge of Sufism. Everyone I asked in Turkey said he was a cook, and nothing more. However, the Westerners who met Dede told very different stories about how wise (and sometimes crafty) he was. I have been unable to resolve this contradiction."

I asked David Bellak about the contradiction, and he replied:

"Sufism is not a dry academic or intellectual concept to be 'studied.' It is a living breathing organism of its true followers. Dede himself said on more than one occasion, 'You know a tree by the fruit it bears.'

"There are few people who truly recognize Dede's station," David continued. "We know him as a *sheikh*, but he was also a

11. Dyer, Daniel Thomas, www.patheos.com/blogs/livingtradition/2018/03/book-review-rumi-comes-america/

murshid, about which he spoke to me on one occasion in private in late 1975. I offer this not out of any misplaced loyalty, but from objective knowledge of the heart that Süleyman Hayati Dede was a true servant of Hazrati Mevlana. He was an embodiment of both the Masnavi and Rumi's teachings. Though one may hold title and position, that in itself doesn't mean that such a one can understand and know.

"Dede was a master of himself and a master of his worlds. He was fully educated in the Shariat (law), versed in Koranic scripture, and could quote surahs from the Quran and passages from the Masnavi. One moment he would play the perfect village idiot, then in the next hour,

Dede cooking fish outside his home.

display mastery of esoteric knowledge and Mevlevi tradition. By dint of my connection to him, I also became steeped. Perhaps together we were dinosaurs in a changing world.

"I am aware that there are those in Turkey who regarded Süleyman Dede as just a simple cook. On numerous occasions, he alluded to cooking for the Çelebi household, as well as for *Atatürk* on one or more occasions. He also referred to cooking in a 'poor kitchen' outside the Konya Dergah, the original lodge of the Mevlevi Dervishes, when it was closed by the government in 1927.

"There were elements in Turkey who disliked Dede and who displayed jealousy and suspicion towards him (and by extension to me as well on occasion), perhaps because of the constant stream of foreign visitors coming to his door. Yet he held no public position, nor did he attract attention to himself — quite to the contrary, he avoided it.

"Conversely there were elements who kissed his feet and sought his blessings. Those alive with the inner eye of truth knew who he was. There were some interesting women who called on him, to whom I served tea in perplexity as he held court and engaged in deep discussions of spiritual worlds. And, there was a whole group of people, most of whom appeared to be well-educated, wealthy, and of high social standing. When they came to his home to pay respects during of the celebrations of Mevlana's 'wedding night' on December 17, they appeared to be his devoted students or regarded him as a Master of the Way without question.

"I suggest that you can find the answer to your question about these contradictions in Book VI of the *Masnavi*, 2044-2138 — *The Story of the disciple of Shaykh Hasan Kharraqani*."

So, I followed David's suggestion and opened Book VI.

Rumi's story tells the story of a young dervish who makes a long and arduous journey to seek a celebrated sheikh. When the young man arrives, he knocks on the door with high hopes. Instead, the sheikh's wife sticks her head out and utters "unseemly and foul and silly words" to the young dervish. Shockingly, she renounces her husband vociferously, calling the celebrated sheikh a "vain hypocritical impostor, a trap for fools and a noose for leading into error." She also tells the young seeker, "Hundreds of thousands of callow simpletons like you have fallen, through him, into a hundred rebelliousness's."

The dumbfounded young dervish sought to clarify the contradiction, even enlisting the townspeople. Was the man at the center of the story a celebrated sheikh or should the young man believe the wife, that her husband was an impostor? Similarly, I wanted to know if Dede carried the spiritual authority to be Rumi's right-hand man, the transmitter of the Seed, or was Dede just a simple cook?

In the story, the sheikh suddenly appeared, riding a fierce lion with a live serpent for his whip. The sheikh turned toward the young dervish and laughed, saying, "Do not listen to the evil suggestion from the Devil."

The moral: A true sheikh rides a fierce lion without fear. Rumi explains further that this lion *of the soul* may not be visible to the senses, yet the lion is "not concealed from the spiritual eye."

Even if no one else saw Süleyman Dede riding that fierce lion, I did — with my spiritual eye.

Like with all Sufi stories, the contradiction remains. Years ago, a friend of mine visited Konya and was told by the Turks in no uncertain terms:

"That story about Dede and the bacon? It never happened."

David succeeded in his mission to arrange for the construction and backing for an appropriate final resting place for Süleyman Dede.

8

THE IMPULSE

It was on a hot summer night in Chicago's White Sox Park, August 1965, when thirty-seven thousand screaming pubescents exploded as The Beatles took to the stage.

I was too young to fully understand the cosmic significance, but my $2.50 ticket injected me into the generational impulse that was sweeping across the Atlantic. Dubbed the "British Invasion" and the "Sixties," this wave of awakening would ultimately draw me into Vietnam protests and experimental cinema, plunge me into a mountain-top experience of pure consciousness and deliver me into the New Age. The Fab Four were riding the leading edge of that wave – a tsunami of change that would ultimately bring Süleyman Dede into our living room ten years later.

I couldn't make out the lyrics to "Twist and Shout" against the jet-engine decibels of girls unleashed, so I watched the surge in fascination. Even at age 14, I

My ticket to the Sacred Impulse.

knew that the bedlam that night was a harbinger of something bigger.

Years later, Reshad put these forces into a larger context:

"At certain times of history, a movement appears on the surface of the planet," Reshad explained. "This impulse can move through a human being, a small group, or even a society. It is sometimes called the sacred impulse. The problem with a sacred impulse is that it is a neutral energy, and neutral energy can be used for one's own purpose. It can turn for good or it can turn into an involuted spiral that extracts energy and money from other people.

"I am reminded of the great Inca civilization of South America," Reshad continued. "The Incas were a mystical race who considered the planet, and life itself, to be very sacred. But like everything in this world, one thing produces its opposite and along came the Aztecs. The Aztecs were essentially scientists. They invented the calendar and many other things. Gold was of tremendous importance to them. During the time of the Incas, gold was a result of an eternal alchemical process. Next came the Spaniards who took the gold and served it up in rich churches as a symbol of Christ's image — and we know what came of that.

"In other words, whenever a sacred impulse comes, so does its potential opposite. That is when people get caught in the world of attraction — a world appears that appears to be so good that they forget the First Cause."[1]

Genghis Khan rode a sacred impulse, rising from humble beginnings to sweep across Asia and propel Rumi's pilgrimage from Balkh to Anatolia. Seven centuries later, The Beatles also rode the impulse that emerged out of the resurgent hope of post-war Britain.

After this creative impulse crossed the Atlantic and spawned

1. Feild, Reshad, Letter to Peter Cunz

the 1967 Summer of Love, 1969's Woodstock, the New Age movement, and a generational burst of art and spirituality, its dark side appeared as a spasm of cultism in the 1980s. Among the many dark notes were Jim Jones' mass suicides in 1978, the sexual proclivities of Da Free John (Adi Da) who exiled to Fiji in 1983, the 1984 Rajneeshee salmonella attack on restaurant salad bars in rural Oregon, and the 1986 murder of Sulocana Prabhu, a Hare Krishna whistleblower who was assassinated two days after he published an expose of the cult.

After the bloom came off our Rumi *tekke* in Boulder, a quick succession of events in the 1980s signaled that the sacred impulse that brought Rumi to our shores was moving on: Reshad was stripped of his Mevlevi credentials, Süleyman Dede passed away, and radical Islam appeared on the world stage.

It was around this time that Reshad left his family behind in England, moved to Santa Cruz, and married again, this time to Penny Belknap, a young student who became his third wife. Healing, breath, and geomancy formed Reshad's new focus as Rumi briefly took a back seat.

Reshad teaching dowsing in California, 1980.

This was not the first time that Reshad, like a spiritual cat with a nine-pack of lives, deftly set up shop anew, reinvented himself in the moment, and plunged into the unknown. He followed the classic trajectory of the Hero's Journey, forging chapter after chapter of his own myth in a manner that Rumi would understand:

Don't be satisfied with stories, how things have gone with others.

153

Unfold your own myth, without complicated explanation,

so everyone will understand the passage: We have opened you.

Rumi[2]

When I first visited Reshad in Santa Cruz, I was shocked to see the Reshad myth take a surprising turn. Instead of the Mevlevi atmosphere I knew in Boulder, Reshad's students were now drinking beer and playing darts.

In the 11 years that had passed since we founded the Institute for Conscious Life, Reshad had changed residence 13 times, so I wasn't surprised when he embraced an invitation for a book tour in Germany and Switzerland and ultimately left America behind.

Reshad arrives in Santa Cruz, CA, 1980.

Reshad treated invitations as divine signs on his hero's journey – invitations from the sacred impulse itself. The book tour took him to Zurich, Basel, Frankfurt, Munich, Heidelberg, Cologne, Stuttgart, Bremen, and Hamburg.

Reshad wrote to me in 1986 while traveling to Hamburg with Penny and his assistant, Matt Shoemaker:

"It is incredible to realize that we have been in Germany for only ten days. The amount of work with which we have been involved is almost impossible to describe, but it most certainly changes one's normal sense of time. You should visualize the picture. Three tired people, hardly grumpy yet, but working on the breath, with three

2. Rumi, Jalal al-Din. 2004. *The Essential Rumi, New Expanded Edition. Translated by Coleman Barks and John Moyne. Reprint edition. San Francisco, CA: HarperOne.*

(very) large scarcely liftable suitcases of the Feild's, plus the smaller, but heavy case of the Shoemaker.

"But then there is the guitar. To protect it, I bought a case costing £65. The man demonstrated that you could stand on it, but that meant it had to be extra-large. The guitar is too big to fit into the trunk of a taxi, which means we take two taxis everywhere. I'm also armed with books, papers, the inter-continental radio (plus instructions), camera and case, briefcase, a plastic bag filled with nibbly bits for the journey, Penny's purse (always crammed), and two coats.

"The plan for getting onto the train (in the allotted two minutes) involves Reshad, looking like an aged tourist, hanging as much of the small stuff 'round his neck and shoulders, then leaping into the train to find seats. Plunking his things down, he runs back down the aisle to find Penny, bending over and pulling the suitcases up the stairs from Matt Shoemaker, who, by this time, is sweating quite a lot. The next step is to lift the darn' things above head height onto the racks.

"Eventually we collapse, and it is time for lunch — always the same menu: goulash soup, fried eggs, hot dogs. The tea is weak, so I carry my own extra tea bags, plus coffee, slices of cut meat, somewhat tasteless, and thin slices of cheese (also tasteless) and half-cold semi-boiled eggs. The trouble is that it all tends to make our trousers and skirts shrink.

"Hamburg is three hours away. I heard they booked the same ghastly hotel as last year. The bathroom consisted of a hand-held shower in a closet. The two stalwart women who run the place, looking like something out of Wagner's "Ring" cycle, were never available since they suffered from gross hangovers and could be found with their feet up on the only sofas when we wanted a cup of tea. Then there is the public lecture tomorrow night which will be about 300-400 people again, then the two-day workshop, and early the next day we take another train, a long ride to Stuttgart.

"The hall in Heidelberg was packed with around 350 people, and of course, you must remember that everything has to be translated into German. I must wait while the translator is thinking about what I have said, and then I must listen within to see whether he or she is thinking in German, English or American! I must also remember that the Germans need to have everything laid out systematically. My usual 'scatter technique' is not good for the German logical mind. And lastly, these German 'spiritual seekers' are far, far too serious, but they love to laugh, and laugh they do when you strike the right note. I have found that a good song, sung from the heart, will melt nearly everyone.

"There are already wonderful memories, as well as the endless effort to exist while trying not to offend more than the average number of people per day. There are gardens everywhere, wonderful manners, almost too impeccable, and a society thirsting for knowledge. They desperately want to do something for the world, especially with pollution [radioactive fallout from the Chernobyl nuclear accident] on everyone's lips. I tell them that the accident in Russia was truly creative, and if they could think positively, much good could come out of it all."

I never imagined that a German book tour would plant the seed for Reshad's life-long vision: a residential living school that blended traditional Sufi teachings, deep esoteric knowledge, and the path of Rumi — all fused in the aristocratic style of a British manor.

But that is what happened. Reshad followed the sacred impulse to move his work to Switzerland — a decision affirmed by Madame Luba, the niece of Gurdjieff who told Reshad with a Gurdjieffian pun, "You should put *all and everything* into Switzerland this year."

Gurdjieff's niece, Madame Luba

My wife, Karen, recalled, "One moment the work was centered in the States, in Santa Cruz, then boom! Reshad left and everything was happening in Europe."

For all and everything to manifest, like a casting agent, the universe pulled people from their habitual lives and trust them into the impulse. In 1986, Peter Cunz was a consulting electrical engineer for large ventures — power plants, electrical grids, and hydroelectric — that included stints in the Middle East and Africa. Later, he held director positions in Alcatel, Bull Ltd, and the Swiss Federal Office of Energy. In addition to his corporate life, Peter had cultivated a life-long interest in esoteric pursuits. Peter described his journey:

"After attending university, I left the church and made an eight-month trip to India and Nepal — searching for what's behind this visible world," Peter recounted. "I traveled internationally, but also made an inner quest. I did yoga, studied Theosophy, Gurdjieff, and Ouspensky. When I met my first wife, I discovered Islam — her father was an imam. Through Islam, the Koran united what I was searching for in India — the Unity of everything. The fundamental message: whatever you do, don't forget the final source, Allah."

"In 1986, a local pastor friend invited Reshad to Spreitenbach in Switzerland," Peter continued. "He asked me to simultaneously translate. I said, okay, why not? I was impressed by some snippets in Reshad's talk which touched my heart. I remember his words, 'A teacher's teaching finishes with his death.' That impressed me."

Peter's wife, Anne Cunz-Regard also remembered the talk:

"During one of the sessions, Reshad began to get on my nerves," Anne recalled. "I found him too selfish and very chaotic in his talking — yet for some unknown reason, Reshad's words touched me very deeply and I burst into tears.

Penny, Anne, and Peter, 1986

"After the seminar, we had tea. Reshad wanted to show us a mystical object. I now know that Reshad was a master in the art of charming people, but this was all new for me. He unwrapped a Chinese jade sword that was engraved with chakra-like circles and I felt myself get pulled into his description of his magic stone."

"During our tea, Reshad complained about his German publishers," Peter continued.

Reshad with the sacred jade artifact

"Reshad had always wanted to offer a 24-day seminar that

followed the 24-day practice program offered in his books, but his publishers felt the financial risk of 24 days was too great."[3]

"Reshad also complained that he needed tickets for a trip to Spain," Anne added. "I am a very efficient, organized person, so I dropped everything I had thought about Reshad during the seminar and kindly offered to help him in whatever way."

"A month later, I translated for Reshad," Peter said, "and again sat for tea afterward. Reshad complained again about his publishers and the 24-day seminar. We listened politely without committing to anything."

Anne continued, "A few weeks later, we received a letter from Reshad. A third time, he griped that his publishers wouldn't sponsor a 24-day seminar. By this time I was getting fed up with the complaints. Completely out of the blue, I said to Peter, 'Let's do it. Let's just move.'"

Peter remembers the moment: "Anne just set fire in herself. It took a moment for her words to set in, and then I said, 'Okay if you wish, why not?'"

Just like that, a door opened for the impulse to bring Rumi to Europe.

Anne explained her decision process: "It was spontaneous – no different than if you asked me to get some vegetables at the market. We sat at the table and planned the whole event. I discovered that our local village had four houses in Valbella for children's ski vacations that would be unused during the summer. So now we had a place. We created a flyer and sent a few off. But we hardly had any addresses."

---

3. The 24-day practice program from Reshad's book, *Here to Heal,* offers a series of morning, afternoon, and evening breathing exercises and visualizations. Many of the practices came from *A System Of Caucasian Yoga* by Count Stefan Colonna Walewski.

Peter continued: "Valbella had room for 85 and we needed 40 people to break even. Someone I knew in Germany offered, 'I'm sending a mailing to 10,000 people and if you want, I can include a little pamphlet.' But they added a strong warning, 'You

Alpine views at Valbella

are crazy to do that with Reshad. You will see what will happen. Impossible!' And just like that, 84 people signed up for the 24-day program."

Anne's unexpected fire and Peter's consent were all it took. The impulse had been invited to Switzerland.

Describing Reshad's 24-day event as a seminar doesn't do justice to his method for accelerated change. Reshad fashioned an energetic crucible that was like immersive theater, or better, a greenhouse where the correct amounts of light, moisture, and nutrient can grow an orchid, or even better, a braising pot where slow heat in a covered vessel breaks down the tough connective gristle in the meat.

In the Reshad school, the covered vessel required four ingredients:

1. *Beautiful impressions:* In addition to the natural setting, the vessel needed glorious floral arrangements, consciously prepared food, and a meticulously cleaned space.
2. *Attention:* Students were asked to breathe consciously while cooking, cleaning, listening, and performing practices.
3. *Impeccable timing:* Yes, the Octave.
4. *The Ingredient:* This is what Reshad called grace or the Third Force.

Reshad's charismatic presence transmitted this mysterious fourth ingredient. It was an awakening energy that functioned like a catalyzing yeast. Guitar in hand, Reshad invited people to leave their wounds behind, cross the "great water" (the dividing line between the lower chakras and the heart), and open into the immediacy of the heart.

One newcomer described the effect: "I noticed a little flame glowing in the center of my heart. The feeling stayed there and was still there after three days. And it still remains."

Another student experienced it as "an awakening into the fullness of human possibility."

Valbella's breathtaking peaks, crystal lakes, and verdant valleys offered the first ingredient. The elusive fourth ingredient could come through Reshad's voice. Imagine blending the royal gravitas of Sir Laurence Olivier, and the bad-boy sauciness of Peter O'Toole, plus the romantic earnestness of Richard Harris, with the antic impishness of Benny Hill. That was the ingredient.

At Valbella, the other ingredients were a bit of a crapshoot. Reshad didn't have an experienced team to maintain the braising heat needed to transform the emotional gristle of eighty-four newcomers. All he had was Richard Rozsa, a young helper from California in his twenties.

"I was by far the youngest everywhere we went which was quite awkward for me," Richard remembers. "But I took my position

Richard, Reshad, and Penny.

161

seriously. I remember someone setting the table and dropping a fork. The person bent down to put it back when I caught him with my eye. I was walking around like a drill sergeant the whole time.

"There was also this massive physical effort," Richard continued. "All the tables had to be moved out of the main room for class and then moved back for lunch, then out again for an afternoon class, then in for dinner, then out for evening class, and back in for the next

Richard teaching Reshad's Movements in Sound.

day's breakfast — in and out like that for 24 days. I was also teaching Reshad's "Movements in Sound" plus the Turn of the dervish. Remarkably, I didn't find myself getting exhausted. It was just lovely. It was exquisitely beautiful. Susanne and I had this room off the kitchen which had a window looking out across a field and toward the mountains. Oh, my God, it was just so beautiful. It's by far the most beautiful place I've experienced in my life. Really, really it was shocking."

How Susanne Hauenstein, who Richard met on the trip, snagged a prized bedroom off the kitchen at Valbella comes with a story — a story that speaks to Reshad's defining trait: an aerialist who worked without a net.

"While planning the event, Reshad told Peter and Anne Cunz that he wanted someone who does 'natural cooking,'" Susanne recalled. "Reshad's understanding of *natural* meant cooking of the region, what people eat in the area. Peter and Anne, not surprisingly, understood *natural* differently, so they hired a macrobiotic cook, a very nice lady who flew in from Holland. The cook ordered all sorts of rice, seaweed, and macrobiotic foods. I was helping her in the kitchen, and following her very complicated way of cooking, when Reshad discovered what kind of cook she was. He stormed into the pantry and exploded, screaming at the cook, 'I don't want your thought-forms in my brown rice!'

"And what he meant, was 'I don't want your concepts' — your macrobiotic ideas — in the food. So, on day one of the 24-day seminar, with eighty-four people to feed, the cook was paid and let go immediately — thrown out. Somehow, I knew that I was going to lead the kitchen. I knew it before Reshad even asked. I said to Richard, 'I will probably be the one.'

"I wasn't a professional cook; I was a painter, an artist. But, now I had to prepare three-course meals for what grew to 90 people. This meant that the rolling food carts had to enter the dining room precisely at 1:00 p.m. — everything on time. The people helping in the kitchen weren't cooks either; one was a retired judge. And, I confess, the chicken was a little raw on one occasion which made Reshad quite upset.

"I worked my ass off for seven days, with two to three hours of sleep per night, always planning the menu and calculating the ingredients for the next day or two. Oh God, it was hard! I would even do the shopping in the morning. This was at a time when I was insecure in myself. Even though it was exhausting, and eventually I couldn't do it anymore, I took on the challenge. There aren't that many times in your life when you experience that level of intensity, that level of energy — and this was on top of the energy and learning of the whole seminar."

Richard and Susanne – a rare moment of rest.

Peter Cunz also faced the "aerialist:"

"Before coming to Valbella, Reshad had broken his hand," Peter recalled. "It became increasingly clear to me that our 24 days would begin with Reshad in the hospital. Anne was getting ready to take Reshad and Penny to the hospital in Chur, but rather than getting into the car, Reshad said, 'First, I need to receive everyone who comes.'"

"Reshad personally greeted everyone as they pulled up," a student recalled, "even telling them that he was a Muslim (which he wasn't), presumably to put them off. He fetched suitcases from the ladies (with his working hand) and carried them to the house. It was all very touching and heartfelt."

With Reshad headed to the hospital and the seminar about to begin, Reshad turned to Peter, paused to let the moment sink in, and announced, "Peter, you have to sit on the chair and teach."

"I was a bit scared as this was the first time I had confronted such a challenge," Peter remembered. "I was a little unsure about what I was being asked to do, but still I felt it was okay; I will try. I cannot do more than I can.

"Earlier in my life, I had a teacher, the author Elisabeth Haich, who wrote the book, *Initiation*. Elisabeth helped me discover the certainty of my deeper self. She taught me that if a situation arose where I had to take a stand, I should tap into this feeling of deep inner stability. This helped me be with Reshad over the years because, with Reshad, I always felt off-balance."

Elisabeth Haich described this attitude in her book, *Initiation*:

"I have learned that it is wrong to want to apply the thoughts of another person in one's own life. [My teacher said to me,] 'I don't want you simply to follow me on the path... Go your own way on the path you select for yourself, corresponding to your own innermost inclinations. Don't accept any statement because I made it. Even if

it is true a hundred times over, it still is not your truth, it is not your experience, and it will not belong to you. Bring truth into being, and then it will belong to you."[4]

Valbella launched an annual tradition – the International Summer School. The following summer, a second school was held in Beatenberg, Switzerland. For Richard Rozsa, helping to run Valbella and Beatenberg was like hanging on to a wild horse.

"I held the reins tight because this thing was galloping," Richard said. "Nobody knew what Reshad would do next. Even though it was tough, it was also quite easy. Despite continuous shuffling of tables and all the rest, there was always room for it — space and time emerged for what needed to happen. People just jumped in and did it. We reached a point where this overflowing love began to come through.

"Looking back, I see Valbella and Beatenberg as expressions of love, but I also see myself as a young man, completely overwhelmed, demanding a military-like perfection from people. Reshad kept asking me to soften, to lighten up. And then one day, at Beatenberg, he blasted me – blasted me

Susanne honored for her role as the Valbella cook.

hard, blasted me to the point that my sense of pride or specialness was gone – saying, 'You think I need you. I don't need you! You're here to fulfill a function. You're not special at all; I can replace you at any time, blah, blah, blah.' He went on and on and on.

4. Haich, Elisabeth. 2000. Initiation. Aurora Pr.

"I tried to get away from the scene because I didn't know what to do," Richard continued. "Everyone saw me get blasted, so they gave me a wide berth.

"Reshad announced that there would be initiations. He was going to initiate Peter Cunz and a Swiss psychologist as Mevlevi sheikhs. Reshad wanted me to turn, but since I had an injured foot, he asked, "Can you turn?" And I said, "If you ask me, of course." In effect, I was answering the call to turn to my Lord.

"After being blasted, I had nothing left to give at that point, but I started to turn anyway. I began to turn and turn and turn and turn and turn. I didn't stop turning while people received their initiations.

"When I stopped turning, I was completely spent, ready to collapse. As I caught my breath, Reshad turned to me and said ever so gently – and I'll never forget the moment – 'And you, Richard... you are a dervish.'"

It's worth pausing here to share Süleyman Dede's definition of *dervish*:

"The word dervish means *der*, as in *door*, and *vish*, as in *sill*," Dede told our group in Los Angeles ten years earlier. "A dervish is in a humble state, like a sill on the ground. The dervish is also the door. If the door does not open, how will we enter? From the window? Will we drill the ceiling? First, we open the door, and the dervish will enter," Dede said. "Therefore, it is the custom for the dervish to not step on the sill, but to step over the sill. It is out of respect. The dervish is with the ground, so humble, soft-hearted, saying *Eyvallah* to everybody. Therefore, being a dervish is crucially important. Being a sheikh is easy. A sheikh is someone who sits on the post, the sheepskin in the *sema*. But a dervish is needed! *Eyvallah!*"

Reshad explained to us at Valbella: "There is a saying, 'All dervishes are Sufis, but not all Sufis are dervishes.' The Sufi way has nothing to do with people whirling about. In this school, we are not following Mevlana, but we are following what Mevlana followed."

Valbella group photo

This was the context to understand the hundreds of people flocking to Reshad in Europe. They were not looking for Rumi; they were responding to the little flame glowing in the center of their hearts. The impulse had awakened a deep spiritual hunger, a collective longing that lifted Reshad onto a bigger stage – but that stage came with a price. Unlike the States, where handfuls of students came in and out the door, hundreds of seekers were now latching their aspirations onto Reshad.

As his closest students, we held the faith that Reshad – our hero on this journey – could ride this bigger wave. But for someone as sensitive as Reshad, bigger waves also cause spectacular wipeouts.

9

THE ABYSS

We were living in Los Angeles when our good friend Julie called us from Atlanta on a Friday afternoon.

"Jonathon and I drove by this old two-story house and thought of you. It could use a bit of work, but it's a unique historic Southern home."

The words "immediately thought of you" put my synchronicity sensor on high alert because Karen and I were keen on leaving L.A. for a more family-friendly place to live.

"Listen," Julie continued. "There was something about a developer. You need to call the owner."

"Like now?" I asked.

"Yes, call him."

Tim, the owner, explained the situation. He needed to move. A sleazy developer had made a low-ball offer but postponed signing the deal because the notary was closed until Monday.

"Can you come over?" Tim asked.

"Like now?" I asked.

"It would be great if you could."

I turned to Karen: "The owner wants to know if we can come now."

"Fly across the country to look at a house?"

"I could go."

"No, we all have to go together," Karen insisted.

And with that Karen, our toddler, and I headed to LAX to purchase three walk-up fares for the red-eye to Atlanta.

Eight hours and 1700 dollars later, we pulled up to the house straight from the airport. The cracked columns, peeling paint, and sketchy roof teased us in the dawn light in a beguiling way, "Hey, big boy, want to have an adventure?"

After breakfast, we toured the house.

"What do you think?" I asked Karen. "It's a lot to take in."

It feels like fate," Karen observed.

"Well, I'm game," I ventured.

Toasting our new purchase.

"So am I," Karen agreed.

And just like that, we were all in. If Peter and Anne could invite Rumi to Europe with the ease of buying vegetables, Karen and I plunged into our own life-changing adventure without much thought.

We justified our purchase as being "for the Work." For this reason, before we unpacked or even had jobs, we decided to invite Reshad and his American students to a seminar in our home. We

170

hoped to rekindle the work in the States, but in our enthusiasm, we didn't realize that the impulse had pushed Reshad onto a much bigger stage and that the bigger spotlight had increased the stress in his life as well.

No one had hosted a residential seminar in their home before, but with our boundless Sufi enthusiasm, Karen and I did just that. Unlike Valbella with its endless mountain vistas to release steam from the crucible, our home could barely absorb the psychic strain. There would be non-stop cooking, cleaning, and furniture moving, plus the added demands of raising a toddler in the seminar space. Complicating matters, Karen and I had hoped to blend into our new neighborhood as affable folks – and not as weird Sufis from California.

When Reshad and Penny arrived, this hope quickly collapsed when Mary Beth, our socially Southern and genteel piano teacher friend, brought along her new boyfriend, John. Hardly a card-carrying Sufi, John was a Vietnam vet auto mechanic who bristled from simmering trauma.

On day three of the seminar, Mary Beth introduced John to Reshad in our intimate study. As we sat quietly in the circle, Reshad asked the pointed question: "Do you have any guns?"

"As a matter of fact I do," John replied without a trace of menace — that is if you understood Southern culture and guns, which of course, we did not.

I'm not exactly sure what happened next, but some well-meaning student, acting in "characterized obedience" to the sheikh, made a phone call. Within minutes, our street was ablaze — end to end — with squad cars and flashing blue lights. The police looked in John's trunk, harsh words followed, and John left indignantly. Like all things with Reshad, the forces at play were not what they appeared to be. John and Mary Beth became happily married.

But pressure in the crucible continued to climb.

The next day, I heard a commotion erupt outside the kitchen, so I quickly turned to look. Reshad's wife, Penny, stood in the driveway, her face etched with grief, sobbing, screaming, "You're killing him. You're killing him! Can't you see? You're killing him!"

The two 2-liter bottles that Karen and I had dutifully purchased for Reshad were now dumped on the pavement in a puddle of gin and vodka. They told a tragic tale like two cars leaking fuel after a collision.

I'm not sure if it was hours or minutes later, but a car pulled up driven by Jonathon and Julie. The two had pulled out of the school's spiritual quicksand a couple months earlier, making them perfect drivers for the getaway. Penny opened the door, stepped in, and was whisked away. That was that, except it wasn't.

Reshad had introduced us to "the emotional tone scale" – a way to understand human emotions as a range of vibration. Devised by L. Ron Hubbard in 1951 as an auditing tool for Scientology, Reshad discreetly offered this teaching "for students only." Similar to the electromagnetic spectrum which measures frequencies of light and radiation, the emotional tone scale measures human emotion in a similar fashion. At the high end is pure consciousness and bliss. The darker, heavier end is characterized by shame, depression, apathy, and failure. Reshad added "comatose" in his version as a final coda. The teacher's job is to coax the group energy up the scale.

Penny's exit punctured our tone scale like a gut punch. I wasn't prepared to see Reshad sink into a whirlpool of grief — or was it shame, or depression, or failure? Garden-variety grief would have been tough enough, but as I watched my 1000 watt spiritual teacher descend into an unknowable pain, I felt powerless to help. Every spark of light in our household sunk into a black hole as Reshad slumped into a force-field of despair in the middle of our kitchen.

The moment was complicated by the fact that Reshad was

scheduled to speak that evening to a heavily-advertised gathering at the Quaker Meeting House — an event that many from the Atlanta psychological community would attend. Reshad was barely able to eat, let alone speak to a discriminating crowd.

"I must... fulfill... my promise," Reshad sputtered like a mortally-wounded dragon.

My Sufi friend, Daniel Ellis, and I headed to the event, set up the room, and kept the guests engaged with Sufi banter, all the time peeking out the window to see if Reshad had arrived, which he hadn't.

As ten minutes late turned into twenty, and maybe even forty, I approached the lectern to deliver my apologies. Suddenly, I saw two headlights head down the drive. I gave Daniel a thumbs-up sign of relief. But then the car stopped. Even worse, the car shifted into reverse. I watched in panic as the car backed up the drive. My panic turned again to relief when the car stopped again, this time at the top of the drive. Then the cosmos shifted again when Reshad and driver finally made their way to the Meeting House.

By nature, Reshad carried a palpable presence whenever he entered a room. I likened his force to the Mystery Spot, the gravitational anomaly located in the redwood forests near Santa Cruz, California where up becomes down, time distorts, and feelings magnify.

A Swiss friend of mine described the effect: "Whenever Reshad came in, suddenly everything would change, making it very difficult to stay centered."

This was the default Reshad-enters-the-room experience. Add to this, the effect of Reshad's marital separation six hours earlier and you have the complete Mystery Spot sense of what awaited the audience. As Reshad staggered through the door, Halima, a sweet-hearted member of the local Sufi community, blurted out:

"Oh my God, he's drunk!"

Reshad collapsed into his seat without a trace of stage presence or regard for his audience. To underscore the "what-you-see-is-what-you-get" quality of the moment, Reshad began to tear up his lecture notes — not as a dramatic bit of stage business, but into tiny paper wads. He dipped each pea-sized paper projectile into his drinking water and flicked it into the audience, bonking therapists and well-meaning seekers like a mischievous school child.

"I don't think anybody had ever seen anything quite like it," Daniel recalled. "In fact, I think there was a method to the madness. The people getting bonked were pompous in some way, or asleep, or maybe needed a jolt of self-awareness. It was outrageous but hardly pointless.

"The extraordinary aspect was the talk," Daniel continued. "Reshad described the nature of the mind, and how the mind had an energetic shape, like a semi-circle interlaced with nodal points. If you could get over the circumstances and the crazy stuff going on, Reshad's ideas were really right on, dead on, profound."

Over the next few days, Reshad's attendants leaped into action, preparing consciously-cooked entrees as an antidote to his pain. He would bite into a lamb chop grilled with rosemary and mustard sauce, spit it out, and sink deeper into despair. Not surprisingly, his taste for alcohol didn't diminish, so I attempted my best man-of-the-castle impression to kick our boorish guest out of the house, which again, was like pouring flea-watts of light into the Mariana Trench.

Out of my depth, I prayed that some photons of light remained in the depth of Reshad's emotional chasm. I hoped for a resurrection, but my bandwidth had also collapsed. I handed the scene over to our beloved saint-in-residence, Elizabeth Bolton, a grits-and-gravy, no-nonsense, street-strong psychotherapist who planned to cook Thanksgiving dinner for Reshad while everyone else struggled for air at the bottom of Reshad's tone scale.

Karen and I abandoned our sense of guilt, loaded our son into the car, and drove to Tennessee. It would be my first Marshmallows-and-Jello Thanksgiving, also known as Southern comfort food – praise the Lord. As we backed out the driveway, I felt more relief than remorse. Yes, I had left my beloved teacher dying in battle in the foxhole of love. But Reshad, with his nine-pack of lives, would rise again.

We even managed to take a seminar portrait before the shit went down:

Group portrait, November 1988

10

VALBELLA II

In 1931, a Georgia farmer named Moses Coleman struggled to get a fair price for his crop during the depth of the Depression, so he decided to try his luck with onions. To Moses' surprise, the onions he grew didn't have a biting hot onion taste. They were sweet! His farmer neighbors quickly followed suit and began to fetch top dollar for these mysterious mild sweet onions.

Today, thirteen counties in rural Georgia produce the Vidalia onion. Blessed with a warm, moist climate and low sulfur soil, this fortuitous combination of weather, water, and nutrients produce a unique sweet and juicy onion without the volatile sulfuric acid that makes you cry.

I tell this story as a parable about soil, and also because I was startled to see our good friend and travel companion, Eleanor Hand, lug a 25-pound bag of Vidalia onions toward our gate as we boarded the Swissair flight to Zurich with our young son.

Six months after Reshad's meltdown in our kitchen, Eleanor,

Karen, and I were headed to Valbella II — the reprise of Reshad's first European summer school two years earlier. We would be the first Americans to participate in Reshad's 24-day residential adventure as students.

Eleanor grew up in Vidalia, Georgia and through serendipitous timing, Vidalia's annual onion harvest had begun the week before. Eleanor wanted to make a cultural gesture by carrying Vidalia onions from her home soil to the Valbella kitchen. In truth, it was an onion experiment in reverse — to discover if our hot American temperaments would transplant into the sweetness of the Swiss soil.

Ruedi and Simone, two flower shop proprietors from Basel, met us at the Zurich airport. We loaded up children, three hundred pounds of luggage, our welcoming flower bouquets, and the onions into two cars and raced up the mountains to Valbella.

As we stepped into the crystalline air of Valbella, a stunning silence overwhelmed our senses. Except for the gentle clang of cowbells, Valbella's deep, geologic quiet offered the slow braising we would need to cook from within. As Americans, we were just one

Hillside view from our chalet

ingredient in a mix of students from several nations, so we decided to lay low and see how our personalities would fit in.

Eleanor headed to the kitchen and graciously presented her onions to the Swiss kitchen staff.

"Thank you," the Swiss replied feeling befuddled. "We have no shortage of onions."

Our Vidalia onions weren't allowed to feel special and neither were we. Despite her massive jet lag, Eleanor was quickly dispatched to toilet duty. I was given a reprieve from the dirty work, so I quietly observed how Reshad's teachings transplanted into Swiss culture. All the hallmarks of his school — visualizing time, person-of-the-day, greeting the guest with flowers, stepping over the threshold, clearing thought-form by burning Epsom salts and alcohol were in play.

Like a new breed of onion, Reshad's work had taken on a decidedly Swiss flavor: The students stood up when Reshad entered the room. And like with the famous trains, the gears of the day moved with absolute precision. This was possible because, unlike Reshad's American students, the Swiss and Germans didn't instinctively resist Reshad's direction. This new regime was altogether different in a mature way. I had lived through so many gin-fueled nights watching Reshad push the Octave through an escalating string of hazards, so I was stunned to see his evening class finish on time, then off to bed.

The Valbella staff asked me to write a question for my interview with Reshad. As a crusty American with fifteen years under my belt, I asked:

"What is the motivation to take the next step in this work – especially when it is so easy to reach a comfortable stasis?

My question was heightened by the fact that Karen and I — desperate in our financial struggle — couldn't afford Valbella. So when Ruedi and Simone, a couple we didn't even know, invited us to come, tuition paid, my internal resistance crumbled. I felt like the Sufi in the desert who, in Rumi's tale, sets up the perfect test to discover if one's daily bread truly comes from God. To make the test, the Sufi laid down in the middle of the desert, teeth clenched, and prepared to shrivel in the sun. After laying there for a time, a passing caravan spotted him from a distance. As Rumi tells it:

They came on and touched him with their hands. That venerable man deliberately said nothing. He did not stir, he did not even move his head or open his eyes, because he was making a trial.

Then they said, "This poor disappointed man has had a stroke of apoplexy caused by hunger." They fetched bread and food in a kettle that they might pour it into his mouth and down his throat. Thereupon the man purposely clenched his teeth to test the truth of that promise.

They felt pity for him and said, "This man is starving and perishing with hunger and at the point of death." So they brought a knife and hastily made a rift in his closed teeth. They poured soup into his mouth and forced into it fragments of bread.[1]

After Reshad's class, I wrote in my journal: *"Like that Sufi in the desert, God is force-feeding me to swallow the finest gourmet fare."*

Out of concern for my American friends being left behind by the impulse crossing the Atlantic, I poured my experience into a detailed journal. This was pre-Internet, yet I managed to upload it each night through a squawky modem. Here are some of my notes:

It is quite a shock to see Reshad in such a different setting. The best word to describe his manner is "tempered" — both as in "temperance" with respect to alcohol and "tempered steel." I have always known his teachings to be infused with his personality and his passion, but now instead, the weight of his teaching comes through being.

I wanted my American friends to understand that an entirely new octave had emerged. I wrote:

The feeling here is deep and contemplative. With so many new people in a foreign setting, this depth of feeling seems partly from fear and awe, and partly from the overwhelming natural beauty and deep respect. But there is something else — a sense that this is an entirely different cycle, as if so many demons have been finally laid to rest.

---

1. *https://archive.org/stream/RumiTheMathnawiVol5Vol6/Rumi_The-Mathnawi-Vol-5-Vol-6_djvu.txt*

Let's stop right there. You should be wondering, *"Demons laid to rest? What about six months ago? The abyss, the emotional tone scale, the irrepressible black hole, and the spitballs? What about the whirlpool of grief and the force field of despair? What happened to the demons?"*

Good question.

Valbella II stands as the exemplary moment in Reshad's career when his teaching, his marriage, the Alpine setting, and the Swiss team forged together like tempered steel. This was all the more remarkable when you looked at the timeline: Six months earlier, I left Reshad dying in the foxhole of love.

Reshad sporting my son's propeller cap with Penny and me.

How did this miraculous transformation come about?

A clue appeared the next morning in the form of a Kundalini yoga class — a surprising addition to our Rumi school, especially since Reshad eschewed all forms of physical exercise and feigned disdain for the white-turbaned Kundalini Sikhs who frequented the Institute for Conscious Life in L.A. as "Huffle Puffles."

So here we were, high in the Swiss Alps huffling and puffling — *mulbanding* our rectums and fire-breathing Kundalini up our spines. As it turned out, Reshad had a fondness for Yogi Bhajan back in Los Angeles. With Reshad's marital life and physical state collapsing, Reshad sought out Yogi Bhajan to help him move back up the tone scale.

Yogi Bhajan's "SuperHealth" substance abuse program in Arizona combined three hours of Kundalini Yoga each day, plus meditation classes, a detoxification diet, Ayurvedic and Bach Flower remedies, a vitamin and herbal regimen, therapeutic massages, Humanology sessions (applied psychology from the perspective of Kundalini Yoga) and counseling.

During this time, Reshad wrote from the desert:

The best way to approach the gate of freedom is to make a list, in total honesty, of all the mistakes we have made in our lives, the people we have hurt, knowingly or not, but which we still remember... We need courage to reach that gate!

We make a loving and honest inventory of as many things as we can find in our subconscious, and then, whether in dreams or after meditation or whatever, when memories come into our consciousness, add them to the list until we feel that we are as clear as possible of the past.

Next we consciously forgive ourselves to make room for God's Forgiveness, which can then fill our hearts with His Light, which is the Light of Pure Understanding. [2]

Whether it was the list of mistakes, or SuperHealth, or Penny, or a big dose of Grace, Reshad emerged from the tempering heat of the desert as an exemplar of his teaching — startling proof that it is possible to move up the tone scale and transform the pattern of your life.

Here are snippets from my notes:

Reshad's Opening Talk — Friday, June 9

Reshad discussed seven aspects that formed the curriculum of the school:

1. *Reciprocal Receptivity — We must hold the inner question using the energy of thought, but not by thinking.*
2. *Triad of Freedom — Through commitment, willingness, and*

2. Feild, Reshad, *Spiritual Psychology: Notes from a Desert Retreat*, Chalice, Switzerland, 1990

agreement, we are placed in a stream of service to participate in the manifestation of being.

3. *The Art of Spontaneity* — If we are spontaneous, but at the wrong time, it is not the "art" of spontaneity. True spontaneity requires the ability to sense which note of the octave we are in at any moment.

4. *Education* — This is a school for continuous education, not a school for "information being stuffed down."

5. *Respect* — Re-spect means to see again. Can we see through a completely new eye (inner and outer) — (or is it a completely new I?)

6. *Spiritual Practices* — Practices build an inner body that can receive the energies of the work.

7. *Balance* — Keeping all the centers in balance — thinking, moving, and feeling.

It was past midnight when I finished my notes to upload to my friends:

Moonlight bathes the valley as church bells mix with an endless cadence of cowbells. All of us are still awake as our bodily clocks fight being reset. Much love to all. Good night.

I hot-wired my modem to the Swiss phone system, logged on to Telemail, and sent chapter one of "Valbella Journal" to my American friends.

Sunday, June 11

Three real quotes from today's Valbella Journal:

"I love the laundry, I could work in the laundry the whole seminar." Karen.

"There are other things I'd rather do than clean toilets all day." Eleanor.

"The toilets are really very important. That's where it's all coming out." Jonathan.

I also wrote: "*The food is literally four-star quality. Each night, the four-course menu is formally announced. Last night it was escallops de veal Milanese with tomato sauce. The previous evening was medallions of lamb with sorrel sauce. Tonight, poulet au citron. Afternoon tea was equally amazing. Instead of tea and biscuits, they wheel out a cart of pastries filled with fresh strawberries and cream. Being Switzerland, every meal has copious amounts of cream, cheese, or butter. Hardly a weight-loss summer camp.*

Monday, June 12

Reshad discussed what it means to live in the question: "*The art of finding the right question is to want to know the answer. The nafs, or ego, does not want to know. The heart always wants to know.*

"*Why is this important? Think about how many times the story of your life keeps repeating itself until you understand it.*"

Ain't that the truth. My struggles around money certainly keep repeating. What part don't I understand?

Tuesday, June 13

Reshad discussed the possibility that the Virgin Mary was trained in a highly esoteric school, explaining: "*Despite the image of her on the back of a donkey, she was from the House of David and was incredibly rich.*"

He quoted a further paradox: "*Ever since the time of the Virgin Mary, there is no more need to think.*"

Reshad was the master of these little koans — what he called "snippets." On paper, his snippets may seem incomprehensible or even ridiculous, but in the teaching moment, they awaken an inner understanding. Without fail, usually minutes later, the realization would be gone. Reshad elaborated further:

"*What this means is that ever since the time of Mary, any woman can produce a Jesus — not in the literal sense, but in the inner meaning. At any moment of pure consciousness, with the Breath, it is possible that a child is being born in the formative world. A child is being born at this moment. Perhaps this is what the Golden Age is all about.*

Reshad told the story of how at the *Annunciation,* when the Archangel Gabriel approached Mary, Gabriel appeared in the form of a beautiful man. Concerned that this man wanted to know her carnally, Mary tightened, but Gabriel whispered to her, "*Beshara,*" Aramaic for "good news." Mary relaxed in that moment, producing a Jesus. As Reshad would tell it, had she not relaxed, "Jesus would be impossible to live with because of his uncompromising nature."[3]

The snippet, "*Ever since the time of the Virgin Mary there is no more need to think*" did not make cognitive sense. In the inner understanding, we are asked to become like Mary, becoming suppliant to the spirit of pure consciousness rather than pushing against that current with thought. This is lovemaking on the most subtle level.

Reshad added a further coda:

"*Every number has a quality. Seven is the esoteric number of the Virgin Mary, the Octave of manifestation, the matrix of this world, the mother's breath, and the womb of the moment. How do you know if you're awake in pure consciousness? You will see what the need is, and what action to take.*"

Hence, no more need to think because life is interconnected.

Wednesday, June 14

Today, Reshad spoke at length about healing, explaining that "*people get cancer very often and lose it without knowing they've got it.*"

He added a zinger:

"*If you sound the Hu with all the love in your heart in a room full of chaos, it is likely that the room will calm down.*

---

3. Beshara was the name of the school Reshad founded in 1971 in England with Bulent Rauf. http://beshara.org/history-archive/

Years ago, I witnessed this phenomenon with the author/trickster E.J. Gold at the legendary Hollywood restaurant, Musson & Frank Grill.

"Place your attention on the chaos," E.J. instructed.

I closed my eyes and focused on the cacophony of drunken banter and kitchen dishes. For a brief moment, the decibels subsided.

Reshad continued:

This is very much like giving healing without permission. Similarly, if you visualize light to hold someone in the light, you'd also have its opposite. The real light of healing has no opposite.

As a new-agey type who routinely holds people in the light, my first thought was, "Ohhh..."

Here are Reshad's four rules of healing:

1. *Don't ask to become a healer.*
2. *Don't say you are a healer. It's okay to say you're a therapist.*
3. *Prepare yourself to perform healing work in the same way you prepare for prayer. You will get more sensitive along the way and can "pick things up."*
4. *Never allow people to give you treatments unless they are at least at your level of consciousness.*

Reshad also mentioned to the consternation of the therapists in the room:

"*When you become a true seeker, you will quickly lose your clients if they aren't prepared to face real change.*"

Friday, June 16

Today, I gave a workshop on the octave that included a consciously-timed outdoor expedition. After my talk, people were instructed to gather impressions from the Swiss countryside. The aim was to experience the octave in the flow of events. As we headed to our cars, Reshad called out, "When will the note Fa arrive?" Jokingly, I blurted, "12:43!"

After a fruitless search for the perfect picnic lunch spot, we finally noticed a path fronted by a "Do Not Enter" sign. Brazenly, we turned the car onto the dirt path, went under a viaduct, and emerged into a resplendent field of wildflowers reminiscent of Ralph Vaughn Williams and "The Lark Ascending." It was 12:43 p.m.

Saturday, June 17

Question and Answer

Student: *"I am grateful, but it hurts. Why?"*

Reshad: *"A rose needs pruning. It only knows it needs pruning when it becomes a rose. When it becomes a rose, it becomes grateful. A human being has the essence of the rose within. We have the possibility of being grateful for the pruning. This is the meaning of conscious suffering. Or a better term, conscious sacrifice."*

Student: *"What hurts when you are becoming grateful?"*

Reshad: *"When the lower emotions are becoming part of the higher emotions."*

Student: *"Why is emptiness so frightening?"*

Reshad: *"Emptiness is not frightening, but the step across the abyss is frightening. We do not know what is on the other side. You come into this world as a man or a woman, but, in Being, the question doesn't even arise. Beyond Being is Not Being, and beyond Not Being is the Absolute."*

Student: *"Why are there people who can't say thank you?"*

Reshad: *"We are offered the opportunity again and again. It's like with parking angels. If we don't say please and thank-you you will end up with a ticket. We can pay these tickets over and over, but eventually, we go bankrupt. If we declare bankruptcy to God, we can start again."*

Student: *"Why do we forget about breathing?"*

Reshad: *"Because we are thinking. Ever since the time of the Virgin Mary, there has been no more need to think."*

Tuesday, June 20

I wrote: *"We seem to be in the note Sol, a most interesting note — even more interesting than the Mi-Fa, because the note Sol is the crux of the matter. With the focus on the nafs [ego], people seem to be aware of the constricting nature of their personalities. It's as if a very powerful mirror has put our failings into focus like a collective lump in the throat. I'm not painting a negative picture because people are earnestly facing themselves and asking to see the way through."*

Reshad explained: *"The way to work with our negative aspects is to make them your friends. How can we do this unless we recognize that all gifts come from God?"*

The Sema performed in the tent.

Thursday, June 22

Tonight, we performed the *sema* in our large mountain-top tent. During the fourth *selam*, Reshad stepped into the center which coincided with a crashing, thundering downpour of rain — the first rain in weeks.

During class, Reshad likened our life journey to the passage of two trains: The first train carries our accumulated experience forward through the events of our life in sequential time. We are unaware of a second train coming at us – the future coming in. Ideally, the trains pass, we integrate our past, and all is well. More often, as evident in a mid-life crisis, the trains collide. The unconscious unredeemed past collides with the necessity to face oneself within the constraint of our lifetime.

Reshad explained: *"Our death comes in at a different rate than the present moment going out. Time is coming in, and time is going out. This gives us the ability to forecast, up to a certain point, the pattern of our lives."*

As we age, we notice this acceleration of time. Suddenly, our grade school children graduate, a spouse asks for a divorce, or we realize that we forgot to plan for retirement. The universe appears to be cruel, but actually, the train coming in is preparing us for the Light.

A young person approached me after the *sema* and observed, "I think the two trains passed tonight." I was taken off-guard that a young'un would know much about anything, but after sitting with it a bit, I realized he was right; we crested the peak. We could all sense that the future was coming in — faster than we were prepared for. I wrote:

The end is coming; the end is coming. Today, for the first time, the recognition of the completion is within view. There is one week to go, but we've already crested the summit. I already sense the sadness that will come when it's time to leave this rarefied environment. Tonight, during sema, I made a decision to take advantage of every remaining moment here. This school offers a rare access to knowledge that is not available in our workaday lives.

Reshad further explained:

All the knowledge in the world is useless if we are dead. The only time we're alive is when we're here. The purpose of a living school is to get people here.

Friday, June 23

Reshad: "*You are never given more pain than you can bear. Most people think in terms of physical or emotional pain. Perhaps knowledge is the greatest source of pain. If God is the All-Knowing, we have to make room for God's Knowledge. Knowledge anchors love.*"

"*There is something greater that brought us together than anything we can imagine. We are being drawn toward an inevitable sense of completion. God does not want separation from us any more than we want separation from Him.*"

Saturday, June 24

At 12:30 a.m., exhausted and yearning for bed, I stuck with my decision to create this journal and wrote:

Tonight, I staged and hosted a cabaret evening, flirting with the opening of Pandora's box. After the usual skits, some musical numbers, and a play, we started dancing — the joy released was quite extraordinary. But for one critical moment, the energies got out of hand and two people clunked heads. This left me quite shaken about the wisdom of releasing this kind of energy.

Snippets from Reshad's class:

"*Life is like a mystery play — you don't understand the answer until the last line.*"

Dance performance at Valbella

"*There are many deaths in life; each time a little weight is taken away.*"

"*God made man impatient. If we weren't impatient, we wouldn't go for the Truth.*"

Sunday, June 25

The work at Valbella has continued to defy my expectations of the drama and intensity of the past. Several people were in tears during the Sunday service. It's as though Reshad's work has reached such a refined pitch, like with homeopathy, that a subtle dose is stronger.

The head cook described the differences between Valbella this summer and Beatenburg a year ago: "At Beatenburg, Reshad would regularly storm into the kitchen to confront a variety of ills. This year, Reshad has come into the kitchen only once — to get a little milk for the cottage."

People have implemented what they've learned and now are able to hold the space with a palpable awareness of energy. Every inch of this property is cleaned and ordered several times a day. This has freed Reshad to work from a higher station. As the cook put it, this year he is like a "scholar." The only unattended situations are those "inside."

I talked to another woman who came to Valbella with great stubbornness and now saw her life through a new lens. "Coming to the point of total respect has enlarged my life completely," she explained.

After dinner, everyone left the room except at Reshad's table where guests continued to listen to his stories. I motioned to Peter Knecht, the head of the room set-up team, that we only had 20 minutes until class.

"Don't you think we should begin clearing the chairs and tables?" I asked.

"We mustn't start until Reshad has finished," Peter replied. "There is nothing we can do. He is our guest."

I noticed this attitude of respect again when Penny fell ill with a mysterious fever. Every evening at meditation, out of respect, the Swiss would lay out a cushion and blanket where Penny normally sat. I wish I had the words to paint the inner subtleties of this attitude, but it is through respect that space opens for the light of knowledge to enter.

Monday, June 26

Reshad spoke at length about the change coming into the world:

"It's not hard to see, if we're courageous, that in regard to stopping the ecological decay of our planet, it's already too late. In the 1970s, when people began to break out of a rigid system and make a new world, things were not the same as they are now [1989]. The ecological disaster we are seeing now has already happened in the subtle world; it's only now that we are seeing it. Visionaries see it before it happens because there is no creation in the relative world, only the becoming of Being.

"If we don't consciously evolve, there is very little we can do except be part of organic evolution.

"When we are told by scientists that within twenty years we will see a total breakdown of the ecological systems, it is very possible that a large part of the human population cannot be in the right place at the right time. You cannot help everybody. There is a reason that God guided us together, a reason that is greater than we can know. We are totally unimportant in one sense, and very important in another."

That evening, a blizzard of hailstones unleashed its fury on the meeting tent. Crackling shots of lightning and mountain-shaking thunder echoed through the valleys for miles. The next morning, hailstones covered the ground like iced manna from heaven.

Tuesday, June 27

Reshad had the flu and a fever today, yet his teaching didn't appear to suffer. He has been uncharacteristically strong and healthy these three weeks. Considering his sensitivity, and all the interviews, he has clearly tapped into Gurdjieff's "Greater Accumulator" — an energy much finer and more powerful than the "small accumulators" (body energy) we use for ordinary activities.

Notes from class:

Reshad: *"If you cast light onto what you want to see, you can increase your illusion. If you cast your light onto what God wants you to see, you may be granted wisdom. If you start projecting your light, you are projecting the nafs — projecting what you want and not what you need. Listen to the eye of the heart. Once you have a taste of Light, nobody can ever lie to you again."*

Wednesday, June 28

My journal includes an ominous note without explanation: *This day was consumed with many difficulties in my personal affairs.* My memory is fuzzy, so let's move on.

Today Reshad was ill, so Penny gave the class. For three weeks, I watched Penny sit at Reshad's side, in sublimation to his light. Now on her own, her private radiance emerged as a knowing strength — a fiercely quiet knowledge accrued from living on a battlefield we could not know. Penny shared:

"Because we are unique, it is our responsibility to be ourselves and not try to be something else because we are the only person in the whole world to bring forth that unique quality of God. It is such a wonderful relief to realize that you don't have to try so hard to be something you think you should be. All you have to do is relax into who you are."

Thursday, June 29

Today was the big day, the final night. The center was buzzing with rehearsals, guests arriving, and special preparations. With eleven nationalities for dinner, the grace was repeated in Swiss German, English, French, Spanish, Turkish, German, "American," Dutch, and Hungarian.

Preparations for the evening performance.

After the evening presentations and *sema*, I met a gentleman from Germany who, with Reudi and Simone, was responsible for bringing us here. Reshad had mentioned to him that it would be a wonderful thing to bring Karen and me to Switzerland. Without another

Dominique Starck and Reshad

word from Reshad, this German man established an organizing committee to raise the funds and make it happen. Most of the people who paid our way have never even met us. Like the Sufi in the desert, I had to accept that the hand of God extends through the heart of man— *Al-Karīm*, The Bountiful and Generous.

From the class:

Reshad: "*People ask me how they can, to use Rumi's words, 'Die before you die.' It is either gross stupidity or at its worst, utter selfishness. We must know the laws of life before we can die before we die.*"

Friday, June 30

The day started with the disassembly of the tent. *Tent* is a misnomer, for this structure spans 24 feet with enormous steel beams. The tent has been the site for all the practices, *zikrs* meditations, turning,

The meeting tent

evening talks, and the like. So, when the 40-foot truck pulled up the steep drive — the train of the future coming in — we knew the inevitability of completion had arrived.

After dinner, the cooks wheeled out a massive cake decorated with a dervish. When they asked Reshad to cut the cake, the irrepressible showman obliged by throwing 20 knives into the cake from his seat, 10 feet away, each spinning a turn before sticking a perfect landing into the cake.

After a three-hour, 16-act presentation, our Swiss hosts wheeled out another surprise — a multi-colored matchbox train with a carriage from each of the participants containing a note of gratitude to Reshad. The train spiraled outward, some 80 cars, into a tableau of roses. Next, the lights dimmed

The train of thoughts and wishes

and we moved to the balcony to sing Ya Salaam, serenading Reshad and Penny as they walked under an Alpine sky, ablaze with stars, to their cottage.

I hope this doesn't sound maudlin or gushy in my attempt to convey the depth of feeling. More than the feelings of brotherhood, our time at Valbella is better described by the depth of character. As I scanned the eyes in the room, I had no remorse that this adventure had drawn to a close. Any parting sorrow was from the fact that this configuration of people, a complete universe unto itself, would never exist again — a living tapestry of people and cultures with a singular aim — to face the truth of oneself.

At last, what I thought would never be possible had occurred. We all stood on the same soil, in consciousness, as one.

§

Hand-in-hand at Valbella

Valbella ended on a triumphant note — but the impulse did not stand still. While we stood hand-in-hand at Valbella, Uwe Morawetz, a 24-year old German poet and Sun Bear, a Native American medicine man from the States, stood side-by-side at the Berlin Wall.

As the young poet and native elder gazed toward the Communist East, Sun Bear shared a prophetic vision. He saw the East and West come together in a big intercultural medicine wheel gathering where wise people from all cultures and religions could cross borders, learn from each other, and find ways to heal the wounds of war and Mother Earth.

Sun Bear.

Six months later, at midnight on November 9, 1989, the impulse staged its coup de grâce. At the border put in place by Stalin, Churchill, and Truman, throngs of West Berliners started running to the Berlin Wall. Spurred on by Free Berlin radio broadcasts, they chanted, "We want in!" and *"Tor auf!* Open the Gate!" The border guards had planned for a change in visiting policy to begin November 9, but they didn't expect hordes of East and West Berliners to swarm the wall, drinking beer and champagne, and flooding through the checkpoints.

More than 2 million people from East Berlin visited West Berlin that weekend. One journalist, sensing the epochal nature of the impulse at work, called it "the greatest street party in the history of the world." People used hammers to knock away chunks of the

The Berlin Wall, November 9, 1989

Wall while cranes and bulldozers pulled down section after section.

One month later, Reshad's students staged the first public *sema* in Europe. As Reshad addressed the audience, he described the transmission of the sacred impulse:

"Tonight we are celebrating the mystical marriage. As we dance together, our personal differences disappear in the fire of love.

"This is indeed a historic occasion for us all. How did this

Sema ceremony, Zurich Switzerland, December 17, 1989

come to be? I would like to explain. About 25 years ago, when one of the works of Mevlana Jelaluddin Rumi came into my hands, I touched the book and cried, as though my heart was burning and singing at the same time.

"From that moment on, having been introduced to the words of Mevlana, I began to be consumed by the fire of love itself. I visited Konya and I turned and I turned. There, the lovers of Rumi embraced me into their circle and said, 'Reshad, take the turn from Konya to the West.'

"So I went back to England, and then on to the States, Canada, and Mexico, where I lived for seventeen years. Now I am back in Europe once again. The turn continues as it has from the first day of creation itself."

In May 1991, Sun Bear's vision was realized. Uwe Morawetz staged the "The Power of Visions" festival in Potsdam, former East Germany, where Stalin, Churchill, and Truman ended the War. Uwe invited Buddhists, Christians, Native Americans, Hindus, Muslims,

Participants at the Power of Visions Festival

Jews, artists, scientists, and cultural leaders to attend. Eight thousand people from all over the world gathered to participate in a once-in-a-generation moment of unified purpose. Sun Bear died shortly after, but a new movement towards peace was born out of his vision.

Uwe invited Reshad to speak at the event. Reshad wrote to me from Potsdam:

Dear Bruce,

At the end of the last war, the Potsdam agreement was signed around a table when Stalin, Churchill and your president had the audacity to divide Germany into sectors. They divided Berlin in half in order to stop Germany from uniting in the future. What a stupid thing to do. Walls will always come down when love prevails...

The Big Event was the result of a vision that Sun Bear had of a medicine wheel built of stones in Germany. It's not difficult to see why he saw it in Germany — his mother was half German and half Norwegian! Sun Bear shared this vision with a young man, Uwe Morowitz, who devoted the next two years of his life to making it happen. At age 26, he gathered together a willing team and a 1.5 million DM budget to make the vision come true.

It was an extraordinary achievement and Uwe was a living example of the Work, just 26 years old, yet never wavering throughout the whole of the festival.

What attracted me to being one of the speakers was that we were not going to be paid. We were invited as true guests, given our tickets, good food, wonderful hotel accommodations, and if anything further came, it came as a gift. You cannot pay for Truth!

If there was one word to describe the whole event it would be the word TRIUMPH. This sense of triumph produced a sense of hope — objective hope for the future. That energy is still available as I dictate this letter.

That energy is the impulse. There is no way to measure it, track it, or predict its effect — but its impact can be seen in the unfolding nature of world events. The year 1989 brought Valbella II and the fall of the Berlin Wall. It also brought the massacre of 10,000 students at Tiananmen Square.[4]

The impulse emerged again and again, notably in 2010 when a wave of riots, coups, and civil wars erupted throughout North Africa and the Middle East — a spontaneous yearning for democracy called "The Arab Spring."

The impulse appears as a game-changing shift – neither "good" nor "bad" – that no one sees coming. Using Malcolm Gladwell's tipping point metaphor, the impulse emerges as a moment of critical mass, often insignificant, that triggers a boiling point. In this way, the impulse expresses God's attribute, *Al-Fattah: He Who Opens All Things.*[5]

4. https://www.independent.co.uk/news/world/asia/tiananmen-square-massacre-death-toll-secret-cable-british-ambassador-1989-alan-donald-a8126461.html

5. Gladwell, Malcolm. 2002. *The Tipping Point: How Little Things Can Make a Big Difference.* Boston: Back Bay Books.

Where will the impulse emerge next? The continuing story of Uwe Morawetz offers a tantalizing clue:

In 1999, Uwe Morawetz established the International Peace Foundation. With the support and participation of world leaders, Nobel Laureates, artists, and celebrities, Uwe's Foundation sponsored more than 700 programs around the globe with 600 keynote speakers, 100,000 participants, and 700 staff members over the next two decades.

In 2016, Uwe, acting on his instincts, made a bold move:

Reuters: May 7, 2016 | Brushing aside objections, Nobel laureates visit Pyongyang

A group of Nobel laureates visited sanctions-bound North Korea over the last week despite objections from South Korea, saying they wanted to extend an olive branch by bringing non-political, academic diplomacy to the isolated nuclear-armed state...

Uwe Morawetz, the foundation's founding chairman, told reporters... that before going, he had met with South Korea's ambassador... "We have been asked by the South Korean ambassador to postpone our visit... [but] the

Uwe Morawetz, center, with Nobel laureates in North Korea.

Nobel laureates are very busy people... So we made it clear that we will go ahead with the visit but we have never been contacted by the U.S. government."

[Sir Richard J. Roberts, a Nobel laureate for medicine who was

part of the visit to North Korea], said, "Maybe the U.S. government just needs prodding," he said.[6]

One year after Uwe undertook his under-the-radar mission to North Korea, a cascade of events unfolded: Amid escalating provocations, North and South Korea stopped talking. President Trump derided North Korea's leader as "Little Rocket Man" and Kim Jong Un threatened to "tame the mentally-deranged dotard with fire" and ignite a hydrogen bomb above the Pacific Ocean. South Korea's president was thrown out from scandal and a reconciliation-focused Moon Jae-in replaced him. Moon dramatically changed course, announcing that he would meet with North Korea "anytime, anywhere." Moon also proposed sending a unified Korean team to the 2018 Winter Olympics in order to pull the two Koreas away from the brink of war. Six months later, North and South Korea marched at the Games under one flag. Kim Jong Un reciprocated with a personal invitation via his sister Kim Yo Jong for a meeting at the DMZ as a gesture of peace:

"I hope Pyongyang and Seoul get closer in our people's hearts and move forward the future of prosperous unification," Kim's sister said at the Games.

One month after the Games, and after a year of mockery and threats, Donald Trump accepted Moon's invitation to meet Kim Jong Un. In June 2018, Trump met the ruthless dictator in what was derided as a syrupy stunt for its recklessness. Regardless of the ultimate outcome, the calculus between North Korea and its neighbors had changed. The stimulating force of the impulse – *Ya Fathah* – often wreaks havoc to heal our world.

If Genghis Khan's barbaric sweep across Asia brought Rumi

6. *https://www.reuters.com/article/us-northkorea-diplomacy-nobel/brushing-aside-objections-nobel-laureates-visit-pyongyang-idUSKCN0XY040*

to Konya, and if Atatürk's draconian decree ultimately brought Dede to Los Angeles, is it possible that a burst of conscious energy zig-zagged its way through Valbella, the Berlin Wall, Potsdam, Uwe, Moon, Kim Jon Un, and even Trump to reshape our world?

J.G. Bennett saw the footprints of history in this epochal light:

"The more we move along the path of transformation, the more evident does it become that our puny wisdom and our modern science fall very far short of being able to understand how human history is being directed." [7]

7. Bennett, J. G. 2017. Transformation. CreateSpace

11

JOHANNESHOF

My Valbella Journal contained an ominous note:

Wednesday, June 28: This day was consumed with many difficulties in my personal affairs.

I struggled to understand Karen's unhappiness with the state of our marriage while we were at Valbella. After we returned home, Karen reached out in multiple directions seeking light for what seemed to be an impossible relationship. We had a "spiritual marriage," meaning we probably wouldn't have hooked up at a party or a pub. We were brought together on a blind date set up by, guess who? – *Reshad* – who married us in a magically chaotic backyard wedding in Los Angeles one year after he and Penny got hitched overlooking the Pacific near Santa Cruz, CA.

Karen and I enjoyed sharing our status with Reshad and Penny as "Sufi couples" in the school. What's more, Karen felt a sisterly connection to Penny. She often sought Penny's wisdom for how to "hang in there" with a difficult marriage. This was the impetus for Karen to ask Penny about a teaching moment in her marriage when one of the most mysterious figures of the Koran and the Mathnawi suddenly appeared:

Dear Karen,

Thank you very much for your letter. The mail here is rather slow, and things have a way of going around the block several times before we actually receive them.

You want to know about the little man on the bench? Let's see if I can write it without making it too lengthy.

Reshad and I were living in Santa Cruz, California. We had been together a little over three years and it was a difficult time. I had faithfully followed the practices I had been given, but it was a time when all my "ideals" of what I thought to be spiritual work and its demands weren't matching the "reals." My trust, which had carried me over many waves up to that time, was beginning to weaken and nothing seemed to make sense to me. I wondered if I had made a big mistake. Reshad as my teacher was also my husband and our personal problems were flaring up as well.

That particular day was a culmination for it all. After an enormous argument the night before, Reshad spent the night in a motel and had now returned to the house. We talked briefly and planned to walk together by the sea to help clear the air.

When it came time for our walk, Reshad wasn't feeling well, so he decided to stay in bed and rest. In despair, I decided to go on the walk as planned. I walked along a high road which winds along a cliff above the bay. It was a beautiful day. Every hundred yards or so there was a bench to sit on. I stopped at an empty one and enjoyed the wildflowers along the cliff. As I was standing in front of the bench, I whimsically thought to myself, "I wonder if I'll ever be able to see the 'little people?' I know they are out there, but they live in another geometry than most can see."

Because of my sadness, I didn't dwell on this thought. Instead, I began to recite the St. Francis prayer to myself: "Lord, make me an instrument of Thy peace."

I couldn't remember all the words, so I started a second time, really saying them with every cell of my body. Lord, make me an instrument of Thy peace."

Suddenly I felt a presence on the bench behind me. I turned around and found an old man, a little scruffy, with his belt not properly in all the loops. His first words were, "Yeah, there sure are a lot of little people out there! There is Old Man Jackrabbit in the desert and Mr. Coyote."

He went on and on, hardly letting me get a word in.

Suddenly he started asking me questions, "Have you ever been to...?" Every place he mentioned I had been to. Then he would say, "Ah, that's where the men are men and so are the women!"

On the one hand, he seemed completely bonkers, but on the other, everything he said had relevance to my situation or my thoughts.

Suddenly he asked emphatically, "Are you married?"

"Yes," I replied.

"Where is your husband?"

"Sleeping."

"Are you going home mad?"

I didn't tell him that we had had a fight. By that time, he had made me laugh so much that I had forgotten a lot of my woes. I told him so.

He continued rambling. He talked about a place of many steps and that I hadn't begun to climb them yet, but that my husband had been up to the top and down the other side again.

"Are you going home mad?" he asked again, and again and again throughout the conversation.

The whole thing was outside of time as I had ever known it. I don't have any idea how long I was on the bench with him. I never mentioned anything about the difficulties with Reshad.

Finally, I felt that it was time to return home. I told him so and he smiled at me.

"Do me a favor. When you are walking home, stop and buy something nice and give it to your husband for me."

I laughed. "All right."

So, I stopped and bought Reshad a funny card on the way home.

Reshad was still sleeping when I walked into the house, but he opened one eye as I came into the room. I wasn't quite sure what to say. Inside, I was asking myself if that could have been Khidr.

"I just had the strangest experience," I said.

Reshad smiled. "You have met Khidr," he said.

I gave Reshad the card and told him the story. The ice was broken and somehow I was given the courage and the trust to continue on the Road of Truth.

So that is the story, Karen. The passion of my inner question was so strong that I gained a lot from that experience that I have been able to continue to put to use.

With all best wishes.

Much love, Penny

Penny's dual role as wife/ student brought double blessings – and double trouble. You can throw a plate at your husband, but not at your teacher.

Khidr, the "The Green One," represents the freshness of spirit and eternal liveliness. He guides the perplexed and those who invoke his name.

Karen and I also struggled with our Sufi marriage. I had not yet learned how to use the excruciating pressures of marital life to sip from what Rumi called "the Secret Cup."

LOVE DOGS

One night a man was crying, Allah! Allah!

His lips grew sweet with the praising, until a cynic said,

"So! I have heard you calling out, but have you ever gotten any response?"

The man had no answer to that. He quit praying and fell into a confused sleep.

He dreamed he saw Khidr, the guide of souls, in a thick, green foliage.

"Why did you stop praising?"

"Because I've never heard anything back."

"This longing you express is the return message.

The grief you cry out from draws you toward union.

Your pure sadness that wants help is the secret cup.

Listen to the moan of a dog for its master. That whining is the connection.

There are love dogs no one knows the names of. Give your life to be one of them."

Rumi[1]

I knew nothing of Secret Cups or how to transform my pain into the light of consciousness. As a result, three years after Valbella, our ability to "keep it together" finally collapsed.

It was in the seventh year of our marriage (Si-Do), and three and a half years without a real job (Mi-Fa), and smack-dab in my midlife crisis ($6 \times 7 = 42$ years), when all of these octaves and intervals lined up for the two trains to collide. Karen calmly sent our son off to another room, closed the door, and signaled the approaching storm.

"I want a separation," Karen announced.

A chasm opened in my stomach.

1. Rumi, Jalal al-Din. 2004. *The Essential Rumi, New Expanded Edition. Translated by Coleman Barks and John Moyne. Reprint edition. San Francisco, CA: HarperOne.*

"What? What!" I protested. "Where is this coming from?"

"It's just not working for me, Bruce. You're not there for me. You seem... oblivious."

"What?" I protested again. "Why drop this insane bomb now?" I took a breath. "What about our son?"

"He will be fine. The last thing he needs is to grow up in a house where his parents aren't emotionally connected."

"When are you planning to do this?" I asked.

Karen's words faded into the background as I sank into a whirlpool of dread, what the ancient Greeks called *katabasis* — the mythological descent into the underworld where the hero must confront his shadow and overcome the buried darkness of his psyche. Suddenly, Rumi's Secret Cup was no longer a secret.

"Steve Brown offered his rental house. I'll be moving in a few days," Karen replied.

Unlike the tale of the Sufi in the desert, this was not a test. I had one dry run under my belt, so I knew what to do if a caravan appeared out of the blue. I got on my knees.

The caravan appeared in the form of an invitation from Reshad to attend the opening of Johanneshof, his residential school overlooking Lake Lucerne in the Swiss Alps. Johanneshof was the crowning realization of Reshad's forty-year career and the answer to my prayer: "Please God, carry me across this abyss."

I held my prayerful attitude like the Secret Cup. In our Sufi school, we described this receptive state as "living in the question" — an openness to the octave coming in — *the two trains.* You can jump onto this train at any moment by embracing the palpable sense that realistically, the future is unknown.

My efforts to make my life work had backfired, and now I felt trumped by the universe. In times of crisis, we attempt to fix our problems by drawing from experience, but it usually doesn't work. You can't shift from first into second without a stint between gears. Johanneshof let me leap into the *barzakh* – the space in-between.

When I arrived at Johanneshof, one of Reshad's lieutenants greeted me warmly at the door. The magnificent villa offered a glorious space – high ceilings, wall tapestries, gorgeous murals, and abundant floral arrangements. Expansive windows showcased the rose gardens, the Alpine peaks, and the fjord-like Lake of Lucerne.

I smiled to myself, "Reshad, you really pulled it off."

I had been following Reshad's quest for a permanent center – what he called a "seat" – since the day I met him in 1974. Eleanor, my travel companion, also remembered entering Johanneshof:

Johanneshof – *Kastanienbaum, Lucerne* Switzerland

"It was like entering a higher world. Reshad taught his students how to create and hold a space as a chalice for transformation and love – even the love that was put into the food. Johanneshof embodied that higher world."

I noticed how the Swiss team hit all the high marks — the impeccable manners, consciously-prepared food, precision timing, and ripple-free operations. I had seen this show before, so I saw beyond the practiced perfection. I knew that the real teaching would emerge later when the train fell off the tracks.

Announcements at lunch.

In every spiritual enterprise, there is always the hidden half — the buried, sublimated side that must not be spoken of. It's the dark side, the subconscious side of the moon that provides the real juice of a school. The job of the student (and they don't tell you this) is to wrap your head around the light and the shadow; it's a package deal. The excruciating contradiction between shit and Shinola *is* the teaching. This is the Law of Three Forces: Affirming Force, Denying Force, and the Third Force — the Reconciling Force. The Great Work is to open to the third-force – to reconcile the opposites into your being by staying grounded and centered — especially when it all goes south.

In Reshad's school, the hidden half, the denying half, and the unspoken elephant in the room that both fueled and subverted the entire enterprise was the alcohol. In the great tradition of spiritual teachers — Alan Watts and Chögyam Trungpa Rinpoche come to mind — Reshad made a practice of sipping from the font of crazy wisdom to both tame the subconscious and empower the moment.

The rose garden of Johanneshof.

I'm not altogether clear what changed Reshad's temperament after the triumph of Valbella and his subsequent summer schools in the Netherlands. But it was here at Johanneshof, Reshad's long-sought, culminating vision of a seat for the Work, that his faithful and beloved wife, Penny, having traveled to Switzerland from New Mexico to help him launch this crowning achievement, found instead that the dark side of Reshad's moon was ascendant. Without any fanfare, Penny got on a plane, left the scene — and Reshad as well.

And now... on with the show.

In the hero's journey, the protagonist must face a supreme ordeal. The universe, with its subversive sense of humor, usually packages that ordeal in the same wrapping as the hero's crowning achievement. In fact, they're often indistinguishable. Eyeing my surroundings and the circumstances, I wondered if Johanneshof would prove to be Reshad's white whale. Would Johanneshof be the venture where Reshad's nine-pack of lives comes up short?

Reshad made it clear over the years that a spiritual teacher or healer must never engage in the grand work of transformation without the grounding of a partner. The Swiss staff and guests didn't notice this small detail, but I did. I saw the wife-less launch of Johanneshof akin to starting a power plant with a crippled reactor. To be honest, I didn't have a partner either at this point, so I couldn't judge.

Eleanor and I had traveled to Johanneshof for "Geomancy Week," the first big event of Johanneshof — the note Do of Reshad's residential school. By nature, the note Do carries great promise before the Octave deviates according to the physics of vibration. This is the natural tendency of

Dr. Edith Wallace, contemporary of C.G. Jung, with Eleanor Hand.

vibrations. As a result, a conscious decision can easily morph into a mirror-like impostor of the original intention. But for now, Reshad was pulling it off. Despite Penny's absence, the program at Johanneshof was brilliant. Along with the classes, meals, and movements, the Swiss arranged boat trips on the lake, a cogwheel trip to the top of Mount Pilatus, and a motor coach tour for geomantic impressions.

As Reshad delivered his opening talk, I looked out the windows. The towering Alps stood like timeless witnesses to support my journey. Reshad challenged us to contact our original, instinctual essence — what he called *primal innocence*:

Reshad giving a talk at Johanneshof.

> "The baby instinctively knows when it is hungry and where the food is coming from," Reshad explained. "There is a total dependence on the parents, and that alone is a subtle form of communication.
>
> "Later, as we get older, this instinctive gift can easily be covered up and forgotten, and so we cease to realize that we owe our total dependence to God, who is the All-Provider.
>
> "When this is forgotten, that form of communication is also forgotten. In the understanding of our total dependence on God, what we need can be communicated to us from the higher worlds, but we have to be empty of the impediments deep in our subconscious.
>
> "There is also communication between the different worlds within us... They long to tell us things, simple things sometimes, but necessary things. We may have lost the art of communicating with them... We may have lost what I call our primal innocence."[2]

I had come to Johanneshof to erase my old circuitry and find my primal innocence — the loving openness that implicitly trusts the beneficence of life.

---

2. Feild, Reshad. 2011. *The Inner Work*. Books on Demand.

Maybe, I was in my primal innocence when I noticed a quiet woman working alone in the garden, a Cinderella of sorts. I don't think anyone noticed her as she tended to the plantings without stirring a molecule of atmosphere. I was struck by the fact that she

Irmgard in the rose garden.

worked barefoot — marvelously muddy feet. You never see the Swiss without their Bally's or their hiking boots. Her bare feet said, "Hey, I'm connected to my primal innocence. Come, let's play in the mud." So, I approached her.

"Hello," I said.

"Hi," she replied shyly.

There wasn't anything more to say after that, because a different form of communicating took over.

"Hi," I stumbled again.

"Hi," she replied in her best German-English.

The conversation didn't go much further because — poof — I stumbled into my primal innocence.

As it turned out, Irmgard was Austrian, not Swiss. I don't think the Swiss knew what to do with her, she being so shy and sensitive. So, Irmgard was given to tending the garden.

It's not uncommon to stumble into transcendent love at a spiritual retreat. And that's what happened as I faced my barefoot soul mate in the Johanneshof garden a few days before heading back to my thorny marriage in the States. Rumi summed up my predicament:

"All the grief outside the garden is but a tiny thorn. Inside the garden are roses and lovers and running fountains." [3]Rumi, Ghazal 3041

3.

Like all fairy tales, the prince must ultimately face his frog. After a magical twenty-four hours with Irmgard that included hopping from rock to rock atop Mt. Niesen and cycling through a flower-bedecked festival in Peter and Anne's village, my magic carriage returned to its pumpkin state.

I went home to face my life. When I entered my empty home, I found it to be just as cold and cavernous as it was before — maybe more so. But, I also noticed little bubbles of consciousness from Johanneshof that had carbonated my being. Something had shifted.

At about this time, Dr. Bhagwan Awatramani, a former medical doctor from India was also visiting Switzerland. I tell Bhagwan's story in full because it illustrates how teachers and their teachings cross-pollinate and how a synchronistic

Dr. Bhagwan Awatramani

universe sends caravans to starving Sufis in the desert. The tale also speaks to the Buddhist proverb, "When the student is ready, the teacher appears."

Bhagwan's journey to Switzerland began in 1947 with the partition of India. Fourteen million refugees were forced to flee from the newly formed states of Pakistan and India in the throes of genocidal violence. As Bhagwan explained, a half million people died and millions more were uprooted:

We lived in what's now Pakistan, so we had to seek refuge in India. After fleeing, we became a joined family with my grandfather, his three sons, and their families living together. There must have been

217

ten or fifteen of us. Adding to the stress of being uprooted, I was sent to boarding school at age five.

There was tremendous pressure at boarding school to do well. Since I couldn't get affection from my family, I sought affection from my teachers. And they would only give it if you did well. This intense pressure to achieve continued. By the time I was ten, I was getting peptic ulcers — something normally suffered by worried businessmen. And because of that, I knew I wanted to be a doctor. I wanted to understand this pain.

After school, I went to college in Bombay — an enormous, chaotic city of ten million back then, thirty million today. In this chaotic situation, I couldn't adapt; it was too much.

So, I sought help from a psychiatrist to help me with my confusion and stress, and to help me adapt to the new situation. He introduced me to the Indian spiritual teachings. Normally, a psychiatrist wouldn't do that, but he sent me to a spiritual teacher in Bombay.

I attended this teacher's lectures for a year, but he focused on the Bhagavad Gita and the Upanishads. His teaching was theoretical, but it was nice to know that there was a path to follow. My teacher explained that there was no hope that you could overcome your state. Only once in a hundred years does someone get enlightened.

After a year of this, a new teacher appeared in Bombay. This teacher wasn't theoretical; his teaching went straight to meditation. I was just blown by that, so I followed him to the letter, to every word he said.

My new teacher estimated that you could get a glimpse of enlightenment in nine years if you were reasonably interested. If you were very regular, maybe six years. And, if you were extremely devoted, maybe in three years.

I was full of hope, so I followed him to the south of India to his Ashram. It was quite a journey — two nights by train. I stayed there for six weeks and did a lot of meditation.

This second teacher was teaching Ramana Maharshi's teachings. This was unusual because no one did meditation in those days, not even in India. In the medical college, I was probably the only one doing it. It must have been strange for them that I was doing such things. But this particular approach of Ramana Maharshi was also rare. Ramana was not well known, not even in India.

Ramana's approach is called self-inquiry. It tells you to inquire within to discover who you are. Am I the body or do I experience a body? Are you your thoughts, feelings, memories, pain and your struggles? Is that who you are? You inquire and you come to the realization that no, I am not my thoughts. I am the thinker of my thoughts. I am not my body and mind; I am the experiencer of the body-mind.

And when you do this, the mind becomes quiet because you're not fueling the mind. You're not giving attention to the mind, so the mind subsides. And that's the process of meditation.

I started this form of meditation before starting my medical practice. You couldn't earn a living teaching meditation; that was unheard of. In India, meditation was free. So, I had to practice medicine, and of course, I was obliged because I had a medical education.

I practiced in a poor area of Bombay, a slum area, where anyone could just walk in without appointments. They were lined up like in a refugee camp. I charged one rupee per person, approximately two cents in today's value, or about 25 cents back then. So, I had to see a large number of people, on average over one hundred patients per day. The maximum was 160 patients in one day. So you could hardly spend two minutes per person.

To be able to do that, patient after patient, took tremendous focus. If I was in a state of meditation, I could easily grasp what the patient was experiencing, what he was suffering from, and what was the appropriate treatment. This way, I could use meditation to diagnose and treat a large number of people. Meditation gave me the compassion and focus to deal with the stress without any loss of energy.

After twenty-five years of practicing medicine, I felt that was enough.

During this time, I met some travelers from Switzerland who had come to my village in Matheran, India. When they meditated with me, they experienced a different quality of meditation. These same people invited me to their home in Basel, Switzerland where they had organized a gathering.

I traveled to Basel where I was invited to meditate with forty people in their garden. I told the group that we would meditate for an hour, which I now know is too much for beginners. I sat there with my eyes closed in front of forty people. An hour later, I opened my eyes, and they were all gone — all except two Germans.

I asked the two Germans, "Why did you not leave?" And they said, "We were so embarrassed. You came all the way from India and everyone has left so we couldn't leave."

It's a longer story, but the person I was staying with in Switzerland invited me to a birthday party. I didn't know the person, but the party was for Peter Cunz. Peter invited me to stay at his *house. At that time, I was willing to stay at anyone's house because I had no accommodations, no money, no nothing.*

On one Thursday evening, Peter asked if I would like to accompany him to Johanneshof. When I arrived, eighty people were seated in the meeting room. I sat in the back, almost hiding, just to watch what was going on. Up in front, Reshad announced, "Has anyone come here for the first time? Please raise your hand."

I did not raise my hand because I was hiding. Reshad asked again, actually three times. And the third time, he was emphatic: "Please raise your hand."

Reshad noticed me and commanded, "Come here." He introduced me to everyone at Johanneshof and invited me to give a little talk.

I mentioned to Reshad that I was flying to the States the next day. He said, "You must go to Atlanta and meet my friend Bruce."

And with that, the caravan in the desert found the starving Sufi again. This time in the form of a phone call. It was Reshad, calling from Switzerland:

"Bruce, listen to the sound of my voice," Reshad declared.

I had heard this prelude before, always a signal that the train of the future was coming in, so I grimaced, tightened, and waited for the *outside shock.*

"I have fixed it for you," Reshad announced.

Reshad didn't explain what he was fixing. All I heard was that an Indian guru would be landing on my doorstep — some guy named Bhagwan. My inner complainer griped, "Guru not wanted at this time, Reshad. Thank you very much."

My resistance stemmed from the fact that in our Sufi school, receiving a guest demanded a high level of protocol, what is called *adab,* or respectful courtesy and manners. We made a big practice of greeting guests at the airport, putting flowers in their room, and serving cups of tea. We also washed the walls with rosewater, prepared fancy meals — it got crazy. The point was to not "presume" the guest. The traveler represented the Third Force, a vector of opportunity that could open the host's narrow world to something bigger. Conversely, the traveler, having left his normal world behind, had the opportunity to be received in love.

When I pictured myself hosting Bhagwan from my spartan bachelor pad, I realized that full-on *adab* was out of my reach. So, I called Karen who, at this point, lived down the street in a rented apartment.

"Karen, I need your help."

"What is it?" She asked.

"Reshad is sending an Indian guru our way."

I'm not sure if it was *adab* or rekindled *amour*, but Karen jumped right on it.

"Okay," she said, "Let's talk about menu, flowers, rosewater..."

Bhagwan was easy to host — no *adab* required. He spent most of the day sitting on the couch reading the New York Times. In the evenings, he and Karen went to the movies and talked afterward. While they talked in the car in the driveway, I watched through an upstairs window like a doting parent.

I asked Karen what she remembered of those talks.

"We talked about the whole idea of the Lover and the Beloved and the difference between having a lover and marriage," Karen recalled. "Marriage was about having children and having a stable life. Bhagwan explained that there is an ever-changing balance between lover and beloved. In some relationships, you're the Lover and in other relationships, you're the Beloved.

"We saw lots of movies," Karen continued, "including *Forrest Gump*, which was about being in the right place at the right time. In the movie, Forrest fell in love with Jenny, his childhood friend. He adored her, but she would never open herself to his love.

Eventually, after trials and tribulations, Jenny opened to his love, but maybe too late. They got married right before she died of AIDS. But they were very happy."

I dreaded the moment, but one afternoon, Bhagwan asked me if I would like to sit with him. Karen caught me hesitating, so she gave me a stern glance. The word *Islam* means *submission,* and since the universe appeared to have set this up, I had no choice.

I trudged up the stairs to a forlorn bedroom, now emptied of furniture, where Bhagwan sat in a folding chair.

"So, tell me about this woman, Irmgard," Bhagwan asked.

I told him of my experience in the garden of Johanneshof and of Rumi's roses and thorns. I added enough synchronicity to support my case: In short, since Irmgard entered like a divine intervention, why step back into a dark and painful marriage?

Bhagwan was understanding but did not seem moved.

I pleaded my case: "Bhagwan, if there is only One Love, there cannot be two. You can't have all sorts of doors opening everywhere."

Bhagwan paused to absorb my question, then replied:

"This business with one love can be confusing. Yes, there is only One Love, One Beloved, but that love can take many appearances. There is the love you have with a child, or with your parents, or with a guru. And so it is with marriage.

"Let me explain how there can be two and still be One. Do you know the story of Radha and Rukmini?"

I stared blankly.

"There were these two women in Krishna's life," Bhagwan explained. "With Radha, it was a transcendent

Krishna and Radha

love, *mahabhava*, the quintessence of love. It was not a worldly love. It was beyond the ego.

"Rukmini"s love is called *kanta-bhava*, the love of wife. This love is bounded by your duties in the world to bring forth children and have a home. With Radha, in your lifetime, you may never even meet this soul. It's enough to know that this kind of love exists. With Rukmini, this is who you are in this world. You are bound in this love; it' your source of strength."

I think I heard the word, "bound" and not much else. I was still married, so I was bound. Being bound either feels good or it doesn't. At that moment, something let go. It wasn't where I wanted to go, but I accepted being bound.

Jews bind their arms. Chinese women bind their feet. Babies like to be swaddled. Yoga is about being "yoked." Even the expression "tying the knot" comes from a Celtic tradition of binding the bride and groom's hands during the wedding ceremony. In a way, I was relieved. I was bound and I accepted that I didn't have to make a decision.

Karen moved back into the house, we had a fabulous fling at the beach, and then she flew to Switzerland to be with Reshad at Johanneshof for two weeks.

While preparing for full *kanta-bhava* to celebrate Karen's return with a big dinner, our friend, Susan, phoned while I was cooking. I put down the phone and shouted upstairs: "Honey, Susan wants to know what kind of wine to bring."

"No wine," Karen shouted back. "Maybe she can pick up a home pregnancy test."

And just like that, our marriage entered Version 2.0. Reshad had fixed it.

In the meantime, Bhagwan returned to Switzerland. He recalled:

"When I got back to Switzerland, Reshad invited me to stay in Johanneshof. Reshad would make breakfast for me every day in his apartment. I was probably the closest person to him at that time. At one point he confided to me, 'Bhagwan, look, a sheikh needs a wife.' I took this as a hint that I should find him a wife."

It was at this time that Leslie Masters, an American student, was also at a crossroads in her life. She had met Reshad while interviewing him on her Seattle radio show, then moved to Santa Fe to study with him. Like the Sufi in the desert, Leslie was also waiting for her caravan. When Karen and I learned that Reshad was desperate for a secretary — someone hardworking and fluent in English — we helped raise the money for Leslie to fly to Switzerland.

"The original plan was for me to attend as a student," Leslie said. "Within a week, Reshad asked me to take over as his secretary. It was very chaotic working for him. Reshad would announce that something would happen and we would start to set it up. Then he would change his mind and it wouldn't happen. I was constantly managing his changing mind. I knew he had an alcohol problem, but I attributed the chaos to him performing the role of the teacher, the trickster, and keeping us on our toes."

While Leslie managed Reshad's affairs, Bhagwan was helping him find a wife.

"I approached Leslie," Bhagwan recounted. "I said, 'Leslie, look, Reshad wants a wife. So, who should be the wife?'"

Leslie continued: "When Bhagwan asked who would be a good wife for Reshad, I replied, 'Well there's Elena, and Reshad is interested in Renata, and there's me.' And so we talked and Bhagwan said, 'Well, I think that you would be a good wife.' And so I took that as a yes; I'd be a good wife. I told Bhagwan, 'My previous husband was a spiritual teacher – and an alcoholic.' Bhagwan lit up: 'Oh, then you are the perfect one.'"

In Reshad's understanding of the *tekke*, the sheikh's wife held the most important function outside of the sheikh himself. This is because the student must not approach the sheikh directly, but only through the wife. Like concentric buffers around the center, the sheikh represented the esoteric or most inner knowledge. The sheikh's wife served as the *mesoteric* or middle layer, and the *khalif* or executive lieutenant represented the outer or *exoteric* layer who managed his external affairs.

Not having a wife to serve as a buffer placed tremendous stress on Reshad. As one of his students later explained, "The situation was too much actually for a man as sensitive as Reshad."

Andre Gasser, a student and acupuncturist, described the physical toll on Reshad.

"After Penny left, Reshad began drinking quite a lot and his health deteriorated," Andre recalled. "I don't know whether it was because he missed Penny or if he felt free that he could finally drink without being criticized. Either way, the atmosphere in Reshad's little boathouse and in Johanneshof became quite intense.

"Reshad would regularly get exhausted and then call me for acupuncture treatments. He usually recovered quickly. I hoped he would save the gathered energy, but my recommendations to rest were ignored. Rather than recover, he spent it all in the next talk or by giving someone a healing who needed help — and there was always somebody!

"I would get frustrated that he could be so careless concerning his health," Andre continued, "but slowly I realized what it meant to be in complete surrender to the Work."

While Reshad dealt with growing numbers of visitors, he enlisted Leslie and others to help with his marital pursuit of Renata."

"When Renata came, he became moonstruck by her," Karen remembered. "She was beautiful."

"Yes, she was beautiful," Leslie recalled. "But she would also get easily hurt by him and would leave. Reshad would get one of us to get on the phone and convince her to come back."

It was during this time that Reshad asked Peter Cunz to rent a house in Hawaii so Reshad could write a book there while courting Renata as his muse.

Peter recalled: "Reshad said, 'I need $64,000 because I want to write another book in Hawaii and I need my muses and my staff to support me.' I said, 'Reshad, that's against the purpose of the foundation; you cannot have that money.' I insisted that he raise the money privately. This created a big scandal, but I refused."

Leslie continued: "Reshad raised the money and I made the arrangements for him to get away. Unfortunately, Reshad got ill before the trip and as a result, three very expensive airfares were lost. With the loss of the money, everyone was upset about this trip. My intuition said the signs were not good. Maybe he wasn't meant to go. He said not to worry about the money — that he had it covered."

Eventually, Reshad and Renata made it to Maui. Unfortunately, Renata left him again.

"I was summoned to Maui," Leslie continued. "When I got there, Reshad enlisted us to help get Renata back, which we did."

Leslie was in Hawaii for less than a week when she began to experience flu-like symptoms. This was not surprising given her stress and fatigue. Leslie had been working around the clock as Reshad's secretary, traveling around the globe, and now managing the impossible role of a jilted lover helping Reshad court another woman.

Leslie's illness began to worsen, so she was rushed to the hospital. The diagnosis: *streptococcus pneumoniae* — the same rare strep infection that killed Jim Henson, the creator of the Muppets.

Facing a similar threat from the same virulent bacterial infection, Leslie's doctors in Maui administered high doses of antibiotics plus vasopressors to maintain blood pressure to her vital organs — an emergency response that can constrict blood flow in the extremities. The medical effort was not successful and Leslie fell into a coma.

Leslie's setback hit Karen and me particularly hard. Reshad had a history of heading to Hawaii to write books that didn't get written, so watching him embark on this ill-fated mission – one that pulled a student in his service into tragic consequences – shattered my trust in his guidance.

"When Leslie went into the hospital, I went into action," Karen recalled. "This was before HIPAA, and as a nurse myself, I managed to call the nurses on Leslie's floor in Hawaii for regular updates. We organized prayer vigils in the States and Europe in the hope that our collective energies could send a healing force."

Despite around-the-globe efforts, the days turned into weeks, and Leslie slipped deeper into the coma.

"The doctors couldn't keep her blood pressure stable," Karen recalled. "They had given her these life-saving drugs that come with huge side effects, but they couldn't turn things around."

After three weeks in a coma without progress, the doctors had no recourse but to pull the plug from Leslie's life support. The impending loss devastated everyone who had been praying.

One of the nurses asked Leslie's mother if, as a last-ditch effort, she would be open to inviting a kahuna, a traditional Hawaiian shaman, to invoke a spiritual ritual at her bedside. Kahunas understand that by unlocking the powerful grip of the subconscious, the physical being can heal.

"My parents are just as dipsy as I am when it comes to spiritual stuff," Leslie recalled, "so my mom said yes, please, please. Kahlúa the Kahuna came to my bedside and did his dimensional work — a shamanic travel into the different realms. Within two hours, my eyes opened.

"When I first came out of the coma, I was still very much on the other side and I could not bridge the gap between worlds. I couldn't speak and I couldn't understand what was going on. I knew that I was okay coming back into space, but I didn't want to come back into time. I didn't want to come back into time because time held the pain.

"While I was in the coma, I could tell that time and space were being held open through everyone's prayers. I could feel it. The prayers allowed my individuated consciousness to travel — to take the time it needed to go through the different realms until it didn't feel separate anymore. And because space and time were being held open, my individuated self could come back.

"When I came out of the coma, I realized that I had to come back into time too. I lost my connection to being in the *brilliance* — that's the best way of saying it — in the connection, the knowing.

"If I tried to watch TV, I couldn't understand what people were saying or what it meant. But as I got more into knowing what the TV was saying, I would lose all the love, the joy, the brilliance, the 'everything' where I was at. After two weeks, I could understand what the TV was saying — and I was back in space and time.

"Lots of unusual things appeared out of the blue during this period. There was Tony Leitner, a very devout Jewish Buddhist who knew Reshad from Los Angeles. He had been praying for me the whole time, and he made it his mission to fly from LA to Maui to visit me at my bedside. When Tony entered my room, I had never seen anyone so absolutely translucent. He handed me a book, *Joy and Healing*, by Torkom Saraydarian, saying I was ready for it. Torkom was an Armenian musician, author, and teacher who I spoke with while I was still in the hospital. He was an amazing man, as was Tony who died while meditating cross-legged in front of his little altar after he returned to Los Angeles."

From the *Joy and Healing*:

Joy changes the chemistry of your brain and enables you to heal energetically, emotionally, and mentally. All you have to do is learn to release it at a moment's notice. Joy is a powerful energy that you can consciously release into your life on a daily basis. Once you release the joy, you will be able to sustain it longer and longer and realize that no matter what happens in your life, no one can take your joy away from you.[4]

"After I was released from the hospital, Reshad would call me," Leslie remembered. "Sometimes he was extremely encouraging, saying that everybody was waiting for me to join back into the group. Other times he would tell me that I just needed to go back to Seattle and live with my parents, that there was no place for me. It was very back and forth until I didn't hear much from him."

"What do you think this traumatic event was about?" I asked.

"Why did this happen to me?" Leslie replied, pausing to consider. "I feel like I was the gutter through which everything had to flow — or the grounding wire that discharged all the turmoil. I think that's why I lost my toes from the vasopressors. They got blown off.

"Today, I kind of clump along, but I walk, so that's good. I just wish I didn't have the pain. I would love to be able to go on a hike, be out in the woods, things like that. I'm working to find something that will handle the pain."

"You have pain in your feet all the time?" Karen asked.

"All the time. I also had brain damage from the coma and then four years ago, I had a brain aneurysm that bled into my brain, like a stroke."

The conversation paused.

"It's important to understand that I don't feel victimized by what happened," Leslie said leaving room for the spaces. "I feel that I was somehow the point of it or the..."

---

4. *Saraydarian, Torkom. 2011. Joy and Healing. First Kindle Edition based on Third Printed Editio edition. TSG Publishing Foundation, Inc*

Leslie tried to find the right words.

"I was needed so that the point of it could happen. That's what I mean."

While editing this chapter, Karen asked me, "Why are you focusing this chapter so much on Leslie?"

My German publisher also had trouble with Leslie's story, insisting that I cut it because *"it is a tragic personal situation which has so many levels that cannot possibly be analyzed within this book. Who knows what scenes are 'pivotal' after all in the big picture?"*

The job of the writer is to make those decisions. As a screenwriter, Johanneshof was like the critical mid-point in the arc of a movie, the point where the hero asks, "What will I have to do to overcome myself?" The mid-point is the "look-in-the-mirror moment" where the protagonist must face himself in his quest for the white whale.

I explained to Karen, "Johanneshof was like a sea journey on the Path of Return. We all got into little harpoon boats to support Reshad's larger quest. As the individual boats capsized, some people lost their savings, some people lost their marriages, many lost their concepts, and Leslie lost her toes. Leslie understood that each of us come onto the stage to move the bigger story forward — in her words, 'so that the point of it could happen.'"

One week after returning from Hawaii, Reshad gave a private talk to a handful of students. With Leslie still on life support and the school in collective shock, Reshad tried to put it all into perspective. He explained:

"The most dangerous way we manipulate life is with expectation," Reshad began. *"Mevlana said, 'Expectation is the red death.' Expectation affects the blood, which is red. Expectation affects the flow of life energy.*

"Consider that there are people who hasten to make you feel

better. So, you feel better one day and then you want more the next. That doesn't work in our tradition. What we are doing, potentially, is working to find yourself, in yourself, by yourself — because there is only One.

"You must give up expectation, otherwise there is no opening — no opening for what can be given at Johanneshof. Over the last two years, many people have come and then gone on their way. But, there have also been incredible healings — but only when people give up expectation.

"Don't expect that life is a sequence. It doesn't work like that. Yes, there is the sequence where you were conceived, nine months later you were born, and you live, and at the end of that apparent sequence, you die. But that is not real; that is only how it appears. In reality, you live the whole lot in one day of love. In one day of love.

"The misunderstanding from attending a seminar or a workshop is expecting a sequence: 'If I do this, then I will be better.' In fact, you will probably be worse. My teacher used to say to me, there is no 'if' or 'but' on the way of truth. Expectation is the bridge between 'if' and 'but.' Is it not? You need to give up the idea that if I come here, and if I spend my money, and if I live at Johanneshof, I will become better. Because what comes from that sequence is the word 'but.'

"I want you to leave here with a great question in your heart. Who brought you here? It wasn't a book that I wrote or somebody else wrote. There is something called kismet, which means destiny. We were brought together to share together and find out why we are here. Each person has a contribution to make; it's what you call in Swiss German mitenand [together]. And that is what I pray for you *all — that you will get a taste of possibility. In Arabic, it's called dawq – a taste of possibility.*

"I pray that you won't ever feel or believe that by doing this you will get an answer. Because you won't. From this school, you will get a lot of knowledge, a lot of practices, a lot of movements... But, if you serve and turn straight to God, you may get a possibility.

"As far as this Englishman is concerned, I wish you well. Do not feel that everyone at Johanneshof is one of my pupils. They're not. It takes 1001 days to become a pupil because it takes at least 1001 days to discover what it means to be a pupil. After 1001 days, maybe I will take on that responsibility and become your servant. It is not the other way round!"

Reshad used this question: "What does it mean to be a pupil?" as a frequent wake-up call to his students — that just because you're studying with him doesn't necessarily mean you're his pupil, and just because you're a Sufi doesn't absolve you from personal karmic suffering. But consider the context of his talk. Was he implying that Leslie wasn't a "pupil" to absolve himself from responsibility for a tragic event on his watch?

The responsibility of spiritual teachers to their students has raised long-standing questions of ethics. Is it okay for a Catholic nun to hit a child with a ruler? How about a Zen master hitting a meditator with a stick? What about Sufis? If a God-intoxicated Sufi is not *responsible* for his own actions, how can he responsible for his student? Rumi adds light to the puzzle:

Out beyond ideas of wrongdoing
and rightdoing there is a field.
I'll meet you there.

When the soul lies down in that grass,
the world is too full to talk about.
~Rumi

This was not the end. Leslie added a "look-in-the-mirror" postscript to the story:

"A year and a half after the coma I heard from Reshad again," Leslie recalled. "I've never told anyone about this, but Reshad called and said, 'I want to make contact with you. I want you to know that if I was in any way a cause of this, I want to apologize.'"

§

Johanneshof had its own karmic path and Hawaii was its turning point — one that left a mark on the psyche of the school. For one, Reshad's marital quest quickly came back to earth. None of his three suitors became his wife. Later, at the end of Johanneshof, Reshad entered into marriage number four with Barbara, his Swiss translator. And what became of Penny? She remained a pupil and dear friend of Reshad until the day he died.

More than just a turning point, Hawaii unveiled the unspoken, shadow side of the school. A core precept was to park your baggage — your psychology — outside the door, as Reshad described it, "like a pair of old shoes." I was not used to looking at my own psychology, so I was ill-equipped to fully integrate the shock of what happened. As a result, my faith in the teacher never fully recovered. For other people, the magic and the mania of Johanneshof quickly picked up where it left off.

Andre Gasser described the atmosphere:

Reshad gives a talk at Johanneshof.

"The bending of spoons, dowsing, geomancy, turning, and music all created an atmosphere for healing and transformation. In the midst of this, we received the healings we needed," Andre remembered.

"One day after turning class, Reshad met privately with just a few of us. We enjoyed wine and drinks while Reshad sang and played the guitar. Everybody was quite relaxed. Reshad wanted to cook for everybody and disappeared into the kitchen. When dinner was served, we felt the 'manna' from the food he prepared.

"After dinner, we continued to sing and dance in a circle," Andre continued. "It was at this point — and this is the last thing I remember — Reshad started tapping my shoulder. Suddenly, I collapsed and left my body. Soon I was watching and listening from the ceiling while the group discussed what should be done. Reshad gave instructions.

"One of Reshad's students touched my feet and I returned to being in my body. When he released his hands, I was out again. This lasted for several minutes until Reshad hit my chest and anchored my spirit back into the body.

"Reshad also used one of his radionics devices to clear old patterns that remained embedded in the cellular pattern of my body. Back then, Reshad was inventing all sorts of devices for esoteric healing.

"I remember people wiping me from head to toe with rosewater. Reshad also invited me to sleep in his flat. The next day, I awoke to feel a heavenly peace that lasted for several days. I realized without a shadow of a doubt what was permanent and what was temporary. When you see your body from a distance, you observe consciousness, not the body. I understood that this happens when we die. All that changes after death is that you cannot express your thoughts, emotions or body functions anymore."

Ruth Linauer also remembers this time: "I was ironing in the basement during a summer seminar in Johanneshof when, through a window, I saw Reshad putting iron rods wrapped with copper wire into the earth. I could feel the change of the atmosphere immediately –

The laundry team in the basement.

even in the basement of that enormous house. It was strange what happened next. I was always deeply interested in nature, symbols, forms, shapes, and colors – and at that moment, I knew that I wanted to become a geomancer. A day later, I took all my courage and asked Reshad if he would teach me geomancy. He agreed and I began a six-year apprenticeship with him."

Today, Ruth offers professional geomantic services to harmonize energetic fields in living spaces, enhance land use, and correct negative impacts in the earth.

Josef Huber was another student at Johanneshof who applied Reshad's knowledge of sacred geometry. Today Josef has designed and patented a line of multifaceted crystals for water purification and healing support.

Peter Cunz's path took a different turn.

Preparing a meal.

"With all this chaos, I had to distance myself from what was going on," Peter recalled. "It was not my cup of tea. As a result, Reshad became increasingly unhappy that I was becoming more distant. One day, Reshad phoned me and asked, 'Why don't you support me anymore?'

"And I answered, 'Because, you make a cult around you.' This shocked Reshad and he responded forcefully, 'No, no, no!' three times and then he hung up the phone."

Peter continued: "A little later, I was at Johanneshof for dinner and Reshad stood up afterward and said publicly, 'As from now on, Peter is not part of our school.' It was a shock — unexpected, but not deep or emotional. I felt annoyed. People in the room were terribly shocked; they just stared at me."

Peter left Reshad and became a sheikh in the formal Mevlevi Order.

After Peter's departure, Reshad forewarned his students of the inevitable split:

"Three years ago, when I took nine people to Istanbul and Konya, it became apparent to me that this would be the last journey to Turkey that I would ever make," Reshad remembered. "It was said by Rumi: one day the sun will rise in the West — and not in the Middle East or the East.

Reshad and group at Dede's tomb in Konya, Turkey.

"On that trip, we went to see the head of the Mevlevis, Çelaleddin Çelebi, a very nice old man... We paid our respects. But none of us [except Peter] are Muslims. We may be believers, but we are not doing the five prayers a day and all that stuff. It was on the last three days of the trip that we met the Çelebi –

and then I knew I had made a mistake. We are not Mevlevi... but some people don't understand. I warned everybody: Look out! In a short time, you will get a letter or a communication from somebody in Turkey who will say they want to come here to be sponsored.

"Well, one hour ago I received such a communication: The Çelebi wants to send his representative and a translator. They communicated with Peter because he is a Muslim. So Peter communicated with me, basically saying: 'Reshad, you should sponsor it.'

"And I said, 'No, it is not our way.' So, I will be sending out a fax saying this Mevlevi invitation is coming and if you want to go, then go. And I want you to say 'no' when you have to say 'no.' This is why: Johanneshof is not for that. I have never met a Muslim who understands what we are involved with."

Soon, Peter sent out a letter to people who had left Johanneshof. Twenty people gathered to join Peter in the formal Mevlevi path.

From that point on, Reshad started to declare, "I'm not a Mevlevi sheikh. The formal sheikh in Switzerland is Peter."

Peter began to host a Mevlevi group and sponsored a full sema on Rumi's Urs. Reshad even came to attend. With this, Peter's feelings toward Reshad began to change:

"I had been very negative toward Reshad," Peter said. "Then slowly, slowly, my negative feelings started to disappear. More and more, Reshad's problems and my problem with them disappeared. I started to find my love for him again. My feelings turned toward compassion.

"I started to see Reshad as a person who had been given incredible talents – the ability to open the door into the other world – and to see into that other world. But part of his nervous system was unable to bear that world. His nervous system wasn't trained to handle the energy. At times he would use his access to that world to stir things up, which was necessary. At other times, he would have been better off if he didn't have sight into the other world. The other world is not all angels; there are also devils.

"So, you attract from the other world whatever you are open to receive," Peter continued. "The good and the bad. The other world is neutral. We can attract both — what appears in our world as good and not good.

"I also saw Reshad's suffering, his suffering from all that he was able to feel but not translate into action – a proper action, in a proper way, into this world.

"And, I saw Reshad aging and losing his energy, the energy he had used to command the center, to stay in the spotlight. As he became lonely and lonelier, and even more lonely, my feelings of compassion for this person from whom I learned so much, and who I always loved, continued to grow and grow. And it continues today."

§

On June 13, 1996, Reshad invited fourteen friends to join him and his new wife, Barbara, for one final dinner before Johanneshof would close its doors forever. The dinner was casual, but also very intimate. Reshad talked during the dinner, speaking of his family history, stories from his life, and the task behind his teaching. Tears flowed during the evening, not from sadness, but from gratitude.

Between courses, there was music. Reshad played harmonica, backed by guitar and saxophone, while his dinner companions sang the "Skye Boat Song." Amid the laughter, jokes, deep feelings, there was also a sense of loss. Roger and Helen remembered the moment:

"Closing down did cause some disappointment, regret, and self-reproach. But the overriding feeling was one of mutual understanding and deep friendship. A certainty emerged that we had been granted this incredible gift of witnessing and participating in an indescribable experiment.

"From this evening onward, for both of us, Reshad had taken a firm and permanent seat in our heart — a connection established for eternity."

"He inscribed himself in my heart," Helen remembers. "It was on this evening, that Reshad invited us to witness Life itself — *how it is done* — how we should regard and value life. He revealed the way he taught and how he would leverage his *baraka* to stimulate transformation in people. He demonstrated around the table that he did not teach by words at all (though he used them to attract people in a most convincing way), but rather by sound and pattern. It was his voice, his look, his heart, and his very being which exercised impact and fostered understanding. I suddenly understood that compassion and awareness are the very same thing."

As the room became quiet, Peter Knecht, a master at using music to move the Octave, inserted harp music to punctuate the pin-drop stillness. Then Reshad spoke slowly, reaching between each syllable as if he was rowing toward an inner Isle of Skye that lived in his heart. He said:

Switzerland is an incredible country, so I am grateful. This is our last time.

The one message I put to you is, "What is the meaning of compassion?"

Pray to your lord that you find the meaning of compassion before you die — and then any judgment will go.

We are all unique within the One. Please listen to that — it is the only message I can give you this evening: "What is the meaning of compassion?"

And then you will bow. Bowing to each other, acknowledging the truth from God. Did you hear me bow? It's a sound.

Reshad turned to each person:

I bow to you. I bow to you, and I bow to you. One day you will have to bow to 30,000 people, 32,000 actually.

*This is the secret: Life gives us life, and it's one of the names of God —
Ya Hayy: The One from whom all life arises.*

*That's a great mystery, and a wonderful one to understand — that
Life gives us life, and we have to give it back again*

*And then, when you hear it, you'll stand up proud and never judge
again.*

*There is a light here (pointing), sometimes called the third eye. Imagine
that in the darkness, you can see the light. Don't imagine it, you have
it. You have the ingredient. You can look through the darkness of what
Hazrat Inayat Khan called human ignorance. The energy needs to move.*

*Look towards it, and you will find there is a response. Don't
underestimate yourselves. You have the light within you. You can direct
the light from here, where my finger is, and you can look, but you won't
see what you think you are going to see, you'll find a direction.*

*It's very important that I said this to you. I invited all of you to dinner,
and please, don't underestimate yourselves.*

*Just remember you are a miner — like a miner of coal — bringing up
millions of years of wood from beneath the ground. Miners have suffered
all over the world. You are miners as well, and you have suffered enough.
Let the light shine*

*There's one more thing I would say to you, and I pray you understand.
You don't face death once, you have to face it many times. At the time of
death when the body disintegrates, that is one. There are many deaths.*

*The clearing exercise I give you is a death every night.[5] Death is life.
It's not a once off when you kick the bucket. If you can face life, as I have
faced death all my life, you can help many, many people. Just face it.*

*Completion is not an ending, nor is there any ending to the movement
of truth itself. Completion in a cycle of life is like the wind looping from*

---

5. Part of Reshad's 24-Day Practice Program, a breathing and meditative method to
release the impressions of the day. http://chalicealivingschool.net/en/study-material-
practices

one place to another. Looping from the north, or south, or east, or west. The wind starts from its own beginnings, and then transitions. The end of the cycle is not the end of possibility, it is only the beginning.

Once, when I was young, I was walking long distances in Scotland. I found myself alone on a hill and there was nowhere I could see to go. But then, after many miles of walking in the mountains, I knew where to go — and I went home.

12

IN PRAISE OF SUFI STORIES

Flannery O'Connor once said: "A story is a way to say something that can't be said any other way." For this reason, esoteric knowledge has long been transmitted through teaching stories to reveal the invisible hand that weaves our world. Similarly, the rambling tales and teaching stories of Rumi's *Masnavi* decode the complexities and contradictions of a dramatic universe.

Teaching stories have the power to change people. More than moralistic homilies, a true teaching story lifts your consciousness. If stories existed within particle physics, a *story* would be the smallest unit of transformation. A story is another name for the Octave. From the inciting incident to the conscious shock, and through the inner struggle that delivers the protagonist from crisis and conflict to acceptance and gratefulness, every beat in a teaching story moves the energy toward deeper understanding.

Rumi didn't suddenly appear on Amazon.com. He entered our culture through a story — through the wide eyes and open hearts of a group of young seekers in Los Angeles who were pulled into the drama. Like a Shakespeare play with its many exits and entrances, it took a cast of actors and dramatic scenes to move Rumi's Sufi story forward — from the Mongol invasion to Coldplay's $400 million tour.

Süleyman Dede taught through stories. His tale of a Turkish businessman who was strangely guided to a Turkish bath in the hope of conceiving a child could have easily been plucked from the pages of the *Masnavi*. And, Dede's story of the miraculous recovery of the Istanbul sheikh, challenged our beliefs about diagnosis and destiny.

David Bellak shared one of his favorite Dede teaching stories with me — about cooking and being cooked:

In the Mevlevi tradition great emphasis is placed upon the preparation of food. In Dede's house, which he often referred to as his tekke, the kitchen was a small, neatly-ordered and simple space with a small gas bottle burner, various pots, and a tall terracotta water vessel to hold spring water delivered by a horse-drawn cart to the neighborhood.

There were times during my service to Dede when he would let me assist in preparations, but only after specific instructions and only when he was confident in my ability to follow instructions.

On one such occasion, we carefully washed our hands, donned aprons, and proceeded to cook. Dede chopped the onions, placed a large pot on the burner, poured in some oil, then the onions, and stirred the contents. I stood idly behind him.

Dede turned to me and said, "Davut, you take the spoon. Stir the onions this way – in a clockwise motion – and don't stop, just keep stirring."

My mind began to drift in this "mindless" task. Each time my stirring slowed and restarted in the opposite direction, Dede would peer over my shoulder and gently chide, "No, I told you the other way, like this." He would even take hold of my wrist and guide the spoon back to its clockwise motion.

After a few moments, my mind would wander again, wondering why we should stir that way when a semazen in the sacred dance is meant to turn in a counter-clockwise direction. Thinking that Dede made a mistake, I stopped, and redirected the spoon, sema-like, in a counter-clockwise direction.

Dede had his back to me, yet he instinctively sensed to turn around and barked, "What are you doing? I told you to turn THIS way!"

Taking my arm firmly, he once again sent the spoon clockwise. I was startled and hurt, but I managed to continue until it was time to pour broth into the pot.

Months later while we were having tea, I asked, "Baba, why did you want me to stir the onions that way and not the other?"

Taking a sip of tea and a puff of his cigarette, he said quietly, almost matter-of-fact, "So you will always do exactly as I tell you."

Forty years later, no matter what I am cooking, I cannot stir a pot other than clockwise. My arm simply won't allow it to happen.

Reshad also loved telling such stories – likely because he lived his life as one continuous Sufi story that was as complex and colorful as a tale from the Mathnawi. Reshad likened himself to a Paddington Bear character who bumbled and fumbled into improbable mystical mishaps — all shared as teaching stories. To everyone's vexation, being around Reshad would thrust you into the middle of these scenarios — and yes, they often involved food.

One night, Karen and I took Reshad and Penny out to dinner

at Virgilio's, an elegant Italian restaurant in Los Angeles. As the meal progressed, I struggled to regale Reshad with witty conversation, but I wasn't up to the task. When Reshad started to drift toward the neighboring tables — injecting himself into other conversations and presenting himself as a famous author — the teaching story I stepped into suddenly became surreal.

Karen and I watched in horror as Reshad began to bend the fancy tableware like the psychic Uri Geller. He massaged and bent the shank of a spoon at our table and then moved to the next table, startling the unsuspecting guests. I might have saved the evening if I had taken charge and ushered Reshad home to bed, but I didn't.

"Take me to La Cage Aux Folles!" Reshad announced as the valet delivered our car. I think his actual words were, "I want to go to a drag show!"

Ever dutiful in my characterized obedience, I steered my little Datsun into a sea of stretch limos in front of the famous pink nightclub on La Cienega in Beverly Hills. As the parking valets opened the doors, I knew we were headed down a rabbit hole.

"Welcome to the world famous La Cage Aux Folles," our flamboyant waiter greeted with a suggestive sashay.

We were brusquely seated around the tiny table, and admittingly, I wasn't comfortable with the aggressive theatricality of female impersonation, but in the spirit of Rumi's *Nasuh,* the young man who, in Rumi's words, *"disguised his virility"* to make a living massaging beautiful women, I did my best to embrace the unpredictable flow.

"A little something before the show?" our waiter asked.

"I think I'll have some water," I replied not feeling the swing of things.

"I'd like some... some *champagne,*" Reshad declared channeling the late, great Peter O'Toole.

"Champagne all around?" The waiter's palm-frond-sized eyelashes flipped upward to signal my Sufi test.

Lest we forget, this is a teaching story. In that champagne moment, the aspiring Sufi (me), had to choose between serving the teacher or following my inner prompting — a tough decision when given a split second to ponder.

"All around!" Reshad announced pulling us into his bubbly vision for the evening.

The waiter returned with a silver bucket and stand, then drilled me eye-to-eye (sensing that I was the keeper of the credit card).

"Dom Perignon. One hundred and fifty dollars," he clipped in a no-nonsense business voice.

Ms. Eyelash then flipped 'em skyward to signal decision-time. Back in character, he/she leaned in, eyed my pauper status, and beguiled, "Shall I pop the cork?"

"Ohhh, let's..." Reshad bubbled with glee.

I reached for my inner adult, but couldn't summon the words... POP!!!

And then, (and only slow-motion can render this scene with justice) Reshad's head drooped suddenly southward. Zonked. Snoring. Passed out. He was gone.

"Try to get him to the car while I pay the bill," I commanded taking charge of the scene two beats too late.

Yes, a perfect Sufi story – the challenge, jeopardy, loss, and the lesson. Looking back, I should have submitted the tale to Idries Shah. Title: *Gone Perignon*.

In one blink of an eyelash, I lost $150 for the bottle, plus four cover charges, valet, and my composure in a moment of decision when I didn't predict that my guest of honor would pass out.

J.G. Bennett saw the whole of life working this way – a *dramatic universe* playing out in a sea of uncertainty. In this way, Bennett felt that the most vibrant spirituality was found in life's uncertainties — what he called Hazard. Hazard, by definition, is an event of significance where one can't know the outcome. Bennett explains:

The present moment is in a constant state of flux... It is the scene of unending strife between order and disorder, between freedom and determination, between evolution and degeneration. The outcome of these conflicts is uncertain on the scale of our own experience; and, so far as we can tell, upon the Universal scale also. This uncertainty gives the Universe its Dramatic character and it also makes our individual lives significant.[1]

When Süleyman Dede planted the seed of Rumi in America, letting men and women turn together, eating bacon (maybe), and initiating a bevy of unprepared young sheikhs, he was playing with Hazard. I suspect he understood the power and purpose of what he was doing, but he couldn't know the effects of his actions. Dede couldn't know if, by injecting straight-up Rumi into the eclectic soup of American culture, the Mevlevi line would take hold, dissipate, or distort into something unintended. But, Dede trusted God's hand acting through Hazard when he stated:

"I come to Los Angeles to plant a seed. I come to plant Mevlana's message of universal love in this soil. The way of Mevlana, of Rumi, will grow here in the West in its own way."

Today, an Americanized Rumi has grown, as prophesied, *"in its own way."* But has the Mevlevi marrow survived in this eclectic soup? This leads to an Idries Shah Sufi story:

A kinsman came to see Nasrudin from the country, and brought

---

1. Bennett, J.G. *The Dramatic Universe, Volume 4: History, preface.* Bennett Books

a duck. Nasrudin was grateful, had the bird cooked, and shared it with his guest.

Presently another visitor arrived. He was a friend, as he said, "of the man who gave you the duck." Nasrudin fed him as well.

This happened several times. Nasrudin's home had become like a restaurant for out-of-town visitors. Everyone was a friend at some removes of the original donor of the duck.

Finally Nasrudin was exasperated. One day there was a knock at the door and a stranger appeared. "I am the friend of the friend of the friend of the man who brought you the duck from the country," he said.

"Come in," said Nasrudin.

They seated themselves at the table, and Nasrudin asked his wife to bring the soup.

When the guest tasted it, it seemed to be nothing more than warm water. "What sort of soup is this?" he asked the Mulla.

"That," said Nasrudin, "is the soup of the soup of the soup of the duck."[2]

Idries Shah's "soup-of-the-soup-of-the-duck" was a recurrent theme in Reshad's school. Reshad would pull out the soup metaphor to underscore the fact that, unlike "inferior" schools that dispensed recycled teachings from long-dead teachers, we had a living teacher serving fresh broth in our midst.

The critical question from a Duck Soup perspective was whether Reshad and others who borrow and blend from Rumi are serving fresh soup? Does the spiritual marrow get stronger in an eclectic stew? Do Americanized Rumi teachings transmit

---

2. Shah, Indries. *The Exploits of the Incomparable Mulla Nasrudin*. Octagon Press Ltd, 1983.

something original and alive, or do they water the soup of the original duck?

Not surprisingly, the Americanization of Rumi has fomented controversy among Rumi scholars. In "The Erasure of Islam from the Poetry of Rumi," *The New Yorker's* Rozina Ali challenges the watered-down soup of Americanized Rumi as she writes:

> Rumi himself described the "Masnavi" as "the roots of the roots of the roots of religion"–meaning Islam –"and the explainer of the Koran." And yet little trace of the religion exists in the translations that sell so well in the United States.[3]

Rozini Ali describes the deep weaving of Quranic references in Rumi's Masnavi that scholars feel is inseparable from the poetic narrative. Ali interviews Jawid Mojaddedi, a scholar of early Sufism at Rutgers, who recently completed an ambitious new translation of the *Masnavi*. According to Mojaddedi, "The Rumi that people love is very beautiful in English, and the price you pay is to cut the culture and religion."[4]

This takes me to Ibrahim Bill Gamard. When Bill and his delightful wife, Sherry, arrived in Los Angeles to help launch the Institute for Conscious Life in 1974 – fresh from one of Reshad's spiritual adventures in Tepotzlan, Mexico – I took to them immediately. Both had a fervor for direct spiritual experience and esoteric knowledge. Bill quickly became our most dedicated *semazen*.

But Bill and Sherry's journey with Reshad came to an abrupt end with the pizza tirade on Dede's final night. Bill shared his memory of the moment:

---

3. Ali, Rozina. "The Erasure of Islam from the Poetry of Rumi." *The New Yorker*, January 5, 2017, http://www.newyorker.com/books/page-turner/the-erasure-of-islam-from-the-poetry-of-rumi
4. ibid

*"After we returned home, we made up our minds to leave the group
and to inform Reshad as soon as possible. We felt strongly that to
remain any longer in Reshad's group would be unethical since it
would be a silent assent to such wrongness from a man who had
been our teacher, whom we had loved, and from whom we had
learned so many valuable spiritual teachings."[5]*

After the pizza exit, Bill turned his spiritual focus toward Dede
and the Mevlevi path. Unlike Bill, I continued with Reshad for
another twenty-five years. As a result, I lost contact with Bill, now
Ibrahim, until now.

Ibrahim has made it his mission to translate Rumi *literally*
because, in his words, "there are so many popular books which
distort his words and teachings in an attempt to make them sound
poetic. Literal translations are very much needed in order for
readers to understand, at the minimum, the outward sense of
Rumi's words."[6]

Ibrahim compares the accurate translations of Rumi with the
"distorted" versions popularized by Coleman Barks and others.
Consider the famous Coleman rendering of Rumi that's chalked
on the wall of my yoga studio:

Let the beauty we love be what we do.
There are hundreds of ways to kneel and kiss the ground.[7]

Ibrahim's accurate translation puts Rumi's statement in an Islamic
context:

5. Gamard, Ibrahim. "Memories of Süleyman Dede Effendi." Dar-Al-Masnavi.org
.http://www.dar-al-masnavi.org/dede.html

6. Gamard, http://www.dar-al-masnavi.org/corrections.popular.html

7. Barks, Coleman. Rumi: The Book of Love: Poems of Ecstasy and Longing (San Francisco:
HarperCollins, 2003), 123.

There are a hundred kinds of prayer, bowing, and prostration
For the one whose prayer-niche is the beauty of the Beloved.[8]

Ibrahim Gamard discusses the differences:

The poem involves a mystical interpretation of the Islamic ritual
prayer. The Sufis pray, not just five times a day, but pray to God, the
Source of Love and Beauty, in hundreds of ways throughout the day.
The original Persian does not mention "kissing" or "the ground." It
can be seen that Barks' often-quoted words, "Let the beauty we love
be what we do," are his words and are not Rumi's words at all —
which in this line depict a spiritual devotion toward the beauty of
the Beloved.[9]

I asked Coleman Barks about this passage:

"It's true those are not literal translations," Coleman agreed. "I don't have John Moyne's literal translation in hand, but I was saying that praying to the Beloved is a way of recognizing the beauty all around us – and in us. Prayer is a way of seeing the beauty and somehow, miraculously, doing the beauty. Everything can become part of that prayer. Back in 1977 when I wrote that line, it felt inspired. That's inflated, of course, but I'm glad those lines are on your yoga studio wall."

Two very different translations: One poetic, one literal. Coleman's poetic translation evokes a universal longing, a reverence for the existence that sustains us, and a longing to transform one's life into the expression of beauty.

Gamard's literal translation captures Rumi's Islamic context because *prostration* is uniquely Islamic. In the literal translation,

8. from Rumi's Quatrain no. 81, translated by Gamard, Ibrahim and Farhadi, Ravan. *The Quatrains of Rumi. Sufi Dari Books, 2008.*
9. Gamard, Ibrahim. *http://www.dar-al-masnavi.org/western_views.html*

Rumi asks the reader to transcend ritual prayer, because true prayer can take many forms. Rumi takes a metaphysical leap when he challenges us to look beyond the *mihrab,* to look beyond the physical niche in the wall aligned to Mecca, thousands of miles away, and instead, awaken to the immediacy of the beauty that surrounds us as an expression of the Beloved.

Both versions challenge the reader to stretch their sense of the sacred. Is this controversy surrounding "literal versus poetic" simply a matter of preference? Or should we ask, "What is the purpose of poetry?"

One of John F. Kennedy's final speeches before his death was to honor Robert Frost and reflect on the power and purpose of poetry:

> *When power corrupts, poetry cleanses, for art establishes the basic human truths which must serve as the touchstones of our judgment. The artist, however faithful to his personal vision of reality, becomes the last champion of the individual mind and sensibility against an intrusive society and an officious state. The great artist is thus a solitary figure. He has, as Frost said, "a lover's quarrel with the world." In pursuing his perceptions of reality, he must often sail against the currents of his time...*[10]

Rumi and Frost were both lovers quarreling with the world. Rumi quarrels with the faithful as if to say, "Wake up Muslims; look beyond the tiles on the wall. Embrace the totality of your experience; embrace the beauty of the Beloved."

Then what about Coleman Barks?

For starters, Coleman is not a translator, and he is not a

---

10. *President Kennedy's Convocation Address, Amherst College, October 26, 1963.*
https://www.amherst.edu/library/archives/exhibitions/kennedy/documents

religious scholar. He is a poet and like Frost, a lover quarreling with the world.

Coleman reworks scholarly translations of Rumi's poems into what he calls "a language that is more in the tradition of American free verse, of spiritual searching poetry. We have a tradition that is known throughout the world for its elegance and delicacy and its plain-spokenness."[11]

Coleman is completely upfront that he does not translate from the original Persian:

"My theory is that you can't be a poet in a language that you didn't hear in the cradle," Coleman explains. "All I heard was this Southern that I'm speaking."

The origin story of Coleman Barks as the foremost American proponent of Rumi is a Sufi story in itself – a story where one thing inevitably led to another. Coleman did not choose "Rumi Studies" as a degree program, nor was Sufism part of his Chattanooga childhood. A year after Robert Bly asked Coleman to "release these poems from their cages," Coleman received what could be considered a Sufi initiation in a dream. He explains:

In 1971, both of my parents died within six weeks of each other. At that point, my dream-life became luminous. I began keeping dream journals. I still do.

In 1977, I had a dream where I was sleeping on a bluff on the Tennessee River right where I grew up, although I never slept out there on that bluff.

I was sleeping there, and I woke up in the dream. I was still asleep, but I was lucid. I had a waking state inside the dream.

And this ball of light came off the river from Williams Island and

11. Curiel, Jonathan. "Poet follows his own muse in translating Sufi mystic…" San Francisco Chronicle, April 4, 2002, http://www.sfgate.com/entertainment/article/Poet-follows-his-own-muse-in-translating-Sufi-2855984.php

clarified above me. There was a man sitting inside the ball of light.
He had a white scarf over his head, and he raised his head and said,
"I love you."

And I said, "I love you, too."

I don't know what would have happened in my life if I hadn't
said that. But it wasn't a decision that I made. I simply responded
that way.

I don't think I said it out loud. It was something telepathic going
on between us.

And that's the end of the dream, except that the landscape felt
drenched with dew — a very natural wetness. And I understood the
wetness to be love. So, it felt like the whole world was full of love.[12]

Coleman's dream was a transmission — a transmission from a ball
of light. But the story doesn't end there. Coleman shared what
happened next:

"My friend Milner Ball was teaching at the law school at
Rutgers... I sent him some of these rephrasings of Rumi and, for
some weird reason, he read them to his class in the law school.

"One of his students, Jonathon Granoff, came up and said,
'Who did those poems?'

"So, Milner gave Jonathon my address. This was before email,
so Jonathon started writing these long letters saying that I had to
come meet this teacher who lived near him.

"In September of 1978, I went to Philadelphia on a poetry
reading trip. Afterward, Jonathon took me to meet his teacher. I
walked into a room, and there was the man who was in the dream
— Bawa Muhaiyaddeen. There is no way that I can prove that.
Bawa and I were the only ones who knew it.

---

12. *From the interview: Coleman Barks - The Man in the Dream, produced by Jason Scholder, Reel*
Change Films, Jun 10, 2012. https://www.youtube.com/watch?v=m8TLbowWpPc

"Bawa used to come to me in dreams and teach me things. I would start telling a dream to him, and he would say, 'You don't need to tell me the dream; I was there.'

"Another time, he said, 'You know, I know Rumi and Shams, but not like people from a book. I know them as I know you.'"

So how did a renunciant master living in the jungle of Sri Lanka end up playing a central role in the spread of Rumi? From the Bawa Muhaiyaddeen Fellowship:

Little is known of the personal history of M. R. Bawa Muhaiyaddeen prior to his emergence from the jungles of Sri Lanka over fifty years ago at which time he was asked to teach. He rarely spoke of himself in any way, never deviating from his focus on the one God.

Since Truth has no limits or boundaries or compartments, it can never be confined to or owned by any religion. Thus, although totally unlettered, to a Hindu he would talk about God in detailed terms of Hinduism; to a Jew or Catholic he would talk about God in detailed terms of Judaism or Catholicism, to a Muslim in terms of Islam. But to an atheist who was a car mechanic, he might talk about God in terms of cars – in whatever terms the individual could best grasp the explanation. His actions were a living example of the Truth about which he spoke. He was the example of that Truth, in whatever form might be needed for the moment. He sometimes described himself as an "ant man," or as a being tinier than the tiniest ant. [13]

13. Bawa Muhaiyaddeen Fellowship, "The History of the Fellowship." http://www.bmf.org/fellowship/history/

Coleman takes the story of Bawa's role in the spread of Rumi further:

Guru Bawa

"Early on, I took some of my first translations of Rumi, some quatrains, to Philadelphia, to Bawa's room, and read them to him," Coleman recounted. "I asked him if I should continue with this work.

Bawa said, 'It has to be done.' I remember that moment very clearly. As I have often said, Bawa is my only valid credential I have for working on the words of Rumi, this great enlightened being. I was in the presence for nine years... visiting this man, Bawa, who like Rumi also spontaneously sang songs and praise of existence. That is the main strand that connects me with Rumi. When I work on these poems, I am strengthening the friendship with my teacher."

The first time I met Coleman, I was struck by the way he wore his soul on the outside. I could imagine him reading a Southern menu with the full Rumi effect: "*Catfish, collards, and hush puppies please... and bring me a side order of Shams-i-Tabriz.*"

If you believe in prophetic dreams, Coleman received a direct transmission from Bawa Muhaiyaddeen. This inner permission transformed a University of Georgia English professor to become the Rumi jazz poet for our time.

Consider the parallels of Coleman's Rumi rephrasings with the rephrasings by jazz giant, John Coltrane. Coltrane took a beloved tune from Rogers and Hammerstein's *The Sound of Music*, "My Favorite Things," and transformed it into a genre-defining triumph — a sound that firmly established the spiritual dimension of jazz.

In another parallel, consider the life-changing gift Coleman Barks received from Robert Bly — "Release these poems from their scholarly cages." Coltrane also received a life-changing gift when Miles Davis gifted him with a soprano saxophone. It was the shift from tenor to soprano sax that lifted Coltrane's musical orbit into the spiritual realm.

According to Miles Davis:

"I was going with a girl who was an antique dealer in France. She gave this soprano sax to me, and I gave it to Coltrane. I gave that thing to Trane, man, and it's probably still in his hand. He probably died with it in his mouth! He never did take that thing out of his mouth."[14]

Coltrane revived the mostly-forgotten soprano sax from its "cages," and took the straight horn into new territory — a foreshadowing of the spiritual journey he was about to take through his music.

Musicologist Porter Lewis described Coltrane's approach through the jazz classic, "A Love Supreme:"

Coltrane more or less finished his improvisation, and he just starts playing the Love Supreme motif, but he changes the key another time, another time, another time. This is something very unusual. It's not the way he usually improvises. It's not really improvised. It's something that he's doing. And if you actually follow it through, he

14. Sorene, Paul. "John Coltrane's Notes For A Love Supreme And Miles Davis' God-Given Gift." *Flashbak.* http://flashbak.com/john-coltranes-notes-for-a-love-supreme-and-miles-davis-god-given-gift-363960/

ends up playing this little Love Supreme theme in all 12 possible keys.[15]

For the artist and poet, the act of creation is improvisatory, and it's sacred. Whether from a straight horn or a straight pen, every poem — musical or written — is an improvisation, an awakening, an opening. In this way, Coleman and Coltrane operate in the same terrain.

Coleman describes Rumi's poetry as "the mystery of opening the heart," something so profound, yet subtle, that "you can't say it in language."[16]

Yes, Coleman takes liberties; he is a poet — an artist who coaxes feelings out of words and opens the heart by marrying ideas together. This is Coleman's unique American gift to Rumi.

1976 was a pivotal year for Coleman Barks, and for Ibrahim Gamard, and for me. Each of us received gifts from Rumi. One of us became a poet; another became a sheikh and a scholar. My gift was different. Let me explain:

After locating a magnificent house for the Institute for Conscious Life, we didn't know what to do next. Reshad instructed us to turn to E.J. Gold for support. E.J. was America's foremost spiritual prankster, and at the time, E.J. presented himself as "Mr. G" – a self-styled, funhouse version of Gurdjieff himself.

I eyed the sign, "The First Sufi Church of Christ" in front of E.J.'s modest bungalow on Alexandria Street. Someone let me in, and I took a chair in the circle. One by one, we offered our introductions. A tall, skinny guy went first:

"Hello, my name is Selim."

Followed by, "My name is Hakim."

15. Porter, Lewis. *John Coltrane's "A Love Supreme": Jazz Improvisation as Composition, Journal of the American Musicological Society, Vol. 38, No. 3 (Autumn, 1985).*

16. Ali, Rozina.

Next, a dreamy-cute girl who studied with Reshad in England shared, "My name is Jamila."

Feeling a bit self-conscious, I spouted, "My name is Bruce."

E.J. turned toward me and penetrated my naivete with a mischievous glance:

"Bruce... when did *you* get your Sufi name?"

Something went *bzzt* in my brain, and no, it wasn't Shams in the bazaar or Bawa in a ball of light, but I received a genuine transmission: *I realized that my spiritual self was complete without additive or adjustment.*

My second gift came during a picnic with Süleyman Dede in Palisades Park overlooking the Pacific. As we sat on the grass, Reshad strummed the opening bars to an old Ewan MacColl folk song. Without prompting, Dede rose from his seat and Reshad began to sing:

"I met my love by the gas works wall
Dreamed a dream by the old canal..."

Dede gently grasped his lapel and began the sacred turn of the dervish, ever so slowly, round and round on the grass.

"I kissed my girl by the factory wall
Dirty old town
Dirty old town."

Reshad sang this song all the time, but Dede's prayerful embrace of the bawdy lyrics strangely freed me from religious form. Yes, kissing one's girl in a dirty old town can be an act of prayer. Thank you, Dede.

Years later, that moment came back to me when I began to experiment with the *sema* music, the music that accompanies the whirling ritual. The traditional Ottoman Turkish *makam* music,

Ayin-i Şerif, is composed to strict rules of tonality, rhythmic structure, and melodic scale.

The structure of the *sema* takes the whirler through a journey of inner vibration. Up, up, up, the whirler releases the veils, releases egoic identification, and finally turns "on one's own axis," gravitationally free from the solar system represented by the sheikh as the sun in the center.

Sweat and stamina can take the *semazens* on this transformational journey, but higher feelings must also awaken. Over the years, I felt that American audiences were missing something as we turned. The Mevlevi music could sound foreign and funereal and it didn't seem to elicit higher emotions for American ears. I feared they were being left behind.

I desperately wanted the audience to take a soul journey, so I did the unthinkable — I scrapped the Mevlevi music. My memory of Dede turning in the park to "Dirty Old Town" gave me a sense of permission – like Coleman Barks taking his permission from his Sri Lankan guru.

For the next ten years, I pulled from pop, rock, new age, ethnic fusions, Turkish *ney* and heart-pounding *zikrs* — layering and layering sounds in my software. People were coming to celebrate Rumi, so I mixed in some Rumi, lots of Rumi — Rumi read by Coleman, Deepak, Madonna, Debra Winger, Reshad, and others. The soundtrack began to mirror the political zeitgeist. [17]

To a traditionalist, I created a heretical mishmash. But, an octave of transformation emerged which, surprisingly, mimicked the rhythmic form of the original. A local Turkish jeweler and his wife remarked, "We saw the Whirling Dervishes in Konya, but your *sema* was more faithful to the spirit."

And that brings me to Mira Hunter.

---

17. You can see hometown Rumi lovers turning to the soundtrack at youtube.com/ ithoutv: *Rumi Celebration - Third Selam. https://www.youtube.com/watch?v=yywimoFG5Qk*

I've never met Mira, but I knew her dad, Raqib Brian Burke. Raqib and I were both introduced to Dede in Los Angeles.

Raqib Burke

When we began to learn to turn, many of us waddled like penguins, but Raqib took to it instantly. He would float 'round and 'round as if on a spindle of light, a perfect 360. With each revolution, his right foot would nail the landing spot with conviction. Arms raised, he tilted his head into a majestic pose that few others could master.

As the years turned into decades, the original batch of *semazens* fell away from the practice, but Raqib continued as a teacher and performer of the turn. More importantly, he found a star pupil — his daughter Mira.

Mira's journey to become the first Mevlevi performance artist speaks to Dede's prophecy — that the seed of Rumi would grow here "in its own way."

Mira recollects:

"My father, Raqib Brian Burke, began studying the *sema* before

I was born, but it was his intention for my sister and me to be raised without any strong religious links so that we would be able to make decisions on faith without a nostalgic bias. For this reason, early on, my imagination, music, and nature became outlets for my spiritual experiences.

"My father made me a mix tape when I was three years old. I wore a dress that had been made just for dancing, with a large flower print skirt. I think then it was Paul Horn and his golden flute, the Penguin Café Orchestra, and the last track was a recording of my mirrored ballerina music box.

"By the time I was twelve, the mixtape included King Crimson, Led Zeppelin, and Roxy Music. Every profound ecstatic experience of my life has been somehow connected to music."

Mira's childhood prancing took a serious turn when, as a Waldorf High School student, she had to choose a topic for her Grade 12 project.

"I chose to explore death and the afterlife," Mira recounted. "I called it *The Graduation*. I set out to prove that after life ends, we all end up in the same place, but our lived realities make that shared experience appear unique. For the project's artistic component I asked my father to teach me the turn of the dervish.

"I always wanted to learn to whirl," Mira said, "but I did not have the inspiration until I started my thesis. I have childhood memories in the North Vancouver *tekke*, of whirling feet and the smell of rose incense, and chanting and candlelight and the hems of dervish skirts in motion. Süleyman Dede even held me as a baby, and my dad feels that Dede's transmission gave me the will to turn."

Mira's school experience, fusing the sacred rite with her Grade 12 project, opened the door to Mira becoming, in her words, "the first female whirling dervish who dances to Turkish electronica."

When I stumbled on Mira's videos, I was immediately transfixed. The inner ecstasy of whirling is normally hidden behind static arms and a vertical torso. Mira unleashed the inner experience for the audience to see. She would fold like a flower, gather deep forces, and explode her arms upward. She challenged the physics of a rotating body while her white skirt sparkled with sewn-in lighting and reflecting mirrors. Her flowing movements would suddenly switch from jerky to forceful to fluidity. With torso bending, hands in prayer, then hands like doves, her arms punched through dimension. Faster and faster, she surrendered to the hypnotic beat of fusion artist, Mercan Dede.[18]

"When I was living in Istanbul, I met a young abstract expressionist painter from Washington State, who had moved to Istanbul," Mira recounts. "Tuesday Frindt and I had so much in common; we were both independent young women, visual artists, and whirling dervishes, but before Tuesday saw me whirl, she had never thought of pushing the rigid and specific boundaries of the traditional form in any way.

"At that point, I didn't understand the history of the practice nor the restraint in the traditional movement. But my Waldorf background in Eurythmy, Rudolph Steiner's approach to movement, had already pulled me toward expressive movement. Eurythmy is a movement that makes the invisible visible, makes sound visible. I was learning Eurythmy and the Turn simultaneously, and the cross-pollination between these two forms felt like a natural progression. Today, my father continues to radicalize the turn in his own deeply unique way, and he acts as my greatest defender, especially when I'm dismissed as a tea house dervish."

Mira took the whirling ritual beyond the sacred *sema* dance floor to evolve into a form of performance art. In her 2008 installation piece, "Time Machine," she and her husband Derek

18. "Mercan Dede & Mira Hunter." Youtube.com. https://www.youtube.com/watch?v=cJYFNwtBi2s

Hunter mounted 65 disposable cameras activated by electromechanical solenoids to immerse the audience into an animated whirling experience.

Mira's "Public Whirling Project" went further by exploring whirling as a healing ceremony for the world. Each ritual was performed in a depressed environment, as she explains, "to bring that energy to places in need." Sites included shipyards, subway platforms, derelict neighborhoods, and even Vancouver's Stanley Park after it had been devastated by a storm.

"After storms leveled much of the park, Derek and I wanted to whirl there. The ground was uneven from the fallen branches, upturned trees, and underbrush, but I managed to whirl anyway, tearing holes in the soles of my prayer slippers as I moved in a careful circle, surrounded by the cameras."

Mira Hunter inside Grand Central Station

Mira's Public Whirling Project culminated inside New York's Grand Central Station with two hours of whirling in full dervish costume. The video shows Mira turning courageously as various street people are drawn to her energy, careening, cavorting, and nearly colliding with her.

The stationmaster can be heard off-camera, sternly warning her husband, Derek, "If I see this and I don't do something, and she falls, I lose my job." If careening street people couldn't stop Mira, neither could the stationmaster.

Mira explained her motive: "Over the years, I have had to reconcile what I see as the inner and outer qualities of whirling, the *batin* and *zahir*, the inner devotion and the outer performance. The form I practice on stage begins as a service for the audience, and it is through my expressiveness that I communicate the power of whirling and bring the viewer with me.

"We don't know what to call this other form of the *sema*, this ancient *ragged* form of whirling. What about the Grateful Dead spinners? What about the healing act performed by whirling shamans in Mongolia? This ancient primal *sema* may still be a powerful healing tool today. All I know is that the more physically competent I have become at the physical act of whirling, the more challenging it is for me to access that liminal, ecstatic state."

There is historical precedent for Mira's expressive turn. A Persian form of *sema* existed for centuries before Rumi's time, where expressive movements accompanied poetry, music, spontaneous hand clapping, foot-stomping, hand-waving, and whirling.

Maybe Rumi was the original whirling street performer — awakened by the *zikr* of hammers in the street to give us the turn. But Mira stretched that moment further to discover an ecstatic form that thrust her whirling self as a healing agent into the world.

§

If there's a takeaway from Rumi coming to America, it's that we all fell down the Rabbit Hole – that stream of possibility formed by the inner passages, heartfelt currents, and life-switcheroos that take you to the center of your self. You can't see them, find them, or force them open. These doors are disguised as *everyday life.* If you step into the maze with sufficient trust — and persevere — you are rewarded with a life of ever-deepening revelation.

Reshad followed his instinct when he stepped into the Rabbit Hole — an Octave shift disguised as the London antique shop where he met his teacher. The magic carpet swept Reshad to Turkey, to dervishes, and to Dede.

A few years later, I innocently climbed a set of stairs above a Baskin-Robbins on Larchmont Boulevard and *kawumph,* I landed in a "real school" that was being readied to launch the "Second Cycle of Mankind."

When Coleman accepted Bly's challenge to release Rumi's poems from their cages, Coleman was visited by Bawa in a ball of light, and *swoosh,* Rumi soon became a household word.

Even Dede fell into the vortex when he accepted an invitation from some young people in Los Angeles.

My favorite Rabbit Hole story comes from David Bellak. As the first young American to form an intimate connection with Süleyman Dede, David found his way to Rumi without any understandable bearings to guide his journey. David writes:

My travels began in April 1972. I had just completed a photography degree following four years of naval service in the Vietnam War after college. At age 30, my inner life seemed to be in tatters as nothing seemed to be happening at this stage of my life in the way I expected.

With six-hundred dollars, a rucksack, and a basic guide to cheap accommodations, I followed a vision that came to me in a dream where I saw myself in Britain.

After a long flight, I arrived in London – exhausted, confused, and frightened – but with a vague willingness to expect the unexpected. My days in London were spent wandering, thinking, and photographing. I also continued my readings of Carl Jung, Herman Hesse, Carlos Castaneda and others.

One Saturday afternoon, while wandering through the market stalls on Portobello Road, I passed a small church meeting hall where I noticed a lecture announcement on Sufism. My curiosity sparked, I wandered into the hall just as a charismatic Englishman began the talk. What he said impressed me deeply.

Exactly one week later, I happened to pass the church again. Being exactly to the hour, I entered with my companion, a filmmaker acquaintance, to hear the talk. My friend lost interest and departed, but I was filled with excitement as if a spark had been ignited. The words had an urgency that seemed directed to me personally. By the conclusion, I was very moved, perhaps excited and even thrilled to hear something that made sense. More importantly, a feeling arose within that I must do something.

As I was filled with questions, I approached the speaker who stood in a doorway chatting with people. His name was Reshad Feild. Reshad seemed to peer at me and then, without hesitation, said that I would find answers to my questions at a summer spiritual retreat in the French Alps.

Five weeks later, after hitchhiking from London to Zurich and to Chamonix, France, I located the teleferique, or cable car, which would take me to an elevation of 2000 meters from which I would hike to the camp. Rather than stepping into the cable car, I procrastinated and even considered leaving. I wandered back to the village, and sat around until the last car set to leave.

Sufi summer camp in Chamonix

Later, I wrote in my journal notes: "I realized that once I went up there, I would never return."

Sufi Camp, Chamonix, France, 1972

Finally, the last car left, and I was on it. I hiked to the camp where I found young spiritual seekers living in tents, meditating, chanting, and singing. At this point in my life, I had never been involved in a spiritual path or community, so I was constantly asking folks, what is this; what is that?

After a week of uncertainty, Reshad arrived, and I approached him.

"We met in London," I reminded Reshad. "You said I should come all the way here. But why? What am I doing here? Nothing about any of this makes sense!"

Reshad scribbled some words onto a piece of paper and said, "Go to Konya in Turkey, to the Office of Tourism. Ask for a man named Süleyman Dede. But before that, visit Sheikh Fahrud'din in Istanbul; tell him what you are doing. You can find him through a French-named philosophical meeting room, in Taksim Square."

After months of hesitation and resistance, mostly from the absurdity of my decision to travel such a great distance on a whim, I was now filled with a growing determination bordering on obsession to get on with the mystery.

In early November, I arrived in a cold, rainy Istanbul, settled into a cheap hotel, and contemplated how I would find "Le Société of something-or-other" in Taksim Square. Chills, high fevers, and a weakened physical state coupled with the relentless, cold rain kept me in my room. After three days by train through Hungary, Romania, and Bulgaria, my cheap room was a welcome respite.

A few days later, still feeling weak from fever, I set out for Taksim Square armed with basic directions supplied by the hotel. The relentless noise and frenetic traffic made for an exhausting ordeal, but I was determined to follow through on the scrap of an address I had carried from the Alps five months before.

I walked endless streets, alleys, and stairways looking for the

French plaque. After countless dead-ends, and still feeling sick and a bit of a fool, I sensed the hopelessness of the task and finally decided to head back through the rain, desperate for my cheap room, some soup, and bed.

In a moment of capitulation, the reality of my "goose chase" hit me hard. I had failed. Facing the bustling traffic in the cold and wet, I began to cry in despair.

As I turned toward the bus stop, three young men crossed in front of me. One of the group broke away from the others and walked straight to me with what seemed like purposeful intent — as if planned. He asked in very good English if he could help. I showed him the scrap of paper. He dashed in and out of several shops, then returned with a helper.

"It's just around the corner," he assured me.

With the helper guiding, we turned left, walked 40 meters, turned into an alley, and walked all the way to the end where I saw a large oak door. The name of a French-named Society was engraved on a brass plaque.

Since it was Sunday, no one was there. But, after months of grasping at the thinnest of threads, I had been brought to the "door."

Exhausted but relieved, I made my way back to my small room, crawled into bed and into a deep, fevered sleep in preparation for the next day.

The next day, because of a miscommunication, I did not meet Sheikh Fahrud'din, but he kindly sent a message that I should continue to Konya.

After a 14-hour train ride to Konya, I went to the tourism office where I met Mehdi Bey, a fluent French-speaking lawyer. After pleasant greetings, Mehdi Bey promised to convey my message to Süleyman Dede.

Every few days I returned to the tourism office to ask Mehdi Bey if had any reply yet, but none had arrived. The days passed into weeks, and finally, with no word from Süleyman Dede, the futility of the entire exercise was settling in — this wasn't going to happen. As I was still unwell, and with winter coming, I decided to leave on the night train to Istanbul, but first I returned to the tourism office to say goodbye.

"David, the Sufi must be patient," Mehdi Bey counseled. "Plus, there are so many historical sites, so much history to see in Konya. Soon, the Sema will be performed. Surely, you will stay."

"Nothing about this makes sense," I retorted. "I have been traveling for nearly six months — to great extremes, sacrifice, and even danger. I have done everything to fulfill this absurd commitment. And now, I am heading to the station to get my train ticket."

Mehdi Bey seemed resigned to my decision as I turned to the door. Suddenly the door opened. In walked an elderly gentleman wearing a three-piece suit, gold watch chain, and a stylish fedora.

"Dede! Mashallah!" Mehdi Bey exclaimed. After the requisite dervish kisses and much back and forth between the two men, it was decided: I was to accompany this man, Süleyman Dede, to his home for lunch.

"But I don't speak Turkish! I can't go with him!" I objected in French.

"I will speak Turkish; you will speak English!" Dede proclaimed in Turkish after hearing the translation.

Taking me by the hand, Dede led me out the door to the busy street and toward his home for lunch.

Thus, began my association with Süleyman Hayati Dede of Konya, Turkey, on that cold December day in 1972.

Many months after this spontaneous pilgrimage began, I met Reshad again. I was still perplexed by it all, so I asked him, "What does all this mean? What is happening? Why did I go to Konya? "Reshad answered, "Because Mevlana brought you."

His reply did nothing to clarify my perplexity, but it did address my heart. I understood that I must continue this journey to the unknown; I would find my answers within.

§

This business of "rabbit holes," planting seeds, and the sacred impulse awakens questions about time and destiny. A woman instinctively plants seeds when she readies her life to bring a child into the world. Vivekananda also carried seeds when, as a wandering sadhu, he responded to the sacred impulse by sailing half a world away to the World's Columbian Exposition in Chicago.

I like to believe that we all plant seeds, but because of the way seeds work, we can't know the effect of our actions. We can't know if a seed will take to the soil, if it's the wrong season, or if people will even desire that crop.

My wife, Karen tells the story of Sharon, a woman who attended our Rumi study group years ago but quickly disappeared from our lives. Twenty-five years later, Karen bumped into Sharon again and discovered that because of that earlier encounter, Sharon made a total life change, went to nursing school, and became a nurse – just like Karen.

This entire phenomenon, of seeds and weeds, and its tangle of luck, volition, synchronicity, and destiny – can be described as *fortune*. Fortune is a grandiose word for *why stuff happens*. It explains how seemingly random events reflect a synchronous world – a *Masnavi-like* picture of life as a continuous interwoven teaching story.

Recently, I wrote a book about *fortune* in an attempt to detangle a difficult stretch in my life. The book took three years of work and twenty-one chapters of exposition to come to the same realization that Süleyman Dede generously offered me forty years earlier: Why does stuff happen? Because "God made you do it."

By living a life of humility, Süleyman Dede opened a very big space for us all. He cooked for the poor, prayed for the sick, and opened his "desolate house" to Rumi lovers from all over the world. He even (reportedly) ate bacon to show respect to his American hosts.

Süleyman Dede's generosity didn't get him into the official Rumi history, and his munificence didn't get his grave site into the travel guides. Many Turks remember Dede as nothing more than a simple cook, perhaps even a wayward sheikh who stepped out of his depth.

But, stepping out of one's depth is the whole point. By diving into the deepest end of the pool at an age when most people eschew the high dive altogether, Dede invited Hazard to reinvigorate Rumi's legacy after fifty years of suppression in Turkey.

Reshad also challenged Hazard. By following Bulent from a London antique shop to Turkey, and then starting schools in England, the U.S., Canada, and Switzerland, Reshad opened the door for Rumi to come to the West.

This is surely the best metric to measure a man: Dede and Reshad got the job done. They shifted Rumi's story across time and space by pulling off the ultimate sleight of hand, a seed-planting gamble, nurtured by the love in their hearts, to keep Rumi's message of unconditional love alive for the generations to come.

Süleyman Dede at Claymont, West Virginia

Epilogue - In the Barzakh

Karen and I paddled our kayaks up the lazy Edisto River, upstream from where the famous tea-stained "blackwater" empties into the sea in South Carolina. Our guide knew these parts well, timing our journey through massive oaks draped in Spanish moss to coincide with the slack tide — the midpoint between ebb and flood. As we reached our stopping point, a heron dive-bombed to snatch a fish — the perfect punctuation to our upstream journey. I closed my eyes to feel the stillness of wind and water. This was the moment of *barzakh* — neither ebb tide nor flood, but the space in-between.

Reshad would often say that *the space in-between* was terribly important. I never understood why, so I laid my paddle across the gunwale and waited for the current to offer a clue. When I opened my eyes, the slack water began to swirl. Can a human actually feel the moon tugging at the tide? Maybe. As the tidal current reversed course, fresh water began to replace the salt, slowly propelling us downstream.

If you study hydrology, the sea water is laden with dissolved salts and minerals, making it heavier and prone to travel in its own current beneath the surface. Freshwater, being less dense, flows closer to the surface as it heads toward the sea. These two currents, fresh and salt, are in constant flux, creating an estuary that is rich with marshes and marine life. Each species swims in its preferred salinity to thrive.

There is no dividing line in a tidal flow, no point where this is salt and this is fresh. The cosmic rhythm creates an ebb and flood — a fluid dividing line, and a mixing of worlds.

Esoteric Sufism describes *barzakh* as the dividing line — translated as *isthmus*. Theologically, *barzakh* describes the state after death, the purgatory between this world and the next like the *bardos* of Tibetan Buddhism. But unlike an isthmus, the *barzakh* isn't static. It's not a place on the map for the soul to visit before heaven or a halfway house on the way to hell. *Barzakh* is a fluid region where the tides pull at the subconscious, coaxing us to return to the sea.

The Quran describes *barzakh* as a fixed demarcation between worlds. From the sura Ar-Rahmān:

He bringeth forth the two seas, which meet; between them is an isthmus (barzakh), which they do not go beyond.

And from the sura Al-Furqān:

He it is who bringeth forth the two seas; one is fresh and drinkable, the other is salt and bitter, and He hath made between the two an isthmus (barzakh) and a closed barrier.

The Sufi mystic Ibn al-Arabi (1165–1240) understood *barzakh* differently. Arabi's *barzakh* resolved the implicit duality between God and the world — the nettlesome fact that on the surface, both can't be one and the same.

Getting on your knees and praying to God invokes the *space in-between* — the *barzakh*. Through call and response, the *barzakh* opens and reveals, even if briefly, that there is no separation; there is only one.

Scholar Salman H. Bashier describes Ibn al-Arabi's understanding of *barzakh*:

Barzakh is a term that represents an activity or an active entity that differentiates between two things and (paradoxically) through the very act of differentiation provides for their unity... Ibn al-Arabi thinks that the Limit [barzakh] is the essence of each thing...

The problem, according to Arabi, is that when one of the parts is identified with one limited thing and the other part with another limited thing, a duality results. As a result, a new limit is required to resolve this duality. For example, the *barzakh* where the freshwater zone and saltwater zone meet is a new zone called *brackish* — which is itself a limited thing. Somewhere upriver, we could establish yet another zone; let's call it Lightly Salted, and so on.

This process can go on indefinitely until we arrive at a concept of the Limit that meets the two limited things... with two faces that are one.[1]

Faces or vase?

The gestalt image of the vase (figure) and the two faces (ground) demonstrates the paradox of two limited things that are one. *Barzakh* describes the demarcation line between the two entities, but in fact, there is no actual line — just solid and void. This is like the age-old question: Is light a particle or a wave? Since normal human perception can't see the unity, we experience the world and its forms through opposites.

In the mind, foreground and background oscillate between the faces and the vase. In this way, *barzakh* is the dance between ebb and flood, fresh water and salt, manifest and unmanifest, seen and unseen, and matter and spirit. This space in-between creates a longing because it points toward the unity behind it. When the space in-between opens, change can happen. This describes how the *sacred impulse* beckoned my New Age cohort like a spiritual tide, pulling a generation of seekers straight into the *barzakh* so that Rumi could come to America.

---

1. Bashier, Salman H. 2004. *Ibn Al-'arabi's Barzakh: The Concept of the Limit and the Relationship Between God and the World.* Albany: State Univ of New York Pr.

Barzakh describes a love affair, the push and pull of lover and beloved, Shiva and Shakti, Bruce and Karen, Jenny and Forrest Gump, and the yearning to transcend limits and merge in ecstatic love — a merging that always remains just out of reach. Like Friday night street racers hurtling head-on into the Light, our generation tried to discover how far and how fast we could floor it into the *barzakh* — toward the vague promise of enlightenment without crashing into a tree.

Our leap into *barzakh* was more than a flirtation. We plunged toward the Light with the all-in madness of a red-hot love affair. Limits be damned!

As Rumi lovers, we dutifully embraced the full checklist of abandonment: Submit to the teacher — *check*. Sufi name — *check*. Study religious texts — *check*. Whirling, chanting, and prayer — *check, check, check*. Cast your fate to God— *check*. We expected each step to take us deeper into the *barzakh*, but no one warned us: When you drag your baggage into the *barzakh* without sufficient preparation, strength of character, and inner will, the wheels fall off, the teacher gets blamed, and suffering results.

Defined as neither this nor that, the *barzakh* is messy. As a result, a long list of gurus appeared on the New Age scene and fell prey to the seductions of power. As my mentor, Bhagwan Awatramani, explained to me, "Becoming a spiritual teacher is the ultimate trap."

Even though the impulse left a trail of collateral damage across the new age landscape, the wreckage didn't make the effort any less valiant. Today, millions of people embrace Mindfulness Training without any need to connect the dots to Chögyam Trungpa Rinpoche and his sex parties in Boulder in the 1970s.

As I interviewed old friends and pupils to write this book, I found few people who could find comfort in the irreconcilable tension of the *barzakh* — that within the unity of *teacher*, sinner and saint rightfully co-mingle.

My favorite understanding of the *barzakh*, with its implicit reconciliation of *sinner* and *saint*, comes from my beloved wife, Karen, who explains: "Things that don't go together, somehow go together."

Peter Cunz spoke to this dynamic tension:

"I had been very negative toward Reshad. Then slowly, slowly, my negative feelings started to disappear. More and more, his problems and my problem with them disappeared. I started to find my love for him again. My feelings turned toward compassion."

And God bless Leslie who, with tremendous courage, moved beyond blame to understanding when she shared:

"It's important to understand that I don't feel victimized by what happened. I feel that I was somehow the point of it. I was needed so that the point of it could happen."

More characteristic was this exchange:

Shamsuddin: "Ah yes, E.J. Gold, one of the great souls who did his best to help Reshad to be a better human being. But like all the other great men who tried, E.J. had little success."

Christopher: "Ah my dear, therein is a long and somewhat sad tale, which perhaps we do better to forget..."

Roger and Helen offered a different point of view:

"Judging a spiritual teacher by what you assume to be their role or how you expect them to deliver it only mirrors your personal expectation of such a relationship. How can anybody be seriously surprised that a teacher is also a human being? If indeed 'the teacher will come when the pupil is ready,' one may conversely conclude that the pupil gets the teaching he or she deserves in each chapter of their journey."

Can a great teacher also be a sad tale? According to the *barzakh*, the teacher is neither this nor that; the teaching is found in the space in between.

Navigating that journey — through the *barzakh* — requires inner work. It is a process of *integration*. By definition, the river is integrated into the sea. This idea of integration began with Freud.

He recognized that the unconscious mind is the primary source of human behavior and likened it to an iceberg, the bulk being inaccessible to the conscious mind.

Jung went further, describing "individuation" as the process by which our deep wiring (unconscious mind or subconscious) is brought into consciousness (often by dreams) to be integrated into a whole personality.

Sufis describe this as *fana* and *baqa* — *'fana'* (annihilation in God) and *'baqa'* (everlasting subsistence in God).

This is not easy stuff. As Bhagwan explained to me, we would rather be pulled apart by elephants than face *fana*, the annihilation of the "I" — the dissolution of self. This explains why rigorous practice and guidance from a teacher are needed to build the framework for the student to absorb spiritual energies.

Facing fears, exploring boundaries, integrating the past, strengthening resolve, and quieting the mind work together to build *will*. Will is the subtle structure or *Kesdjian* body, that permits dissolution of ego without holy terror.[2] Reshad called this "the gentle way of Mary" as opposed to the "terror of Christ."

Needless to say, Reshad's life story followed the latter — and certainly not by choice. As Peter Cunz wisely observed:

"I started to see Reshad as a person who had been given incredible talents – the ability to open the door into the other world – and to see into that other world. But part of his nervous system was unable to bear that world. His nervous system wasn't trained to handle the energy.

Reshad's teacher, Bulent Rauf, gave Reshad the unexpected and unenviable task to open the door for Rumi to come to the

---

2. J.G. Bennett: "*The possibility is given to us of forming a vessel which will... reach the spiritual world — the body Kesdjan. Gurdjieff describes the state of the substance of the inner world in ordinary man to be like a cloud — amorphous, without any coherence of its own... Many of the exercises that we do are aimed at producing some coherence in this substance. We learn how to use our attention to separate and blend the various energies of which it is made. If we can become quiet enough, the energies settle into their appropriate places in us and can coalesce to form the (Kesdjan) body.*" J.G. Bennett, Deeper Man, p 225

West. Reshad's magnetic charisma and deep sensitivity beckoned us into the *barzakh*, where the subtle realms Rumi described could be experienced in the heart. But the enormity of that task — to lead a generation of young seekers to a realization that rightfully required the wisdom of maturity — was maybe too much to expect. Something had to give. As a result, a common critique of Reshad was that he was an imperfect vessel — someone chosen by God for a role for which he had insufficient psychological preparation.

Even Bulent said of his former protegé:

"O Reshad! He could have become one of the great ones."[3]

There's sadness in Bulent's remark— a recognition of what could have been. But, having navigated the *barzakh* with Reshad for over twenty-five years, I reject that characterization. Reshad *was* one of the great ones. His role in ushering a generational change in consciousness through his books, teachings, and spiritual vision can't be underestimated.

Many times, I watched Reshad melt a room of hardened hearts into tears of recognition. I was similarly touched when he awakened a timeless sense of self in me — awakening my life work to serve God and humanity.

Over the ensuing years, Reshad's command of the present moment, his ability to steer a listing ship through a sea of creative tension, his unparalleled esoteric knowledge, and his abundant and charismatic talent were central to my path.

To appreciate the challenge Reshad faced as the ground-breaker for Rumi, imagine his childhood as Timothy Feild during the deprivations and rationing of World War II in England. Reshad described his true esoteric teacher, not as Bulent, or the Arch Druid, or Gurdjieff's niece — but rather, the family's gamekeeper.

---

3. Reported by Ibrahim Gamard

During the War, rabbit was an important food source. One day, the gamekeeper instructed young Timothy (Reshad) to catch a rabbit in his bare hands — not by going after the rabbit, but by thinking outside of time to where the rabbit would go next.

In Reshad's telling, young Tim followed the gamekeeper's guidance instinctively and caught the rabbit. The gamekeeper then instructed him, "Now kill it."

As Reshad told it, the rabbit's soul departed through his hands, and a world of pure light opened up for him. A "second sight" emerged that could perceive energy and dimension. From this, Reshad became adept at healing the subtle body, restoring the energies of the land, and even dowsing for missing persons for the London police. I can only imagine the challenge Reshad faced growing up with that spiritual sensitivity amid the social cruelty of aristocratic England.

Given today's understanding of addiction, the misuse of sex and power, and the need for psychological integration, one could argue that Reshad was an *impure vessel* for the job. He was certainly not of the generation or social background to "work through" childhood patterns or psychological issues. From Reshad's aristocratic background, a stiff upper lip was all that was needed to navigate an emotional storm.

But if we believe a dramatic universe is working toward a purpose, Reshad was the *perfect vessel* to transmit the redemptive force of Rumi's mystical love. Reshad's esoteric insight, magician-like spontaneity, bawdy humor, bountiful heart, and spiritual inebriation cast a theatrical life that could have been woven straight from the pages of the Mathnawi. During Reshad's most inspired moments, I could imagine what it would have been like 700 years ago to witness Rumi whirling into ecstasy from the depth of his despair or channeling free verse into a poetic masterpiece.

Yes, Reshad's bloodstream was coursing with spirits and the spirit. Ibrahim Gamard describes this in Sufi terms:

It can be said that the real goal is sobriety after ecstasy (symbolized by the term, "drunkenness," in sufism), as mentioned by Shams-i Tabrîzî, Mawlânâ Rûmî's teacher:

"The man who reaches this perfection is drowned in the light of God and drunk in the pleasure of the Real [Haqq]."[4]

Let us not forget Süleyman Dede. Plucked by God for his bountiful heart, deep humility, and wily tenaciousness, Dede was able to get the job done outside the stamp of Çelebi officialdom. What would Rumi think if he could time-travel into today's Mevlevi culture and discover what his son, Sultan Velad had wrought: The robes and formality, the somber music, the hierarchical family, and the recitation of ancient texts? Would this time-traveling Rumi find comfort with Mevlevi formality or with the creative spontaneity that characterized Reshad and Dede's spiritual experiment?

§

I last saw Reshad in September 2001. He invited me to introduce his talk at the Open Center in New York City. The talk had been planned well in advance, but two weeks before the talk, the World Trade Center towers were attacked. For the audience, what might have been a routine lecture now carried profound significance. We were in SoHo, a few blocks from the carnage, and the air was still acrid with toxins, smoke, and shock. Flowers, pleas, and prayers adorned impromptu firehouse shrines in the neighborhood.

---

4. Gamard, Ibrahim. *http://www.dar-al-masnavi.org/defense-of-sema.html*

The New Yorkers wanted a message, some knowledge, a little hope, anything to salve the collective shock and fill their hearts with meaning. Reshad and I sat in the green room, sitting side by side, waiting to go out. I hadn't planned my introduction; I was more concerned, or maybe fascinated, by a side of my spiritual teacher that I hadn't seen before — *he was nervous.*

Was the master showman out of his depth, not knowing how to connect with trauma so raw? Or maybe, his standard Sufi message would be off-pitch after a perceived Islamic attack. Here we were with all of New York collectively in the *barzakh* — straddling the alien gulf between world-class city and dystopian landscape.

I have very little memory of the talk, so it probably didn't go well. I left Reshad's school a week later. It's only now that I realize that these moments of candor and vulnerability with Reshad were precious. Confiding in the Santa Cruz motel, the emotional collapse in my kitchen, and his bout of nerves in the Open Center green room — these weren't character defects; they were revealing glimpses of the man without the teaching hat.

Reshad gave his last public talk in Zug, Switzerland in April 2013, three years before he died in Devon, England. I planned to listen to the talk from a CD during a long drive to Pensacola, Florida where Karen would be conducting a funeral for her Uncle Bill in an airplane hanger. Bill loved to fly.

As we hit the highway, I popped in the CD and savored the words of my beloved teacher at the end of his career. Reshad stepped to the microphone and began to speak:

Can you believe it? We have been on this road together for a long time. Thirty years for some of you... Valbella, Beatenberg, DeVoorde, Johanneshof — we have traveled so far together.

But here we are; we're all getting old. (sings) "When I'm Sixty-Four..." Look at this room... what a beautiful sea of gray.

Being the oldest, I have always preceded you on this journey. There's a certain kind of wisdom that only comes from age, and this time is no different.

Like all of you, I have faced the chapters of my life — including the difficult ones. Thank God, I don't have to whip up the energy anymore, or open anyone, or anything. I can simply be myself — dwelling in the space in-between. Do you remember me talking about the space in-between? For me now, it's the space between my work in this world, and the world to come.

It sounds romantic, but it isn't pretty. It is not easy being nearly 80 and living alone. I am mostly confined to bed these days. Luckily Barbara comes over when she can and spends a week or two to look after me. Apart from her, I have to hire help when I can get it since I can do little for myself. One of my helpers is Mrs. Jenkins.

Mrs. Jenkins serves me breakfast — usually a poached egg, toast with English marmalade, and tea. And then come the pills, ugh, the bloody pills — a basket of them. A pill to keep it all in, and a pill to move it all out. Mostly, they're for the pain — the ghastly pain I've been with for at least a dozen years — actually my whole life. I don't complain, but unfortunately, the pills dull the senses. I've done my best over the years to make the senses my friend, and I do my best to remain grateful. Yes, it's hard, but I'm not complaining.

There comes a time when we have to consciously forgive ourselves to make room for God's Forgiveness — and that is when we are ready to approach the gate of freedom in total honesty.

It's not easy, but that's my work right now. Taking stock, remaining present, asking forgiveness, and saying thank you. That's my work. We each have our work — our individual work.

I left Switzerland because you already had everything you need. And, I am so grateful, so deeply grateful that you continue to support me so that I can have the space to do my work. When you live your life on stage full-time — as I did as a spiritual teacher (chuckles) whatever that means — you don't have the luxury to do your own work.

This time of my life is like one big clearing exercise — instead of clearing what happened during the day, I am looking at the whole of my life.

A few days ago, in the afternoon when I was lying in bed, I had an amazing series of memory flashbacks about the ICL in Los Angeles. What a time that was. And when I sat with the memories and feelings, and stayed present and grateful, without judging — in that quiet prayer, the whole lot of it could be let go.

This may be the last talk I ever give. I don't think I have the energy to do another. I might not make it through this one (jokingly, Reshad looks at his watch). But I want to ask one simple question. Are you ready?

Are you ready to do one big clearing exercise? Raise your hands. (A few hands are raised)

Come on now. This is it, baby. This is the big one. It's not heavy; let it be light. This may be our last time together. Let's let go of this thing, this wonderful, magnificent catastrophe. Remember Zorba the Greek? What did Zorba say? "Wife, children, house, everything, the full catastrophe." Come on, raise your hands. (More hands go up, and more).

If I ever said or did anything that was untoward or hurt you, or I presumed you, or presumed your sacrifice, even for a second, or if I didn't recognize you as who you are, as your self... or if I talked about you behind your back, or didn't make the space or time to recognize you, if I didn't see you in your uniqueness, the Wahid in the Ahad, as the beautiful expression of God... then I humbly apologize.

I love you, I bow to you; I bow to you, and you, and you. You have the ingredient — not for yourself, but for life itself. Just go do it. It doesn't matter what "it" is. Make this a better world.

God, I enjoyed writing that. Of course, it was my fantasy. I made it up. But more than a lark, my made-up speech reflects my yearning, my long-held desire for emotional closure with my teacher. I wanted to hear him say, "Thank you, Bruce. You now have permission to be yourself."

One night, while I was working on the European chapters, Reshad came to me in a dream – a fully conscious veridical dream that was as palpable as daily life. I remember feeling, "Wow, Reshad, you're so warm and humble, and encouraging." I didn't have to make up a talk; my moment of emotional closure with Reshad was real.

To my surprise, Reshad seemed quite happy about the book. Having passed from this world, he couldn't give a twit about his image. In his new world, he could see God's work of transformation and redemption moving along as it should, all according to the Grand Scheme. Any nasty bits in his personal story were an earthly giggle at this point. I liked Reshad being so cool and real. Naturally, when I ran to get my gear to record the interview, I woke up. It was 3:00 a.m.

At that moment, in the *real* world, my phone beeped. A terse email arrived from one of the key people I interviewed in Switzerland. With a quick bleary-eyed read, I went to the kicker: "*I have decided that I do not want to be mentioned in this book. Not at all. I am not sure anymore what the real purpose of it is.*" Another Swiss student of Reshad pulled out an hour later, and a few weeks after that, Reshad's publisher pulled the plug on the whole thing.

As a result, I had to face his question: *What is the real purpose of this book?*

One level was easy enough: I was witness to a story that needed to be told. The next level required some thought but quickly became clear: My purpose has been to pull you into the *barzakh* – to perplex that part of the mind that chooses sides – *sinner* versus *saint* – and share a taste of God's mysterious ways. By presenting the crazy quilt of a real spiritual story, my hope is that you will be tempted to follow what Rumi followed – which in essence is the truth of yourself.

As we continued to Pensacola, I didn't put the CD of Reshad's talk into the player. Nope, couldn't do it. I so desperately wanted Reshad to talk about his breakfast and the pills and bless the full catastrophe that I couldn't push the play button; I hadn't had my dream yet. So Karen and I drove the full six hours without playing the CD.

Karen conducted the funeral in the airplane hanger under a hot Florida sun where Bill's old two-seater was on display. Bill's family and his old fly-boy friends were moved by Karen's words and everyone was grateful. Having bathed in the sea of their gratitude, Karen and I got back in the car, turned onto the Interstate, and then I inserted the CD and pressed Play.

Reshad began:

If you have any special questions, please do ask, but not on should I breathe this way or that way, or should I do it on a Thursday and not on a Wednesday, or what do you think of this book or that book. Anyway, bless you, you've come a very long way, a lot of you.

I shouldn't have been surprised when Reshad jumped into the talk with his trademark charm. Since his earliest days as a crooner on a cruise ship, he had always been a showman. I bet somewhere beyond the *barzakh*, Reshad is still doing the old soft shoe — opening the hearts of angels who politely leave their shoes outside the door to heaven. He continued:

Reshad as a young entertainer in Hawaii.

I'm going to ask you a question. Can you find a question in this room that can help our little course? Has there been a question before you came? Did you come here in order to find a question? I think, yes. I see smiles. Now we're getting somewhere.

Yes, his health was kaput. And it shouldn't have bothered me that he was pulling out the same tired chestnuts like an aging performer. At age 90, my famous PR mother was still out on the street wearing a pretend news crew jacket, in her blond wig, microphone in hand, interviewing children at small-town parades and pet fairs. But I stayed with it:

Most of you have come here to find a question. Good, that's something. If you've come here to find a question, from where would you ask the question that you've come with or you want to find? I don't encourage people to write many letters to me because I have no help to answer them. Most of them have been asking questions which nobody can really answer. But I can guarantee that 99% of all have been writing to me to find the question.

This business about finding a question went on for a full 23 minutes.

How in God, in 23 minutes, are we going to find a question? Any ideas? Why don't I ask you another question? We say, "Give us this day our daily bread," right, not, "Give us this day our daily questions."

I turned to Karen in horror realizing, "I don't think Reshad has a question!"

I'm embarrassed that I couldn't hang in the *barzakh* with Reshad and feel utter compassion for him making one last go of it. I hadn't been hit by my own aging indignities yet. It would be a few months before I would plunge into a sea of compassion after losing my business and almost losing my wife from a brain tumor – both on the same afternoon.

Finally, nearing the end of the talk, Reshad changed gears, softened, and offered the wee bit of the candor I was hoping for:

When I walk out of that door because I'm very, very tired – I'm just holding on – I should go straight to bed. I don't expect God is going to provide an answer for me by breakfast. What I do know, and you can all know, is that in this path, God or whatever words you want, Allah, or whatever expression you want, will provide for us in the present moment, what we need to know, so that love and knowledge become one.

Yes, the *barzakh!* — that ineffable present where love and knowledge become one.

And then, bless his heart, Reshad summoned strength from some untapped reservoir to bring the talk into completion:

I'm going to leave you on time exactly with both the question and the answer in one word... Love.

Let's just be quiet for a minute together. Just breathe love. Know you're loved. Remember you don't have to like somebody to love them. Just be awake, to love. Love has always been here for you and me. As we say, love is the cause and love is its own effect.

I wish you all good things tonight, tomorrow, and for all your lives. I still would like to remind you all that it is up to us, each individual, to be awake. As Rumi said on his deathbed, he could not breathe without God. The breath is the spirit of God. That in a teaching contains so much. You can find it in manuscripts, and from any real teacher, that God is love, and we are loved.

Let us carry this love to a waiting world.

§

This morning, after editing the epilogue, I took Bhagwan to the airport. He had just finished a meditation seminar in our home and was headed to Toronto. Twenty-four years earlier, he arrived on our doorstep to explain the difference between Radha and Rukmini and he has continued to visit Karen and me ever since. Three nights ago, I gave him the manuscript so he could review his part of the story. Naturally, he read the whole thing.

"I'm concerned," Bhagwan advised, "that people will pick up this book expecting to learn something about Rumi, but instead there's this meditation teacher from India, there's Reshad with all his wives, and Leslie in a coma, and the kahuna. Maybe, you should sprinkle in more about Rumi — just so people feel that the book is what it claims... a story about Rumi coming to America."

"Bhagwan," I replied in exasperation, "Rumi has been dead for over 700 years! He never came to America. It's about the seed of

Rumi — how the impulse landed and it created all this chaos, and magic, and love! There is no Rumi — the person. It's what he was carrying and continues to carry across history and into the hearts of his lovers!"

To my consternation, Bhagwan is supremely precise and literal. This can be maddening, but as we pulled up to the terminal, Bhagwan understood my poetic drift.

"Oh, that way," Bhagwan said. "I get it."

Bhagwan does not embrace his students, but I always give him an awkward hug before he disappears into the airport pulling his over-sized suitcase tied with bright red ribbons. As I drove off, I was concerned. Will readers looking for "the beef" complain, "Where's the Rumi?" Will they understand this thing about the "impulse" and planting invisible "seeds?"

And then I remembered a young woman forty years ago in Los Angeles who asked Süleyman Dede an important question:

"How long will it take for Rumi's work to become known?" she asked.

Dede replied with his charming candor, "This I do not know. It may be ten years, fifty, or one hundred years, or even five hundred years. But, one thing I do know is that it will happen. Why? Because we are here, planting the seeds for Mevlana."

Dede and his "angels," Los Angeles, 1976

ACKNOWLEDGMENTS

I would like to thank the many people who filled in the blanks with first-hand memories and scholarship to tell this story.

No words can express my gratitude to David Bellak of Edinburgh, Scotland for sharing his recollections from the 1970s with Süleyman Dede in Konya. In so many ways, David revealed how Süleyman Dede's humanity and humility informed his spiritual insight. I remain indebted to David for sharing the intimate core of this book. The relationship between Dede and David echos history's great spiritual mentorships, including, in so many ways, the story of Shams and Rumi.

Many thanks to Ibrahim Bill Gamard who has dedicated his spiritual career to translating Rumi, researching the history, and fostering the Mevlevi tradition. Ibrahim's scholarship filled a big gap in my historical understanding. Ibrahim's Web site, www.dar-al-masnavi.org, hosts in-depth Mevlevi studies which I have used to help fill out the story. Ibrahim is also the author of *Rumi and Islam: Selections from His Stories, Poems, and Discourses* (2004), and *The Quatrains of Rumi: Ruba'iyat-e Jalaluddin Muhammad Balkhi-Rumi* (2008) co-translated with Rawan Farhadi.

A big thank you to Coleman Barks who I have always considered as a friend. I fondly remember when Coleman graced our dinner table years ago when we were hosting Reshad in Atlanta. Thank you, Coleman for sharing your journey and for allowing me to compare you with Coltrane as the jazz poet for our time.

And thank you Mira Hunter for sharing your artistic vision and keeping Rumi's American story fresh for a new generation of Rumi lovers.

I would also like to acknowledge my friends and fellow travelers who are mentioned or quoted in the story:

Raqib Brian Burke, Lisa Fillingham Oswald, Barbara Jolley, Judith Bergeron, Ivan and Jinny Rhodes, Jonathon Krieg, Lima Wright, Susan Mearns, Vic Garbarini, Jonathon Krieg, Aleta Laria, Niki Mantas, Marguerite Wilson, Sherry Gamard, Mufrida Bell, Hajah Tetley, Penny Webster, Peter Thurrell, and Karen Miller.

And I wish to acknowledge teachers, friends, and loved ones who are part of the story and have passed on:

Reshad Feild, Süleyman Dede, Bülent Rauf, J.G. Bennett, George and Maryam Steffen, Tony Leitner, Hassan Heiserman, and my mom, Nann Miller.

I also want to acknowledge Dede's son, Jelaladdin Loras. We only met once, and very briefly. But Jelaladdin has worked to preserve Dede's legacy and bring Rumi and the sema to a new generation.

I want to add a new round of acknowledgments for the people who made the expanded edition possible and shared their stories from Reshad's time in Europe. They include:

Peter Cunz and Anne Cunz-Regard, Leslie Masters, Penny Russell, Richard Rozsa, Susanne Hauenstein, Matt Shoemaker, Andre Gasser, Ruth Linauer, Eleanor Hand, Daniel Ellis, and my meditation teacher of 24 years, Dr. Bhagwan Awatramani.

Many thanks to Chalice Verlag. They provided the motivation for the new edition, plus much needed editorial support and critique, and provided the source material from Reshad's Swiss talks.

The prime mover of this story and my Sufi teacher, the late

Reshad Feild, requires special acknowledgment. The art of storytelling skews toward the dramatic, and the events I have selected (mattresses, drag queens, pizza, spitballs and the like) paint the picture of a Reshad who pulled out all the stops to open a heart – which he did. But, beyond the dramatic, I want to acknowledge Reshad's spiritual depth as a human being. He carried the substance which brought the people, possibilities, and contradictions together for Rumi to come to America. Thank you, Reshad. You rest in my heart and the hearts of so many.

And finally, my deepest respect goes to the man who planted Rumi's seed in America, Süleyman Hayati Loras Dede. Some people remember Dede as an exemplar of love. For others, Dede was just a simple cook. It wasn't until I worked with these tapes that I realized that Dede was a font of light and wisdom — and a clever one at that. Dede told me not to sell the tapes cheap. So, Dede, I hope I have fulfilled my part of the bargain.

To any young seekers, I hope this book is more than a history lesson. Let it be an invitation to follow your highest angels and be surprised at what unfolds.

Keep turning,
Bruce Miller

PHOTO CREDITS

ABOUT THE AUTHOR

After studying filmmaking and screenwriting at UCLA, Bruce Miller spent the bulk of his career as a brand strategist, media producer, and marketing partner in an Atlanta brand development agency.

In the 1970s, Bruce's spiritual search led him to English author, performer, and teacher, Reshad Feild. Together, they started The Institute for Conscious Life, the Mevlana Foundation, and later, the Chalice Guild. With Reshad, Bruce helped bring the work of Jalaluddin Rumi to America, the story recounted in *Rumi Comes to America*. Bruce also collaborated on *Steps to Freedom, Discourses on the Essential Knowledge of the Heart* based on talks given by Reshad Feild.

Bruce has led residential seminars on the knowledge of the Octave, ideas brought forth by P.D. Ouspensky and G.I. Gurdjieff, and the Law of Hazard, an understanding of risk and uncertainty based on the work of J.G. Bennett.

As an author, Bruce's first book, "FORTUNE, Our Deep Dive into the Mysteries of Love, Healing, and Success," explored the karmic mystery of *why stuff happens*. Bruce is currently writing a small business book: "Brand Story™ — The Step-by-Step Guide to Positioning Your Start-Up Like a National Brand."

Bruce is an active sailor, yoga enthusiast, and teaches the turn of the Whirling Dervishes. His wife Karen is an ordained minister and chaplain educator.

Connect with Bruce at www.ithou.com

Made in the USA
Lexington, KY
03 December 2018